GAY AND LESBIAN POETRY

ROUTLEDGE REFERENCE LIBRARY OF THE HUMANITIES
VOLUME 1874

Ganymede *by Michelangelo. (Courtesy Harvard University Art Museums)*

GAY AND LESBIAN POETRY
AN ANTHOLOGY FROM
SAPPHO TO MICHELANGELO

EDITED BY JAMES J. WILHELM

Routledge
Taylor & Francis Group

NEW YORK AND LONDON

OTHER MEDIEVAL WORKS BY THE AUTHOR

The Cruelest Month: Spring, Nature and Love in Classical and Medieval Lyrics

Seven Troubadors: The Creators of Modern Verse

Dante and Pound: The Epic of Judgement

The Poetry of Arnaut Daniel

Il Miglior Fabbro: The Cult of the Difficult in Daniel, Dante and Pound

The Romance of Arthur: An Anthology of Medieval Texts in Translation, New Expanded Edition

Published by Routledge

711 Third Avenue, New York, NY 10017

2 Park Square, Milton Park, Abingdon, Oxon, OX14 4RN

Library of Congress Cataloging-in-Publication Data

Gay and lesbian poetry : an anthology from Sappho to Michelangelo / edited by James J. Wilhelm.

    p. cm. — (Garland reference library of the humanities ; v. 1874)

    Includes index.

    ISBN 0-8153-1887-1 (alk. paper). — ISBN 0-8153-1886-3 (pbk. : alk. paper)

    1. Homosexuality—Poetry. 2. Gays' writings. 3. Lesbians' writings. I. Wilhelm, James J. II. Series: Reference library of the humanities ; v. 1874.

PN6110.H65G39 1995

808.81'9353—dc20   95-9987

                                          CIP

Paperback cover design by Karin Badger. Photograph: *Ganymede Astride the Eagle* by Benvenuto Cellini. (Courtesy Alinari/Art Resource, New York).

Publisher's Note

The publisher has gone to great lengths to ensure the quality of this reprint but points out that some imperfections in the original may be apparent.

FOR THOMAS STEHLING
WILLIAM HARPER
AND OTHERS WHO DIED TOO YOUNG

Contents

xi   PREFACE

SECTION I
3   CLASSICAL GREEK LITERATURE
DENNIS KRATZ

Chapter 1
5   SAPPHO (ca. 630–ca. 580 B.C.)

Chapter 2
11   EARLY MALE LYRIC POETS

Chapter 3
23   THEOCRITUS AND THE PASTORAL TRADITION

Chapter 4
29   STRATO OF SARDIS *MUSA PUERILIS* THE BOYISH MUSE

SECTION II
85   CLASSICAL LATIN LITERATURE
JAMES J. WILHELM

Chapter 5
87   THE LYRIC: CATULLUS, HORACE, AND TIBULLUS

Chapter 6
107   VERGIL

Chapter 7

111   OVID

Chapter 8

117   SATIRE: MARTIAL, JUVENAL, AND PETRONIUS

SECTION III

135   MEDIEVAL LATIN LITERATURE
      THOMAS STEHLING AND JAMES J. WILHELM

Chapter 9

137   A.D. 300–1000

Chapter 10

153   A.D. 1000–1300

Chapter 11

171   ANONYMOUS POEMS FROM LATER MANUSCRIPTS

SECTION IV

193   ARABIC POETRY
      ARTHUR WORMHOUDT

Chapter 12

195   MEDIEVAL SPANISH SELECTIONS

SECTION V

235   HEBREW POETRY
      NORMAN ROTH

Chapter 13

237   MEDIEVAL SPANISH SELECTIONS

SECTION VI

261   LATE MEDIEVAL VERNACULAR LITERATURE
      TO 1400
      JAMES J. WILHELM

Chapter 14

263   THE *TROBAIRITZ* BIETRIS DE ROMANS (ca. EARLY 1200S)

Chapter 15

265   DANTE ALIGHIERI (1265–1321)

Chapter 16

273   GEOFFREY CHAUCER (ca. 1341–1400)

SECTION VII

277   ITALIAN RENAISSANCE LITERATURE TO MICHELANGELO
     JAMES J. WILHELM

Chapter 17

279   SELECTIONS FROM 1400 TO 1550

327   GENERAL BIBLIOGRAPHY

329   INDEX OF AUTHORS AND LONGER WORKS

PREFACE

When Gary Kuris of Garland Publishing asked me if I would like to edit an anthology of gay and lesbian verse, I answered immediately that I would. It struck me that, until now, the anthologies have largely been done by people who were more interested in a broad, general collection than in showing any depth. From the start the first things to establish were the frontiers.

We decided after long discussion to limit this work to Europe, since the homoerotic literature of Japan, for example, deserves a book of its own, which Garland may issue in the near future. That is why the Arabic poetry is limited to what was produced in Spain—not the Middle East. We also wanted to establish time limits. We decided, therefore, to begin with the origins of European literature, specifically with Sappho and other Greeks, and to end with the height of the Italian Renaissance. We used Michelangelo as a *terminus ad quem*, since he marks a watershed between the Italians and the English, who would most logically begin any successive volume.

From the start we were determined to print as many women as possible, but we soon found that the number before 1500 is extremely small. Sappho stands almost as an island to herself. The Romans produce no one, and even the surprisingly large homoerotic literature of the Middle Ages is almost entirely written by men. It is only in recent times that lesbian literature comes to full bloom.

My fellow editors and I agreed that we would try to walk a line between completeness and diversity. We tried to offer at least one poem by anyone we were aware of. We could have published many more poems by Arab poets, but, once again, that can be handled in a future volume in which all of Arabic poetry is brought together. On the other hand we print the entire *Musa Puerilis* of Strato, and offer generous portions of Martial and many unknown but important Renaissance writers, especially Antonio Panormita and Pacifico Massimi. All in all the reader will receive the most comprehensive collection of this poetry to date.

As for style we were interested in accuracy, but we did not want the work to be pedantic. We annotate where we think it is necessary, but do not try to duplicate what can be found in any authoritative dictionary. We try to direct the reader to other sources, especially original texts, as well as general books, but we never conceived the primary purpose of this work to be bibliographic.

I would like to thank my fellow contributors, who worked with speed and enthusiasm. We felt all the while that we were making a contribution by bringing to light many works that had for too long a time been hidden (often quite deliberately). If we have published some poems in which the affection is Platonic rather than erotic, we felt that we had to allow the reader to decide. We include some homophobic literature, but we felt that a little of that goes a long way.

I have dedicated this book to two young men who died of AIDS: to Thomas Stehling, whose work is represented in Chapter 3 with my editing, and to William Harper, a brilliant student of mine at Rutgers. But there are many more out there, including some who were not very young, who died untimely deaths but who linger on in our memories with affection.

J. J. W.
Rutgers University

GAY AND LESBIAN POETRY

Replica of the Discus Thrower *of Miro. (Courtesy Alinari/Art Resource, New York)*

CLASSICAL GREEK LITERATURE

Dennis Kratz

The treatment of homosexual love in Classical Greek literature reflects the ambivalent role of homosexuality in Greek culture. On the one hand homosexuality is often portrayed positively. As the range of poems presented in this section demonstrates, numerous poets described the pangs and pleasures of homosexual unions. Nor was homosexual passion restricted to poetic works. In two dialogues, the *Symposium* and *Phaedrus*, the philosopher Plato makes homosexual attraction the starting point for his discussion of love as the force that initiates and guides the search for beauty, nobility, and wisdom.

On the other hand Greek literature offers abundant evidence of negative attitudes toward both homosexuality and the homosexual. The comic dramatist Aristophanes made homosexuals, especially those who submitted to anal intercourse, the butt of many jokes. Moreover, homosexual themes and characters are notably absent from Greek tragedy and epic, with the possible exception of Achilles and Patroclus in the *Iliad*. This failure of classical Greek literature other than lyric poetry to offer positive portrayals of homosexual love might be considered further evidence of a general disapproval of most forms of homosexual behavior.

Even lyric poetry, which provides abundant examples of homosexual themes, is for the most part limited to a specific homoerotic relationship: that between a mature male and a preadolescent boy. In this relationship the older man, called in Greek the *erastes* (lover) played the dominant role; but he was expected to extend his relationship with the boy, called the *eromenos* (lover) beyond sexual satisfaction. In many ways, the erastes was expected to mentor his partner, modeling for him and teaching him those virtues valued in a citizen of the Greek polis.

It is the voice of the erastes that we encounter exclusively in Greek lyric poetry from both the classical and the Hellenistic eras. From this poetry emerges a clear view of the rules associated with pederastic relationships. The erastes, smitten by the beauty of a young boy, courts him with gifts and words. The gifts are often conventional and apparently symbolic: a garland of flowers, a ball or other plaything, a bird. Lesbian love poetry from Greek antiquity is limited to the surviving poems by Sappho. Even here, it is the voice of Sappho the erastes, the pursuer rather than the pursued, that we encounter.

The language of homosexual seduction has much in common with the conventions of heterosexual love poetry. The potential lover invokes examples of divine passion—above all, the love of Zeus for the handsome boy Ganymede. The man often warns his beloved of the fleeting nature of his youthful good looks. A common theme of this pederastic love poetry describes the horror of the sprouting beard that will destroy the attraction of the potential eromenos. The boy, for his part, is expected to yield eventually, though not too soon or easily. He should not, however, be too greedy in his quest for tokens of the older man's affection. The complaints of Greek pederastic poetry are divided equally among the themes of avarice, rejection, and infidelity.

As Kenneth Dover has pointed out, Greek homosexual passion seems to have exhibited the same double standard that can be observed in Greek heterosexual relations. The pursuit by the erastes is sanctioned—his success viewed as a triumph. Yielding easily to seduction, however, is regarded as a sign of weakness. In the lyrics we encounter men who vow abiding love for a sequence of handsome youths.

The lyric poetry devoted to this form of homoerotic relationship offers a remarkably consistent picture from the fifth century B.C. through the Hellenistic era. This consistency seems to reflect both the central role of pederasty in Greek society and the conservative nature of Greek lyric poetry, which tends to refine and repeat rather than seek new forms of expression.

The most important work of recent scholarship devoted to the subject of homoerotic passion in Greek society is Dover's *Greek Homosexuality* (Cambridge, Mass., 1978). In her study *The Reign of the Phallus: Sexual Politics in Ancient Athens*, Eva Keuls offers a perceptive, critical analysis of the attitudes of Athenian males toward both heterosexual and homosexual passion. Finally, in *Same-sex Unions in Premodern Europe*, John Boswell argues that Greek society had a far more tolerant view of homosexual relations, particularly between two adults, than is generally assumed.

1. SAPPHO

(ca. 630–ca. 580 B.C.)

An epigram attributed to Plato calls Sappho the "tenth Muse." She is without question the most admired of all the lyric poets of Greek antiquity.

Little is known of her life. She seems to have belonged to one of the leading families of Mytilene on the island of Lesbos. Apparently she married, for in several poems she mentions a daughter named Cleis. Sappho's poetry was widely read in antiquity. In her poetry Sappho portrays herself as a member of an elegant circle of aristocratic women. Her most famous poems are choral wedding hymns and love songs about and to these women. Some are poems of friendship, but in others she sings of passionate, sexual affection. Many of these lyrics are profoundly sensual, especially Sappho's famous description of the physical effects of her passion for another woman (31).

Sappho's language is unusually direct and unaffected. Her poetry is characterized by her presentation of compelling details. The lyrics of Sappho represent the most eloquent and the most artistic expression of female sexuality produced in the ancient world, or perhaps ever.

I have used the edition of Sappho prepared by David A. Campbell for the Loeb Classical Library, *Greek Lyric,* Volume I (Cambridge: Harvard University Press, 1982).

1

Immortal Aphrodite, on your elegant throne,
daughter of Zeus, weaver of wiles, I beg you
not to crush my spirit, mistress,
with pain or anguish,

but come, if ever before you heard
my voice singing from far away
and listened, and leaving your father's
golden house, you came

in your chariot. And lovely swift sparrows,
wings whirring, brought you over
the dark earth down from heaven
through the air,

and soon they landed. And you, blessed one,
a smile on your immortal face,
asked what was wrong with me again,
why I was calling again,

and in my maddened heart what I most wished
to happen to me: "Whom must I persuade this time
and lead back to your love? Sappho,
who is wronging you?

If she flees, soon she will pursue;
if she does not take gifts, soon she will give them.
If she does not love, soon she will love,
even against her will."

Come once again to me, release me from
my grief and pain, fulfill all that
my heart desires. You yourself
be my ally.

16

Some say an army of horsemen, and others
a fleet of ships is the most beautiful thing
on the black earth. But I say
it is whatever a person loves.

It is easy to make everyone understand this.
The woman who far surpassed all mortals in beauty,

Helen, leaving behind the very best
of husbands,

sailed off to Troy without a thought for her child
or her dear parents, but [love]
led her astray . . .

. . . .
lightly . . .
reminding me now of Anactoria,
who is not here.

I would rather see her lovely step
and the radiant sparkle of her face
than the Lydians' chariots and
armed infantry.

31

He seems to me the equal of the gods,
the man who sits facing you
and, near you, listens to
your charming voice

and your alluring laugh that makes
my heart flutter in my breast.
When I see you, even briefly, then
I cannot speak,

but my tongue is silenced; a slender
flame slips suddenly beneath my flesh;
my eyes see nothing, my ears
are roaring,

sweat drenches me, trembling
seizes my entire body, I am paler
than grass, and I seem
almost dead.

But I must endure, since . . .

47

Love shook my heart like a wind
in the mountain smashing into oaks.

48

You came, and I was longing for you,
and you cooled my heart that was aflame with desire.

94

... "I wish that I were dead."
She was sobbing as she left me

and said this to me:
"How terribly we have suffered,
Sappho. I leave against my will."

And I replied,
"Farewell, remember me,
for you know how we cared for you.

If not, I want to remind you
... of the happy times we shared ...

Wreathed with violets, roses
and crocuses ... by my side ...

and around your tender neck
... garlands woven from flowers ...

and with exquisite myrrh ...
fit for a queen, you anointed ...

and on soft beds
you satisfied your longing for ...

There was neither ... nor shrine ...
we failed to visit,
... no sacred grove" ...

105A

As the sweet apple reddens on the highest branch,
on the top of the topmost branch, and the apple-pickers
have forgotten it; no, not forgotten,
but they could not reach it.

121

But if you are my friend,
choose the bed of a younger woman.
I could not bear to live with you,
if I were the older one.

168B

The moon has set,
and the Pleiades:
the middle
of the night,
the hours slip by,
and I sleep alone.

2. Early Male Lyric Poets

ANACREON (ca. 570–485 B.C.)

Anacreon was born in Teos in Asia Minor. He traveled to Samos, where he entertained at the court of the tyrant Polycrates, who ruled from 533–522 B.C. There he earned a reputation as a composer of elegant, sophisticated poetry. When Polycrates was assassinated, Anacreon's fame induced the rulers of Athens to send a warship to bring him to their court.

Anacreon gained particular fame as a composer of monody, or lyric poetry recited by a single person. Sadly, few of his poems have survived; but evidence of the admiration in which he was held is provided by the more than sixty extant imitations of poems by him that were composed between 200 B.C. and A.D. 500. I have used the text of the fragments of Anacreon provided by Denys Page in *Poetae Melici Graeci* (Oxford: Clarendon Press, 1962).

PMG 357

Lord, with whom Love the subduer
and the dark-eyed Nymphs
and lustrous Aphrodite
play, you that wander over
lofty mountain crests:
I pray to you, come
to us gently, hear our prayer,
may it be acceptable to you.
Dionysus, please give to Cleoboulus
this wise advice: accept our love.

PMG 359

Cleoboulus I desire,
Cleoboulus I praise,
at Cleoboulus I gaze.

PMG 360

Boy who casts a girlish glance,
I am pursuing you,
but you don't listen,
not knowing that
you hold the reins
of my soul.

PMG 400

I was fleeing love when I
returned to Pythomandrus.

IBYCUS (fl. ca. 540–530 B.C.)

Little is known about the life of Ibycus other than that he was born in
Rhegium, in southern Italy, and entertained during the 530s at the court of
Polycrates, who ruled Samos from 533–522 B.C. At Samos he presumably
knew Anacreon. Only a few fragments of his poems remain, and these con-
firm his reputation in antiquity as a poet of passionate love. Fragment 287,
in particular, presents an idea of passion that was widespread among the
Greeks: love is a dangerous and maddening force that cannot be evaded.

I have used the edition of Denys Page, *Poetae Melici Graeci* (Oxford:
Clarendon Press, 1962).

PMG 287

Love, staring under dark eyebrows,
melts me with his gaze again.
Using every kind of charm,
he entangles me in Aphrodite's nets.
I tremble at his coming
just as a stallion who has borne the yoke,

a prizewinner now approaching old age,
goes to the race of speeding chariots
against his will.

PMG 288
Euryalus, child of the bright-eyed Graces,
favorite of the Graces with the lovely hair,
Aphrodite and gentle-eyed Persuasion
nursed you among the rose blossoms.

THEOGNIS (fl. ca. 550 B.C.)

Theognis was a noble from the Sicilian city of Megara who lived, according
to tradition, in the middle of the sixth century B.C. He wrote a number of brief
elegiac poems expressing the values and the anxieties of an aristocrat who saw
his privileged position in society threatened by new political and social devel-
opments. Most of his poetry was didactic in nature, giving advice to a young
man named Cyrnus about the behavior proper to an aristocratic citizen.

In the fifth century the collected works of Theognis seem to have been
expanded into an anthology that contains approximately 1,400 lines of el-
egiac poetry. This collection was attributed to Theognis, although many of
the poems were certainly composed by others.

In the Middle Ages the final 150 lines of this anthology were set apart
as "Book II," and this division persists in all the surviving manuscripts. The
poems of the second book all deal with the love of boys. Although they pur-
port to be by Theognis many were composed by other poets. The poems are
all addressed to an unnamed boy. Many of the poems complain about the
boy's infidelity while describing the depth and the honorable nature of the
poet's affection. I have included as well several poems from Book I of the
anthology that the ancient editors failed to recognize as erotic in their sub-
ject matter. The value of the collection lies in part in its presentation of what
may fairly be considered works typical of the poetry written in the sixth and
fifth centuries for symposia and other social settings.

I have used the text of the poems published by J.M. Edmonds in the
Loeb Classical Library: *Elegy and Iambus*, Volume I (Cambridge: Harvard
University Press, 1931). The line numbers of the Greek do not always coin-
cide with the lines of the translations.

Book I

371–372

Don't drag me, goad me to the yoke against my will,
Cyrnus, by driving me by force to loving you.

695–696

Heart, I cannot give you everything that you desire. Be patient.
You're not the only one in love with beautiful boys.

949–954

I did not drink the blood of the fawn that I, like a lion
sure of his strength, seized with my claws from a deer.
I scaled the walls but did not sack the city.
I yoked the horses but did not mount the chariot.
I did it and yet did not, reached my goal and yet did not,
acted but did not act, finished but did not.

959–962

As long as it was I alone who drank from the darkwater spring,
the water seemed to me sweet and delicious.
Now it has been fouled, the water mixed with mud.
I will drink from another spring, an unsullied one.

Book II

1231–1234

Cruel Love, the Frenzies cradled you and nursed you.
You caused destruction of Troy's citadel.
You destroyed great Theseus, the son of Aegeus,
and Ajax, son of Oileus, with your recklessness.

1235–1238

You, boy, who have mastered my passion, listen.
I will tell you a tale neither unconvincing
nor unpleasant to your heart. But try
to understand my point. You are not compelled
to do anything that you find disagreeable.

1238a–1240

Do not abandon the friend you have to seek another,
persuaded by the words of vulgar men.
They will tell me many lies about you,
and tell you many about me. Don't listen to them.

1241–1242

You will be delighted by this love when it is over
and no longer under your control.

1243–1244

We have been lovers a long time. Find others now.
You are devious and disloyal.

1245–1246

Water and fire will never mix. And we
will never be faithful to each other.

1247–1248

Ponder my hatred and your transgression.
Know in your heart that I
will exact the best revenge I can.

1249–1252

Boy, you are like a stallion.
Now that you are filled with barley,
you come back to our stall
looking for a good rider, a lush meadow,
cool water and a shady grove.

1253–1254

He is wealthy who has boys to love, single-hooved horses,
hounds and friends in foreign lands.

1255–1256

Whoever does not love boys, single-hooved horses
and dogs is never truly happy.

1257–1258

Boy, you are like those who fly wherever the wind blows.
You are well disposed now to some, now to others.

1259–1262

Boy, you were born handsome, but a wreath of
stupidity crowns your head.
You have the disposition of a darting kite,
seduced by the words of other men.

1263–1266

Boy, you paid back my kindness with evil.
You have no gratitude at all for favors.
You never helped me. Despite my many acts
of kindness, I receive no respect from you.

1267–1270

A boy and a horse think alike. The horse
does not weep for its rider lying in the dust,
but it takes on the next man once it is filled wih barley.
Likewise a boy loves the man who is handy.

1271–1274

Boy, you have driven me mad with your whoring,
and you have become a disgrace to our friends.
You have given me a brief respite, and with night approaching
I have found a haven from the storm.

1275–1278

Love also rises in season when the earth swells
and blossoms with the flowers of spring.
Then Love leaves Cypris, that beautiful island,
and travels among men scattering seed on the ground.

1278a–b

Whoever advised you concerning me and urged you
to give up our love and go away . . .

1279–1282

I have no wish to hurt you, even if, dear boy,
the immortal gods will prefer it.
I sit in judgment on no petty crimes,
but beautiful boys escape punishment for their misbehavior.

1283–1294

Boy, don't do me wrong (I still want you
to like me), but pay close attention to this:
You won't fool me with your tricks.
You have won for now and hold the upper hand,
but I will get you as you run away, even as they say
the daughter of Iasius once fled, though ripe
for marriage, rejecting marriage to a man.
She girded herself and accomplished nothing:
fair-haired Atalanta forsook her father's house,
fled to the lofty mountain peaks,
fleeing the delights of marriage, the gift
of golden Aphrodite. Despite her opposition,
she knew how it would end.

1295–1298

Boy, don't arouse my heart with agony.
Don't let my love for you bear me off
to Persephone's domain. Beware the wrath
of the gods and what men will say
and devise a kinder plan of action.

1299–1304

Boy, how long will you flee from me? How closely
I pursue you! If only your anger would come to an end.
You flee because you are greedy and stubborn.
You have the nasty disposition of a kite.
Stop and grant me your favor. Not much longer
will you have the gift of violet-crowned Aphrodite.

1305–1310

Knowing in your heart that the flower of exquisite boyhood
is quicker than a footrace, understanding this, free me
from my bonds. You might be fettered too, mighty boy, and just

as I do now with you, might encounter Aphrodite's harsher side.
Beware. Some cruel boy might conquer you some day.

1311–1318

I know that you cheated me, boy. I'm on to you.
Your new friends, the ones with whom you're now so
tight and loving, the ones for whom you scorned
and cast away my love: you were not their friend before.
But I thought that of all my friends I had made you
the closest. And now you have another lover.
I who served you well lie in the dust. No one on earth,
seeing you, would wish to fall in love with a boy.

1318a–b

I am in despair. My sufferings have made me
a pleasure to my enemies, a burden to my friends.

1319–1322

Boy, since the goddess Aphrodite gave you such alluring
gracefulness, and your beauty bothers all the young men,
listen to these words and for my sake take them to heart,
knowing how hard desire is for a man to endure.

1323–1326

Cypris-born, end my suffering, scatter the cares
that burden my mind, make me content again,
end these terrible anxieties, grant that I may act
with wisdom now that my days of youthfulness are over.

1327–1328

Boy, as long as you have smooth cheeks, I will
never stop courting you, not even if I have to die.

1329–1334

For you the act of giving is noble. For me, the one in love,
asking is no disgrace. On bended knee I beg you,
handsome boy, show me respect and grant your favor.
If ever it is you who crave the gift of Aphrodite
with her violet crown and must approach another, may
the goddess give to you the same response that I receive.

1335–1336

Happy the lover who exercises, then, when he comes home,
sleeps all day with a gorgeous boy.

1337–1340

I am in love with the boy no more. I have shaken off
dreadful sorrows and joyfully escaped crushing woes.
I have been freed from my passion by Aphrodite
of the lovely wreath. Boy, you do not appeal to me.

1341–1344

Poor me, I love a smooth-skinned boy who mocks me,
against my will, to all his friends. I will endure
many insults, nor will I hide. For I have been tamed
by a boy who is in no way unattractive.

1345–1350

Loving boys has brought delight since Cronus' son,
king of immortals, fell for Ganymede,
seized him, brought him to Olympus and made him
a god in the lovely blossoming of boyhood.
So, Simonides, don't be surprised if it is revealed
I too have been tamed by the love of a beautiful boy.

1351–1352

Boy, don't go carousing. Pay attention to the old saying:
"Carousing is not good for a young man."

1352–1356

Bitter and sweet, enticing and harsh, Cyrnus,
the desire for youths—until consummated.
If you get what you seek, it is sweet; if you pursue
without achievement, it brings the worst pain there is.

1357–1358

Always on the neck of boy-lovers lies a yoke
that is heavy, a chafing monument of promiscuity.

1359–1360

Trying to seduce a boy into loving you is like
putting your hand into a fire of dry branches.

1361–1362

You are a ship that struck a rock and missed the harbor
of my love, boy, and you grabbed a rotting rope.

1363–1364

Never will I hurt you, even when I am gone. No one
will persuade me, as you have tried, to stop loving you.

1365–1366

Loveliest and most desirable of all boys,
stand here and listen to me for a while.

1367–1368

A boy has a sense of gratitude. A woman lacks
fidelity. She always loves the man who happens to be there.

1369–1372

Passion for a boy is fine to feel, fine to discard.
It is much easier to find than to satisfy.
A thousand evils and a thousand goods accompany it,
but even the uncertainty has a certain charm.

1373–1374

You never waited for my sake,
but you always rushed off to every message.

1375–1376

Happy the man in love with a boy who does not know the sea
and does not worry as night descends upon the deep.

1377–1380

Though handsome, boy, your mind is worthless and you spend
your time with vulgar men. You are harshly criticized for this.
Although (despite my efforts) I have failed to win your love,
at least I know my behavior was worthy of a citizen.

1381–1382

Men thought that you came bearing the gift
of the golden goddess born on Cypris . . .

1383–1385

. . . the gift of the violet-wreathed goddess becomes
the harshest burden for a man, unless the goddess
grants deliverance from hardship.

1386–1388

Cypris-born Aphrodite, weaver of wiles, Zeus honored you
by granting you this extraordinary gift.
You master the cleverness of men, and there is no one
strong or skilled enough to flee from you.

PLATO (428–347 B.C.)

The philosopher Plato made love—the force that lures humans to seek
understanding of the eternal idea of Beauty—central to his philosophic
vision; moreover, he made homosexual attraction the starting point for his
metaphysics. It is not surprising, therefore, to find that several epigrams
attributed to Plato in antiquity address homosexual themes. Although some
of these brief poems are excellent (above all, the epigram that describes the
ecstasy of kissing Agathon), unfortunately none of the love poems can have
been by Plato. Such epigrams on the subject of love simply were not com-
posed prior to 300 B.C. The following poems are in all likelihood products
of the Hellenistic era, that is, the third century B.C.

I have based my translations of the epigrams on the text in the Loeb
Classical Library *Elegy and Iambus*, Volume II (Cambridge: Harvard Uni-
versity Press, 1931), edited by J. M. Edmonds.

1 *To Aster*

You gaze at the stars, my star. If only I were the heavens, I would gaze at
    you with many eyes.
[Aster is both the young man's name and the Greek word for "star."]

2 To Aster

Once you were shining, a star of morning among the living,
and now, in death, you shine as the evening star among the dead.

3 To Dion

To Hecuba and the Trojan women as they were born
the Fates assigned tears. Dion, when you
had triumphed by performing deeds of nobility,
the divinities spilled your promise on the ground.
You lie here in the spacious city, honored by the citizens,
Dion, you who maddened my soul with love.

4 To Alexis

Now, when I have merely whispered that Alexis is handsome,
everyone who turns and looks is looking at him.
Soul of mine, why do you show the dogs a bone? You will regret it
afterwards. Is this not how we lost Phaedrus?

6 To Agathon

I felt my soul on my lips as I was kissing Agathon.
The poor thing came there in the hope of crossing over.

3. THEOCRITUS AND THE PASTORAL TRADITION

Theocritus was a native of Syracuse in Sicily. He was probably of humble origin. At some point early in his career he went to Alexandria, where he made the acquaintance of Callimachus, perhaps the most famous and certainly the most influential poet of his generation.

The importance of Theocritus in the history of Greek literature rests on his claim as the inventor of the genre known as the bucolic idyll. These poems present idealized pictures (the Greek work *eidyllion* means, in fact, a little picture) of rustic life.

While homosexual love is mentioned in many of the thirty idylls attributed to Theocritus, it is the main subject of Idylls 12, 29, and 30. These poems differ in tone as well as subject matter from the other idylls. In most of the others Theocritus offers dramatic dialogues spoken by shepherds or other rustic characters. In Idylls 12, 29, and 30, Theocritus speaks in what seems to be his own voice. They are more correctly described as lyric meditations than as idylls. As such they rank among Theocritus's most elegant and alluring works.

Idyll 6 is more representative of Theocritus's bucolic poetry. It tells the story of a singing contest between two herdsmen: Daphnis and Damoetas, who is the younger of the two. Their song concerns another pair of lovers, the Cyclops Polyphemus (perhaps better known as the monster whom Odysseus blinds in the *Odyssey*) and his beloved, a sea nymph named Galatea. The failure of the relationship of Polyphemus and Galatea seems to be offered as a warning by each of the shepherds to the other. The two young men are clearly lovers, as the kiss that concludes their contest (and the idyll) proves.

I have based my translation on the edition of Theocritus published by A.S.F. Gow in his *Bucolici Graeci* (Oxford, Clarendon Press, 1952).

Idyll 6

Damoetas and Daphnis, two herdsmen, drove their cattle one day
through the very same place at noontime on a summer's day.
Daphnis had a ruddy beard; Damoetas' beard was halfway grown.
The two of them sat by a spring, and they began to sing.
Daphnis began the match because he had proposed the contest:
"Galatea is pelting your flock with apples, Polyphemus,
while calling you a goatherd and a lousy lover.
And you (sad wretch) see nothing as you sit there
sweetly piping. Now she's throwing one at your sheepdog!
The dog looks out to sea and barks at the rolling waves   10
you can see him silhouetted against the sea
as he runs along the shore where the water turns to foam.
Watch out or he might charge at her knees as the girl
emerges from the deep and rip her delicate flesh.
Now she's showing off again. She is as prickly as
the leaves left on the thistle in the heat of summer.
She flees you when you love her and pursues when you do not.
She moves her pieces boldly in this game. How often,
Polyphemus, love has made the foul seem fair!"
Then Damoetas lifted up his voice and sang in answer: 20
"I saw, Pan be my witness, yes I saw her when she threw them.
It did not escape my notice, I swear by my one sweet eye.
May I see with it until I die, and may the prophet Telamus
take his curses home with him to keep for his own children.
But I don't mind because I too know how to irritate, and say
that I have another woman now. As soon as she hears this,
she is filled with jealousy and from the sea she spies
on my cave and my sheep like a woman driven mad with love.
I was the one who caused my dog to bark at her; when we
were courting, he would place his muzzle on her lap   30
and whine. When she has seen enough, perhaps she'll send
a messenger; but I will bar my door until she swears in person
to sleep with me as man and wife on this my island.
I am not an ugly man, despite what people say.
I looked at my reflection in the glassy sea
and found my cheeks and my one eye rather handsome.
My teeth gleamed back at me whiter than Parian marble.
To keep evil away I spat three times toward my chest
just as the witch Cotyttaris taught me."

When he had finished singing, Damoetas kissed Daphnis,   40
then gave him a pipe and a pretty flute too.
Damoetas played the flute while the herdsman Daphnis piped,
and the heifers began to dance on the tender grass.
Neither was the victor; both emerged unvanquished.

Idyll 12

You have come, dear heart. As the third day is dawning,
you have come; but one day apart makes lovers turn gray.
By as much as spring is sweeter than winter, as apples
are sweeter than plums, as the ewe is fleecier than her lamb,
as a maiden is preferable to a thrice-wed wife,
as a fawn is nimbler than a calf, as the clear-voiced
nightingale is the most musical bird of all, by so much has
the sight of you delighted me, and I have run to you
as a traveler runs from the scorching sun to the shade of an oak.
I wish that equal Loves would animate the two of us,   10
and we would become a legend and a song for posterity:
"Among our ancestors were two godlike men,
one called, in the Spartan tongue, Inspirer
and the other, as the Thessalians say, Beloved.
They loved each other mutually. In those days men
were made of gold, when the beloved loved in return.
Father Zeus and you unaging gods, grant this:
a thousand years from now may someone meet me
at the bank of Acheron that cannot be recrossed and say,
'Everyone, especially the young, talks about   20
the love you shared with your Beloved.'"
This is in the hands of the heavenly gods,
whatever they wish. But when I praise you,
no liar's warts will sprout on the tip of my nose.
For if you ever cause me pain, you heal the hurt at once
and give me a double reward, and I depart enriched.
Nisaean Megarians, you who are masters of rowing,
may you live prosperously, for having honored
the Attic stranger Diocles, a lover of boys.   30
About his tomb every year in early spring
your youths engage in a kissing contest:
the one who presses lips to lips most deliciously

returns to his mother crowned with garlands.
Happy the man who judges the boys' kisses!
Surely he prays fervently to bright-eyed Ganymede
for lips like the Lydian touchstone, which
distinguishes for moneychangers true gold from false.

Idyll 29

"Wine and truth," the saying goes, dear boy.
And so we must tell the truth when we are drinking.
And I will tell you what is lurking in my mind:
that you do not want to love me with all your heart.
I know it, for I have half my life by reason of
your loveliness, and the rest has perished.
When you wish it, then I spend a godlike day,
or a day in darkness, when you wish it otherwise.
How is this fair, to hand your lover over to grief?
If you, a young man, would listen to me, an older man,   10
you would profit and be grateful to me.
You should make but one nest in a tree,
where no beast of prey will attack it.
You perch on one branch today, another tomorrow,
flitting from here to there. If anyone should see
and praise your handsome face, suddenly you have been
his friend for more than three years. Meanwhile you place
the one who loved you first among your recent acquaintances,
one of those men for whom you have little regard.
As long as you live, love one who is your equal.   20
If you do this, you will have a noble reputation
among the citizens, and you will not be treated harshly
by Love, who easily subdues the minds of men
and has transformed me from a man of iron into a weakling.
By your tender mouth I beg you to remember that
a year ago you were younger than you are today.
We mortals age and wrinkle quicker than we can spit.
Youth, when it has departed, cannot be recaptured,
for it has wings on its shoulders, and we mortals
are too clumsy to capture winged creatures.   30
By pondering this you should grow more compassionate,
and return your lover's affection with no deceit.

When the time comes for you to have bearded cheeks,
then we will be for each other Achilles and Patroclus.
But if you cast these words to the winds
and say in your heart, "Why do you bother me, sir?"
although now I would seek the Golden Apples for your sake
or fetch Cerberus, the guard-dog of the dead, for you,
then even if you stood at my door and called to me,
I would not come out, having been cured of my painful madness.   40

Idyll 30

Poor me! This illness is harsh and painful!
For two months I have been afflicted with recurring passion
for a boy only moderately good-looking; but every step
he takes is filled with grace, and he has a charming smile.
The fever seizes me on some days, some days not,
but soon I'll have no respite, not even when I sleep.
When we met yesterday, he glanced at me discreetly,
too shy to look me in the face, and blushed bright red.
Then Love gripped the reins of my heart still tighter,
and I went home nursing this wound.   10
There I summoned my soul and had a talk with myself:
"Why did you do this? What will be the end of this madness?
Have the gray hairs on your temples escaped your notice?
It is time you learned some prudence. A man no longer young
should not act like those who are savoring their youthful years.
You have also forgotten this: it is better, at this stage
of your life, to avoid the hardships of loving boys.
The life of a boy flows as smoothly and swiftly as a deer.
Tomorrow he will catch a different wind to cross the sea.
For him and his generation the sweet flower of youth abides.   20
For the other what remains are a longing that gnaws at his heart
and a host of dreams at night. A year is not time enough
to cure him of his lovesickness." I used these arguments
and many others to find fault with my soul; but she replied,
"Whoever thinks that he can defeat devious Love might
think as well that he can calculate how many times nine
is the number of stars in the heavens above us. And now,
if I like, I must stretch my neck beneath the yoke
and pull, even if I don't like it. Such is the will of the god

who beguiled the mighty mind of Zeus and even Aphrodite.   30
Poor me! His blast of wind will lift me and whirl me away,
an ephemeral leaf, susceptible to just a gentle breeze."

4. STRATO OF SARDIS

MUSA PUERILIS (THE BOYISH MUSE)

The anthology of homoerotic verse known as the *Musa Puerilis* (The Boyish Muse) is an expanded version of a collection of his own poetry made by Strato of Sardis sometime in the reign of the Roman emperor Hadrian (A.D. 117–138). Around the year 900 a Byzantine scholar named Constantine Cephalus put together the largest and most comprehensive collection of epigrams compiled up to that time.

As part of this grand work Cephalus included Strato's collection; however he also amplified the original work by adding homosexual poems (especially poems on pederastic love) that he found in two other anthologies, the so-called *Garland* of Meleager of Gadara (published in 70 B.C.) and the *Garland* of Philippus of Thessalonica (published in A.D. 40). Each of these anthologies consisted of approximately 800 poems.

The Boyish Muse now forms the twelfth book of the collection of Greek epigrams known as the *Greek Anthology*, which is itself an expansion and revision of Cephalus's work that a prodigious Byzantine scholar named Maximus Planudes made in the thirteenth century.

The *Greek Anthology* is an invaluable storehouse of Hellenistic epigrams, that is, brief poems composed almost always in elegiac couplets. The twelfth book is likewise the most comprehensive collection of epigrams on homosexual love in general and pederasty in particular. The poems range from delicate expressions of affection to crude accounts of rape. Most of the motifs and themes of Greek love poetry can be found here in numerous transformations: the power of passion, the rites of courtship, the pain of a lover's infidelity, the pleasures of shared affection. One theme specifically associated with pederasty appears more than thirty times, a variation on the *carpe diem* ("seize the day") theme that warns the young boy of the imminent appearance of rough hair and a beard.

The *Musa Puerilis* offers as well an opportunity to observe the major images of love: the stormy sea, the weapons of the boy Love (Eros), the fire of passion, and love (or at least infatuation) at first sight. It is a collection of immense importance for anyone interested in homosexual poetry or, indeed, Greek literature.

In addition to 95 epigrams by Strato the *Musa Puerilis* includes poems by a wide range of other poets. The most important Hellenistic poet represented in the collection is Callimachus (ca. 310–240 B.C.). Asclepiades of Samos (fl. 320–290 B.C.) is regarded, along with Callimachus, as one of the two creators and first skilled practitioners of the erotic epigram. Two other poets of note, both contemporaries of Callimachus represented in the anthology, are Posidippus of Pella (a friend of Asclepiades) and Nicander of Colophon.

The careful reader will observe a few poems in the collection addressed to young women (for examples, 82 and 113). How did these poems find their way into the *Musa Puerilis*? The answer would seem to be found in the Greek habit of giving women names that were grammatically neuter. Apparently a later scribe mistook these for the names of young men.

I have based my translations on the text printed in the Loeb Classical Library edition of the *Greek Anthology*, Volume IV (Cambridge: Harvard University Press, 1918), edited by W.R. Paton.

1 Strato (Poems 1–11)

Let's begin, as Aratus once said, with Zeus.
Muses, I won't bother you today.
If I love boys and spend my time with boys,
what business is that of the Heliconian Muses?

2

Don't expect Priam at the altar in my pages.
Don't expect the sorrows of Medea and Niobe,
or Itys in his bedroom and nightingales among the leaves.
Poets have written more than enough about all that.
Look instead for sweet Love united with the happy Graces,
and Bacchus too. Here a frown is out of place.

3

Boys' penises fall into three main types,
Diodorus. Learn their proper names.
Call a penis that is as yet untouched a lalu.
The koko is the penis just begun to swell.
A cock that throbs to the touch of a hand:
call that a lizard.
Now you know more thoroughly what you ought to call them.

4

I enjoy the cock of a twelve-year-old,
but I long for a thirteen-year-old much, much more.
A fourteen-year-old is a still sweeter flower of the Loves,
and a boy just turning fifteen is even more delicious.
Sixteen is the year of the gods. Seventeen?
For Zeus, not me, to seek. But if anyone
desires older boys, he is not playing any more,
but he desires someone to respond.

5

I love them pale; I like them honey-colored. I like
the fair-skinned too, and I am very fond of black-haired boys.
And while I don't ignore the brown-eyed boys,
I adore, oh yes I utterly adore, sparkling black eyes.

6

Proktos [ass] and *chrusos* [gold] have the same numerical value.
I discovered this by putting one and one together.

    [Greek letters were used as numbers and assigned numeric values.]

7

A young girl lacks a sphincter.
She cannot give a simple kiss.
The scent of her skin is not so sweet,
her whispered love-words unenticing.
Her glance is not ingenuous,

her knowledge is not interesting.
They're all so boring from behind and
(this is the main thing) they have no place
where you can put a roaming hand.

8

I saw a boy there, intertwining petals with the berries,
while I was strolling past the garland market.
I did not escape unwounded.
I stood there and I whispered,
"For how much can I buy your crown?"
He blushed redder than his rosebuds
and looking at the ground he said,
"Go away before my father sees you."
I bought some garlands (just a pretense)
and when I reached my house, I crowned
the gods. My prayer: I want him.

9

Now you are lovely, Diodorus, ripe for lovers.
Even if you marry, we will not abandon you.

10

Even if the fuzz is turning into beard
and delicate coils of golden hair
have leapt upon your cheeks,
I will not desert my beloved boy.
His beauty is, despite the beard,
despite the hairs, ours.

11

I spent last night with Philostratus
but could not rise to the occasion
though he (how shall I put it?)
was ready for everything.
Dear friends, count me no more among your friends,

but hurl me headlong from a tower.
I have become a limp Astyanax.

> *[In Greek Astyanax can be read as a pun for "unable to rise."]*

12 *Flaccus*

Just as his beard is sprouting, Lado,
gorgeous but cruel to his lovers,
has fallen for a boy. Nemesis is swift.

13 *Strato*

I came upon some beardless doctors, love-antagonists,
who were concocting antidotes for passion.
Caught in the act, they begged me,
"Keep this to yourself."
I answered, "Certainly, just cure me."

14 *Dioscorides*

If Demophilus, when he grows up,
kisses lovers as he kisses me
(though he is still a child),
at night his mother's door
will not be silent any more.

15 *Strato*

If a plank pinched Graphicus there in the bath,
what will happen to me, a man? Even wood has feelings.

16 *Strato*

Don't try to hide our love, Philocrates.
The god himself is strong enough
to trample on my heart.
Just give me a taste
of your delicious kisses.
The time will come when you
will ask this favor from another.

17 Anonymous

Women leave me cold, but male sparks
kindle burning coals that cannot be
extinguished.
This heat is hotter.
By as much as men
have greater strength than women
by that much
is this desire keener.

18 Alpheius of Mytilene

How sad and loveless life must be for them,
For those devoid of love
words and deeds are difficult.
I, now, am limping, slow.
But should I see Xenophilus,
swifter than a lightning bolt I'd fly.
I encourage every man to seek
and not avoid sweet passion.
Love is the whetstone of the soul.

19 Anonymous

I cannot, though I want me to, be your friend.
You never ask or give me what I ask
or take what I am giving.

20 Julius Leonidas

Zeus must be dining with the Ethiopians
or turned to gold to sneak into Danaë's bedroom.
It would be a miracle if he had seen Periander
and did not carry off that darling boy.
Or does the god no longer seek the love of boys?

21 Strato

How long will we be stealing kisses,
sending secret signals, darting glances

to each other?
How much longer will we talk
without deciding anything,
piling postponement on postponement?
Delaying longer will be the death of beauty.
Phidon! Before the bristles come,
let's turn these words to deeds.

22 Scythinus

Mighty devastation, war, and conflagration have
come into my life. Elissus, ripe for love, has turned sixteen,
accompanied by every charm both great and small:
a voice that is honey to hear, lips that are honey to kiss,
and a flawless little entrance. What will become of me?
He says that I can only look. Oh I shall often lie awake at night
struggling with my hands against this phantom passion.

23 Meleager

Trapped, the one who used to laugh
at the serenades of love-sick youngsters.
Myiscus, winged Love has nailed me to your gate.
The inscription reads "the spoils of chastity."

24 Tullius Laureas

If Polemo comes back to me, safe and sound,
just as he was, Apollo, when we sent him on his way,
I do not refuse to sacrifice upon your altar
the bird, that herald of the dawn, the one
I promised in my prayers to you.
If he returns with more or less of anything
than he had then, my promise is no longer binding.
He came back with a beard.
If he prayed for such a prize himself, exact
your sacrifice from him who made that prayer.

25 Statyllius Flaccus (Poems 25–27)

When I said goodbye to Polemo, I prayed, Apollo,
for his safe return, and I vowed to sacrifice a bird to you.
But Polemo came back all hairy-chinned.
No, Phoebus, he did not come to me, I swear it,
no, he fled from me with bitter speed.
I will no longer sacrifice a cock to you.
Don't cheat me by returning chaff for wheat.

26

If Polemo, the one whom I sent off, returned
undamaged, then I promised you a sacrifice.
But Polemo came back saved for himself.
This person who arrived is Polemo no more.
Bearded, he is not undamaged, not for me.
Perhaps he prayed for such a darkened chin.
Then let him make the sacrifice himself,
since he requested something counter to my hopes.

27

When I bid Polemo adieu (his cheeks like yours),
I promised I would sacrifice a bird to you
if he came back. Apollo, I do not take him back,
not with cheeks rough with malicious bristles.
What a fool I was to make a vow for such a man!
It seems unfair to pluck a guiltless cock in vain,
unless, Apollo, Polemo is plucked as well.

28 Numenius of Tarsus

Cyrus is a lord [kyrios]. So what if he is missing a letter?
I don't want to read his beauty, just to look on it.

29 Alcaeus (Poems 29–30)

Protarchus is lovely,
but he does not want to be.

Later he will want to be,
and his youthfulness races on,
holding out a torch.

30

Your leg, Nicander dear, is getting hairy.
Beware of bristles in your backside.
Then you'll know how fickle lovers are.
Now ponder this: youth cannot be recalled.

31 *Phanias*

By Themis and the bowl of wine that made me dizzy,
your love, Pamphilus, is running out of time.
Your thigh is hairy and your cheeks are sprouting.
Desire lures you toward another kind of passion.
For now, since tiny traces of the spark remain,
don't hoard them. Opportunity is the friend of Love.

32 *Thymocles*

You remember, you remember when
I spoke this holy verse to you:
"Springtime is the loveliest
and the fleetingist season."
The swiftest bird in the sky
cannot fly faster than spring.
Look, now, how all your blossoms
have fallen on the ground.

33 *Meleager*

Heraclitus was handsome when there was a Heraclitus.
Now that he is past his prime a leather screen
deters those who would mount the walls.
When you see this, son of Polyxenus, do not feel too superior.
Nemesis grows in more places than the cheeks.

34 Automedon

I had dinner yesterday with Demetrius,
the luckiest man there is: he serves as trainer
to the boys. One sat there on his lap,
another leaned over his shoulder, one brought
him a bite to eat, another something to drink—
a charming quartet. I teased him, asking
"Friend, do you also train the boys at night?"

35 Diocles

Someone said this to a boy who failed to greet him.
"So Damon, who excels in beauty, no longer says hello.
A time will come when this will be avenged.
Then you'll be shaggy and you will volunteer 'hello'
to those who will not greet you in return."

36 Asclepiades of Samos

Now you are willing when the tender growth is creeping
down your temple and a prickly growth invades your thighs.
Then you say "I like this better." But who would say
that he prefers dry stubble to the tender stalks?

37 Dioscorides

Love, the murderer, was playing when he fashioned
Sosarchus' rump as pliable as marrow.
He wanted to annoy great Zeus because his thighs
are sweeter than the thighs of Ganymede.

38 Rhianus

The Hours and the Graces shed sweet oil on you,
dear buttocks. You disturb the sleeping even of old men.
Tell me, to whom do you belong? Which of the boys
do you adorn? It answered me, "Menecrates."

39 Anonymous

Nicander's light is out. The bloom has left his cheeks.
Not even in name do his charms survive.
And we once counted him among the gods.
Young men, do not ignore the limits of
mortality: hairs are on the way.

40 Anonymous

Do not remove my cloak. Gaze at me as if I were
a statue: the body wood, the rest of marble.
If you wish to see the naked charm of Antiphilus,
you will find a rose-bud growing there.

41 Meleager

Thero does not seem so lovely any more.
Apollodorus, once a flame, now seems a burnt-out torch.
I love women. I leave it to the goat-humpers
to put the squeeze on hairy bottoms.

42 Dioscorides

Visit Hermogenes the boyhawk with your hands full,
and perhaps you will achieve your heart's desire,
maybe even relax the furrows on your melancholy brow.
But if you fish for him and use an empty hook,
you'll pull water, nothing more, out of the harbor.
The spendthrift faggot harbors neither shame nor pity.

43 Callimachus

I hate poems about the same old stories.
I don't like roads that carry too much traffic.
I hate a lover who has been around,
and I do not drink from fountains.
The vulgar and the commonplace disgust me.
Lysanias, you are another lovely, lovely boy.
But before I say that clearly comes
the echo answering "another's lover."

44 Glaucus

Long ago it happened that young boys
who wanted presents were quite satisfied
with quails or balls or knuckle-bones.
But now they want a fancy meal and coins.
The toys of yesterday have lost their power.
Look for something else, boy-lovers.

45 Posidippus

Go on and shoot me, Loves. I stand here by myself,
a target available to all. Don't spare me, silly boys,
for if you conquer me, you will gain immortal fame
as masters of a mighty quiver.

46 Asclepiades

I am not even twenty-two, and bored.
Loves, why this mistreatment? Why set me on fire?
What will you do if I die? No doubt, silly Loves,
you'll go back to playing knuckle-bones.

47 Meleager (Poems 47–49)

A baby in his mother's lap, in the morning
Love played dice and gambled away my life.

48

I'm down. Step on my neck, fierce demon.
I know you, by the gods, I know your weight.
I know your flaming arrows. But if you try
to torch my heart, you'll start no fire.
It's nothing but ashes now.

49

Drink wine, unhappy lover, and Bacchus, the god
who grants forgetting, will lull to sleep
the burning of your longing for that boy.

Drink, drain the cup of wine and drive
the pain that you abhor out of your heart.

50 Asclepiades

Drink, Asclepiades. Why these tears? What's wrong?
You're not the only one cruel Aphrodite has ensnared.
Bitter Love is sharpening his arrows for others too.
You are alive: why are you lying in the dust?
Let's share some wine. Life is but a finger's width.
Shall we wait for the lamp that says it's time
to go to bed? Let's drink, sad lover.
Poor soul, the time is not that far away
when we will sleep the long, long night away.

51 Callimachus

Pour the wine and say again, "To Diocles."
Let the ladles dedicated to the river god
remain untouched. The boy is beautiful, Achelous,
too beautiful. If anyone should disagree,
then I alone would know what beauty is.

52 Meleager (Poems 52–54)

The south wind, favorable for sailors,
has carried off Andragathus, half of my soul.
Three times happy are the ship, fortunate the waves,
and four times blessed is the wind that moves the boy.
I wish I were a dolphin, to bear him on my shoulders
across the sea to gaze on Rhodes, land of honeyed boys.

53

Wealth-bearing ocean ships that sail the Hellespont,
embracing as you go the fair North Wind,
if by chance you see there on the beach of Cos
Phanion looking out upon the glistening sea,
give her this message, noble ships: Desire
brings me there, not on a ship, but walking.

For if you tell her this, kind messengers,
Zeus will at once breathe fair winds for your sails.

54

The Cyprian denies that she gave birth to Love,
now that she sees a second Love, the youth Antiochus.
Young men, love this new Desire; for in truth
this boy has proved a grander love than Love.

55 Anonymous

Child of Leto, son of mighty Zeus,
speaker of the oracles to everyone,
you are lord of sea-surrounded Delos.
But Echedemus is the lord of Athens,
a second Phoebus, the boy whom Love, the god
with gentle curls, illumined with a radiant bloom.
His city, Athens, once ruled sea and land,
but now enslaves all Hellas with his beauty.

56 Meleager (Poems 56–57)

Praxiteles the sculptor carved a marble statue
fashioning the son of Aphrodite, Love.
Now Love, the fairest of the gods, portrays himself
by fashioning Praxiteles, then animating his creation,
so one on earth and one among the gods dispenses passion,
and Love may have dominion over mortals
just as in the heavens. Sacred city of the Meropes,
how blessed you are for nurturing a godborn child,
this new Love to offer guidance to young men.

57

Praxiteles the sculptor made a likeness once.
He carved the stone to form an image delicate
but lifeless, a silent image of the beautiful.
Today's Praxiteles, whose magic fashions living flesh,
has molded in my heart the arch-rogue—Love.

By chance they share a name, but his art is grander.
He has transformed, not marble, but my inner being.
May he be gracious as he shapes my character,
to have within me after he has molded it
a holy place for Love: my soul.

58 Rhianus

Troezen nurtures well. You would not be wrong
if you were to praise the least of her young boys.
Empedocles surpasses every one of them just as
the rose outshines the other flowers in the spring.

59 Meleager (Poems 59–60)

Tyre nurtures gentle boys, I swear by Love.
But the sunburst of Myiscus extinguishes the stars.

60

If I set eyes on Thero, I see everything;
but if I gaze on everything but him,
then I do not see anything at all.

61 Anonymous

Look! Do not dissolve Cnidos so completely,
Aribazus. The stone is crumbling.

62 Anonymous

Persian mothers, you bear lovely, lovely children;
But Aribazus seems to me more beautiful than Beauty.

63 Meleager

Heraclitus sends a silent message with his eyes:
"I will inflame the lightning bolts of Zeus."
Yes, and the voice of Diodorus says, "And I
melt rocks warmed by my body's touch."

Unhappy he who has received a torch from
Heraclitus' glance, and from the other
a sweet flame smoldering with passion.

64 Alcaeus

Zeus, lord of Pisa, at Olympus crown
Peithenor, second son of Aphrodite.
Lord, please do not become an eagle, swooping down
to seize him as replacement for your Trojan boy.
If I have ever brought you from the Muses any gift
that pleased you, grant me that the godlike boy
have thoughts in harmony with mine.

65 Meleager

If Zeus is still the god who kidnapped Ganymede
to have a boy to bear the cups of nectar,
then I will hide the fair Myiscus in my heart
before the god eludes me and swoops down on him.

66 Anonymous

Loves, you judge whom the boy deserves.
If truly he deserves a god, then so be it.
I will not compete with Zeus.
But if a piece is left for mortals too,
Loves, tell me, please, whose Dorotheus was
and to whom he now belongs.
They make it clear that I am favored. But he leaves.
I hope that you are not, like me, enticed in vain to beauty.

67 Anonymous

I do not see the handsome Dionysius.
Father Zeus, has he been snatched away
to be a second Ganymede for the gods?
Tell me, eagle, when your wings beat over him,
how did you carry off the charming boy?
Did your claws leave any marks on him?

68 Meleager

I don't wish Charidemus for myself.
The handsome boy has set his sight on Zeus
as if already serving nectar to the god.
I do not want him. What good would it do me
to compete in love with the king of the gods?
It is enough for me if, as he climbs Olympus,
the boy takes from the earth my tears to use for washing,
a token of our love. Perhaps he might give me
one sweet and melting glance and let me snatch
one fleeting kiss. Let Zeus, as is correct,
have all the rest. And yet, if he were willing,
perhaps I too would have a brief taste of ambrosia.

69 Anonymous

Enjoy, Zeus, your old Ganymede. Lord, from a distance
gaze at my Dexandrus. I don't mind. But if you take
the darling boy away by force, no longer is your tyranny
endurable. I choose death before life under you.

70 Meleager

I will stand up to Zeus himself, Myiscus,
if he wants to kidnap you to serve him nectar.
And yet Zeus has often told me, "What are you
afraid of? I will not destroy you out of jealousy.
I too have suffered. I have learned compassion."
That's what he says, but even if I hear a fly,
I shudder, fearful that great Zeus was lying.

71 Callimachus

Thessalian Cleonicus, you poor poor man!
By the glaring sun, I swear I did not know you!
Where have you been? You are nothing but hair and bones.
Have you been possessed by a demon? Punished by the gods?
I know, Euxitheus has snared you. You rascal,
you were staring at the darling when you came here.

72 Meleager

Sweet dawn is here, and sleepless on the porch
Damis exhales what little breath remains to him.
Poor soul, he has set eyes on Heraclitus.
Standing in the rays from Heraclitus' eyes,
he was like wax thrown onto glowing coals.
Wake up now, Damis the unfortunate! I also bear
the wounds of Love, and I shed tears for yours.

73 Callimachus

Merely half my soul still breathes. The other half?
It has disappeared, seized by Love perhaps—or Death.
Has it run off again to see some boy? How many times
I told them, "Young men, don't let in the runaway."
Go look for it. I know my lovesick soul, my soul
deserving death by stoning, must be somewhere.

74 Meleager

If I die, Cleobulus (for hurled into the flame
of loving boys, I lie here in the ash heap),
intoxicate the urn before you place it in the ground,
and write on it "the gift of Love to Death."

75 Asclepiades

If you had wings, a bow and arrows in your hand,
then you, not Love, would be proclaimed the son of Aphrodite.

76 Meleager

If Love had neither bow nor wings nor quiver,
and did not have the flame-dipped arrows of desire,
you could not tell by looking (I swear this by the winged boy
himself) which of the two is Love, and which is Zoilus.

77 *Asclepiades*

If you grew golden wings and on your silver shoulders
were to place a quiver filled with arrows, then stood
by splendid Love, dear boy, I swear by Hermes that
the goddess Aphrodite would not know which was her son.

78 *Meleager*

If Love should wear a chlamys and petasus, and if
Love had no wings or bow and quiver on his back,
I swear this by the splendid youth himself,
Antiochus would be Love and Love Antiochus.

79 *Anonymous*

Antipater kissed me when my love was cooling,
and rekindled ardor from the tepid ashes.
So I encountered twice (unwillingly) one flame.
Sad lovers, flee! I burn those who come close to me.

80 *Meleager (Poems 80–86)*

Sad weeping soul, why is that dormant wound of Love
again ignited, coursing through your body?
No! No! For God's sake, no! You do not take advice,
but don't stir up the flame that glows beneath the ashes.
You, forgetful of past pain! If Love recaptures you,
a runaway, he will punish you unmercifully.

81

Lovesick self-deceivers, you who know the burn
of boy-love, who have tasted bitter honey,
pour cold water on my heart. Quickly now!
Ice water! Water from newly melted snow!
I have dared to look at Dionysius. My fellow slaves,
before it reaches vital organs, put this fire out.

82

I ran away from Love, but he lit a tiny torch
that he made from ashes, and he found me hiding.
He did not bend his bow but pinched a spark of fire
and threw it at me while I wasn't looking.
From it arose the flames that now surround me.
Phanion, you are the spark who lit a fire in my heart.

83

Love did not wound me with an arrow, nor (as before)
did he light a torch and hold it to my heart.
This time he used a tiny love-torch with a scented flame,
companion to the reveling Desires. He touched the flame-tip
to my eyes. The blaze consumed me. The little torch,
incandescent in my heart, became the fire of my soul.

84

Men, save me! I have just set foot on land,
safe after my first voyage on the waves; and now
Love drags me here by force. As if he held
a torch in front of me, he turns my gaze
upon the beauty of this boy. I follow in his footsteps.
To his sweet image in the air I give sweet kisses.
Have I escaped the bitter ocean just to cross
on foot the far more bitter sea of Aphrodite?

85

Admit me, drinkers! I have just come ashore, safe from
the sea and pirates, only to perish on the land.
No sooner had I placed my first step on the solid ground
than I was captured, dragged here forcibly by Love.
And here is where I saw the boy walk through the gate.
My feet now bear me swiftly on their own, against my will.
I join you, but my heart is gorged with fire, not with wine.
Friends, strangers: help me out a little. Help me,
strangers. In the name of Love, the god of Guests,
admit me. I am close to death and beg your friendship.

86

A woman, Aphrodite, inflames us with desire for women,
but it is Love himself who governs our desire for males.
Which way for me? To the boy or to his mother? I say
that even she admits "the cheeky boy prevails."

87 Anonymous

Cruel Love, you never strike me with desire for women,
but only with the lightning bolt of fever for a male.
Now burned by Damon, now looking at Ismenos,
I am tortured by persistent pain. And these
are not the only ones on whom I've cast my gaze.
My roving eye is lured into the snares of quite a few.

88 Anonymous

Two loves pour down on me and wear me down,
Eumachus. I am battered by two frenzies.
I lean now toward Asander; now my eye,
its vision sharpened, turns to Telephus.
Cut me in half (this would delight me),
divide my limbs by lot, and carry them away.

89 Anonymous

Why, Aphrodite, shoot three arrows at one target?
Why have you buried three weapons in one soul?
On one side I am burning, on the other torn apart.
I have no notion where to turn, and I
am burned to ashes in the fiery turbulence.

90 Anonymous

I love no more. I have wrestled with three passions:
one for a courtesan, one for a girl, one for a boy.
They torture me; for I have labored to persuade
the lady's doors (foes of the empty-handed) to swing open.
I make my bed, all sleepless on the maiden's couch,
and give her just one thing (the most desired): kisses.

Alas! How shall I speak of that third flame? From it
I have earned only glances and vain hopes.

91 Polystratus

A double passion burns a single soul. Oh eyes
that gaze at everything that is remarkable!
You saw Antiochus, glittering with golden charms,
Antiochus the flower of our radiant youth.
Let him suffice. Why also gaze on gentle, sweet
Stasicrates, the stripling of violet-crowned Aphrodite?
Set yourself on fire, blaze, burn down to ashes.
The two of you would not desire a single soul.

92 Meleager

Betrayers of the soul, boy-hunting hounds: my eyes!
Your glances always smeared with bird-lime, you
have caught another Love, the way sheep catch a wolf,
or crows a scorpion, or ashes trap flames smoldering below.
Do what you wish. Why rain down tears and then
go running back at once to Hiketas?
Roast in beauty, burn to a crisp now.
Love is a master chef of the soul.

93 Rhianus

Boys are a labyrinth with no escape. Your eye,
wherever it alights, is snared as if with bird-lime.
Now Theodorus lures you to his plump, ripe flesh,
lures you to the unspoiled blossom of his body.
Here is the golden countenance of Philocles,
not tall, and yet enveloped by a heavenly charm.
But if you turn to look at Leptines, then you
stand still, as if held fast by chains of steel.
Such fire flashes from his eyes that he lights up
from head to toe. Hurrah for handsome boys!
May you all reach the prime of youth
and live until your hair turns white.

94 Meleager (Poems 94–95)

Diodorus is a joy, and everyone stares at Heraclitus.
Dion is sweet-spoken, and Uliades has shapely loins.
Philocles, go on and touch the soft-skinned boy.
Gaze at another, chat with one, and the fourth . . . whatever.
Then you will understand my lack of jealousy. But if
you look with lust at Myiscus,
then I hope you never see the beautiful again.

95

If the Passions and Persuasion of the honeyed breath
and the Graces with their garlands favor you,
my dear Philocles, then may you hug young Diodorus.
May sweet Dorotheus stand in front of you and sing,
and may Callicrates recline there on your knee.
And Dio, may he use his hand to warm the horn
that you are so adept at thrusting, and may Uliades
unfetter it. Let Philo grant sweet kisses
and Thero chatter on while you are squeezing
Eudemus' nipples, reaching underneath his cloak.
And if the gods grant you all these delights,
oh what a Roman casserole of boys you will concoct.

96 Anonymous

This well-known proverb is by no means foolish:
"The gods did not give everything to everyone."
Your shape is faultless, your eyes aglow with modesty,
your breast suffused with gracefulness. With all
these gifts you conquer young men, but the gods
did not grant you the gift of graceful feet.
This boot, dear Pyrrhus, will conceal your foot
and give you joy as you peruse its beauty.

97 Antipater

Eupalamus is rosy red (like Love) down to
his thighs. From there down to his feet
he is no longer ruddy. Now see how envious

Nature, mother of us all, can be.
If he were, down below, as good as up above,
he would be even nobler than Achilles.

98 Posidippus

After Passion tied the Muses' soul, he wished
it to lie down on thorns and held a torch
against its side. The soul, however, since
it had suffered much in books before, ignoring
other pains, told off the ruthless god.

99 Anonymous

I am snared by Love—I, who never dreamed of this,
who never felt a male flame hot within my heart.
I'm snared. It was no wish for anything illicit,
it was a glance in innocence (shame's foster brother)
that burned me to a crisp. Let the protracted labor
of the Muses burn away. My mind is in the fire,
and it bears the burden of a sweet distress.

100 Anonymous

What is this foreign harbor of desire to which
you bring me, Aphrodite, showing me no pity
though you yourself have knowledge of this pain?
Do you want me to feel the unendurable and say
"Aphrodite, alone, has wounded the Muses' sage?"

101 Meleager

I was unwounded by the Passions, but Myiscus shot me,
with his eyes, under my breast. Then he declared,
"I have brought down his insolence. Behold, I place
my foot upon the arrogance of sceptered wisdom that
once adorned his brow." But I regained my breath
enough to say to him, "Dear boy, why your amazement?
Love brought great Zeus himself down from Olympus."

102 *Callimachus*

In the hills the hunter Epicydes follows every hare
and finds the tracks that every deer leaves in the frost
and snow. But if someone should say to him,
"Look, a beast lies here, already shot," he would not take it.
Such is my love: prone to pursue the fleeing game,
it flies past anything directly in its path.

103 *Anonymous*

This I know: to love my friends. This I have learned:
to hate whoever wrongs me. In neither am I inexperienced.

104 *Anonymous*

Let my love abide with me alone; but if
it visits others, Aphrodite, I despise shared love.

105 *Asclepiades*

A tiny love, still catchable, I flew off from my mother.
But from the house of Damis I will not fly off.
Here, loving and beloved without a rival,
I live, not in a crowd, but in harmony with one.

106 *Meleager*

I know one beauty. It is everything to me.
My greedy eye knows one thing only: to see
Myiscus. I am blind to other things.
For me, all things are manifest in him.
Do the eyes, those sycophants, look only
on what offers pleasure to the soul?

107 *Anonymous*

If handsome Dionysius chooses me, then, Graces,
lead him through the seasons, ever handsome.
But if, bypassing me, he loves another, let him be
a shriveled berry, swept out with the garbage.

108 Dionysius

Acratus, if you love me, may you be as fine
as Chian wine—no, sweeter still than Chian.
But if you choose another, I hope the gnats
will buzz about you as they do near vinegar.

109 Meleager (Poems 109–110)

The gentle Diodorus, hurling flames at young men,
has been captured by Timarion's wanton eyes.
Implanted in him is Love's arrow, bittersweet.
I see a marvel: fire blazing, scorched by fire.

110

His sweet beauty flashes, flame darts from his eyes.
Has Love produced a boy armed with the thunderbolt?
Myiscus, greetings! You bring the Passions' radiance
to mortals. Shine on earth, a torch benign to me.

111 Anonymous

Love has his wings, but you are swift of foot. The loveliness
of both is quite the same. Eubius, all we lack are bows.

112 Anonymous

Young men, be quiet. Arcesilaus is leading Love.
He bound him with the purple cord of Aphrodite.

113 Meleager (Poems 113–114)

The winged Love himself was captured in mid-air,
enchanted by your eyes, Timarion.

114

Herald of the dawn! Greetings, Morning Star!
Come back quickly as the Evening Star,
and secretly return her whom you take from me.

115 *Anonymous*

I have drunk pure madness. Intoxicated with my words,
I have armed myself with folly for my journey.
I will carouse there. Thunderbolts and lightning? No concern.
If he throws them, I have love as my impenetrable shield.

116 *Anonymous*

I will go carousing: I am very drunk.
Boy, take this wreath drenched with my tears.
Although the road is long, I will not go in vain.
It is the middle of the night and dark,
but Themison is torch enough for me.

117 *Meleager*

The die is cast. Light the torch. I'm on my way.
Wow: the daring of a drunkard. What's your worry?
I'm off to carouse, I'm off to carouse.
Mind, where are you off to? Does love need explanation?
Light it now! And where is your former concern for reason?
Farewell to long labor devoted to wisdom.
One thing I know and one thing alone:
that Love has defeated even Zeus's resolve.

118 *Callimachus*

If I came here on purpose to party, Archinus,
reproach me at length. If I came, though unwilling,
then observe my compulsion: love and strong wine.
The one dragged me here, the other clouded my mind.
I arrived without telling who I am or belong to.
I did kiss the doorpost. If that's a crime, then I'm guilty.

119 *Meleager*

Your boldness, Bacchus, I swear I will bear it.
Begin the carousing: a god, you govern a mortal heart.
Born in the fire, you love love's flames,
and once more you bind me and drive me, your suppliant.

You are a traitor, a god who is not to be trusted.
You say that your secrets must always stay hidden,
and meanwhile you wish to expose all of mine.

120 Posidippus

I am well armed. I will fight with you and stand my ground,
though I am but a mortal. And you, Love, stop attacking me.
If you find me drunk, then take me captive. But as long as I
am sober, I have Reason in the battle line against you.

121 Rhianus

Cleonicus, now tell me, did the Graces meet you while
you strolled along a narrow path? Did they
embrace you in their rosy arms? My boy,
is that how you became so graceful?
I greet you from a distance. It is not safe
for a dry husk, dear boy, to come too near the fire.

122 Meleager

You Graces looked at handsome Aristagoras,
then placed your gentle arms around him.
Now fire flashes from his comeliness.
He speaks, when the occasion calls, with elegance;
and even silent holds delightful conversations with his eyes.
Please, keep him far away from me. And yet to what avail?
Like Zeus, the boy has learned to cast his lightning from afar.

123 Anonymous

When Menecharmus, son of Anticles, emerged the victor
in the boxing match, ten times I placed a crown on him,
three times I kissed him though he was all smeared with blood.
That blood to me was sweeter than sweet myrrh.

124 *Anonymous*

I stole a kiss from Echydemus, a charmer just about
to reach his prime, as he stole glances from the doorway.
Now I'm afraid. He visited my dreams last night:
he wore a quiver, but he gave me fighting cocks before
he left. He was friendly sometimes, sometimes surly.
Have I touched a swarm of bees, a nettle and a flame?

125 *Meleager (Poems 125–128)*

Love came at night and placed beneath my covers
the sweet dream of a laughing boy, eighteen years old,
still wearing the chlamys. I hugged his tender flesh
to mine, and savored empty hopes. The desire fostered by
that memory still warms me, and in my eyes I keep
the sleep that snared for me that winged phantom.
My unrequited soul, cease, even in your dreams,
to warm yourself, in vain, with images of beauty.

126

The pain has just now reached my heart; for hot Love,
as he wandered by, scratched me with his fingernail.
He smiled and said, "You'll have a sweet wound
once again, sad lover, burned by swirling honey."
And then I saw among the youths the stripling Diophantus,
and I can neither stay nor run away.

127

I saw Alexis walking on the road at noontime,
when summer's fruitful tresses are just being cut.
Twin rays burned into me: some came from the sun,
some were rays of love from the young lad's eyes.
Night put the former rays to sleep; but in my dreams
the rays of love flared up in images of beauty.
Sleep, that releases other men from toil, brought pain:
an imagined beauty that was, for my soul, a living fire.

128

Pastoral pipes, invoke no longer Daphnis in the mountains,
delighting Pan, the goat-mounting god.
You, lyre, spokesman of Apollo, no longer sing
of Hyacinthus, crowned with virgin laurel.
Daphnis, while he lived, delighted Mountain Nymphs,
and Hyacinthus delighted you. Now Dion rules the Passions.

129 Aratus

At Argos, Argive Philocles is "handsome"; the same phrase
is engraved on columns at Corinth and tombstones at Megara.
He is inscribed as "handsome" as far as the baths of Amphiaraus.
That's not so much, and we are left merely with letters.
While stones proclaim the beauty of this Philocles,
Rhianus saw him with his eyes; that evidence is stronger.

130 Anonymous

I said, and I repeated. "He is handsome, handsome."
I will still say Dositheus is handsome and has
sparkling eyes. I did not write this on an oak or pine
or on a wall. Love burned it on my heart. If anyone
denies it, don't believe him. I swear that he's a liar,
and I who say this am the only one who knows the truth.

131 Posidippus

Goddess, you who visit Cypris, Cythera, Miletus,
and the lovely plain of Scythia where hooves resound,
please come in kindness to Callistion,
who never drove a lover from her door.

132 Meleager (Poems 132–133)

Soul, I told you, didn't I, "By Aphrodite, you'll be snared,
you lovesick soul who fly back to the lime-smeared branch?"
Didn't I? And you are caught. Why struggle vainly in
your bonds? For Love himself has tied your wings and placed

you on the fire. He spinkled you with unguents when you fainted
and gives you, when you thirst, hot tears to drink.

133

I kissed the soft-skinned boy in summer (I was thirsty),
and said, once I had slaked my parching thirst,
"Zeus, father, do you drink the nectared kiss of Ganymede?
Is this the wine that he serves to your lips?"
For now that I have kissed Antiochus, the flower
of our youth, I have drunk the sweet honey of the soul.

134 Callimachus

We did not notice our guest's wound. Did you fail to see
how painfully he heaved a sigh from deep within his chest
when he drank that third cup? And all the roses on
his wreaths first dropped their petals, then fell to the ground.
Some fire scorches him. This is not a guess, by god.
A thief myself, I recognize the footprints of a thief.

135 Asclepiades

Wine is the proof of love. Nicagoras denied he was in love,
but all those toasts he made betrayed him. Oh yes, he wept
and hung his head and stared down at the ground.
The wreath wrapped round his head refused to stay in place.

136 Anonymous

Chattering birds, why are you making so much noise?
You nightingales perched among the leaves,
don't bother me as I lie here, warmed by the boy's soft flesh.
You females, sleep, I beg you. Please shut up.

137 Meleager

Dawn crier, bad-news-bringer to the lovelorn, triple-cursed,
you shriek in the darkness, beat your wings against your sides,
smirking there above my bed. You do this now, when oh so brief

a chance for nighttime loving still survives. And now you sweetly
mock my suffering. Is this the thanks I get
for feeding you? I swear by this drab dawn: this is
the last time you will sing your bitter melody.

138 Mnasalcas

Vine, do you rush to drop your leaves upon the ground
because you fear the setting of the Pleiades?
Wait until sweet sleep embraces Antileon, there in your shade.
Please wait, you who bestow all favors on the fair.

139 Callimachus

There is, I swear by Pan, some fire hidden, yes I swear
by Dionysus, some fire hidden underneath the ashes.
I do not trust myself. Do not embrace me. A gentle stream
has often undermined a wall at its foundation.
And now I fear, Menexenus, that stealthy passion
may creep into me and make me fall in love.

140 Anonymous

When I saw handsome Archestratus, I said (I swear by Hermes)
that he was not so handsome. He did not look like much to me.
The words were hardly spoken. Nemesis then seized me,
and all at once I lay there in the fire, while like a boy
Zeus rained his lightning bolts on me. Shall I ask the boy
or ask the goddess for compassion? I think the boy
is stronger than the goddess. Nemesis, goodbye.

141 Meleager

My courageous soul, by Aphrodite, you have stated what
a god would not: to you Thero does not seem handsome.
Thero does not seem handsome to you. You brought this on
yourself, not fearing even Zeus's thunderbolt.
Now somber Nemesis has made you an example (you who used
to talk so much), for all to see, of braggadocio.

142 Rhianus

Dexionicus once caught a blackbird, by using lime,
beneath a plane-tree. He held it by its wings
while the sacred bird cried out in loud complaint.
But I, dear Love and blooming Graces, I would like
to be a thrush or blackbird in his hand.
Then both my voice and my sweet tears would flow.

143 Anonymous

. . . "I met the same fate, stranger. My passion for
Apollophanes is destroying me." "You have passed me,
athlete. The two of us have jumped into one fire."

144 Meleager

Deceiver, why the weeping? Why have you removed
your savage bow and arrows, folding up your wings?
Does invincible Myiscus burn you also with his eyes?
How hard to learn by suffering what you once did to others!

145 Anonymous

Boy lovers, cease your vain endeavors. Rest from your toil,
you madmen. We are insane with unrequited hopes.
To seek the love of boys, why that's to bail the sea
onto the shore or count the grains of desert sand.
Yet gods and men both find their haughty beauty sweet.
Look at me, everyone! My futile efforts in the past
have been like pouring water on an arid beach.

146 Rhianus

I lost the fawn I captured. After all my careful work
in setting up the traps I'm left with empty hands.
And those who did not work at all leave with my quarry.
Love, I hope that you treat them severely.

147 Meleager

Kidnapped! Who is cruel enough to hurt her?
Rash enough to challenge Love himself?
Quick! Light torches! Wait—a footstep.
Heliodora's! Heart, climb back into my chest.

148 Callimachus (Poems 148–150)

I know that I come empty-handed, but please, Menippus,
by the Graces, don't tell me my dream. It hurts
to hear the bitter tale from start to finish.
Of all the ways you treat me, this is the most unloving.

149

You will be caught, Menexenus. Try to escape. I said this
on the twentieth of August. On September—what?—the tenth,
the ox accepted, of his own accord, the yoke. Well done,
my Hermes! The twenty days it took is no cause for complaint.

150

What an effective charm for lovers Polyphemus found!
By Mother Earth, that Cyclops was no ignoramus.
The Muses make a lover waste away, Philippus.
Wisdom is the medicine for every illness.
The only thing that hunger has to recommend it
is that it cures the sickness of our love for boys.
I have good reason to declare to Love,
"Your wings are being clipped, young fellow.
I'm not afraid of you, not in the least."
At home I have both charms for that deep wound.

151 Anonymous

If you saw among the boys the one who was the most
desirable, without a doubt you saw Apollodotus.
If once you saw him, stranger, you were not inflamed
with passion, then you must be a god—or made of stone.

152 *Anonymous*

My darling Heraclitus is a magnet. He attracts
not iron to a stone but my soul to beauty.

153 *Asclepiades*

Once Archeades liked to touch me. Now he hardly turns
my way, not even when we're playing. I'm so unhappy!
Not even honeyed Love is always sweet. But often he
becomes a sweeter god for lovers by tormenting them.

154 *Meleager*

The boy is sweet; his name is even sweet and full of charm:
Myiscus. What reason could I offer for not loving him?
He is beautiful, by Aphrodite, beautiful in every way. And if
he hurts me, Love likes mixing bitterness with honey.

155 *Anonymous*

Don't say that again. (How is it my fault? He sent me.)
You're repeating it? (I'll repeat it. He said: go.
Please don't delay, they're expecting you.) I'll go when
I see them. I know from before what comes next.

156 *Anonymous*

My love is like a thunderstorm in springtime, Diodorus,
responding to the gloomy sea. At times you show
me darkened clouds, at other times the heavens clear;
you smile, and a gentleness flows from your eyes.
Like a shipwrecked sailor in the turbulence, measuring
the waves that blot the sky, I'm battered by the awful storm.
Show me a landmark. Indicate your friendship or your hatred.
Let me know what kind of sea this is in which I swim.

157 *Meleager (Poems 157–159)*

Aphrodite is the pilot. Love controls the tiller,
holding in his hand the rudder of my soul.

Passion is the grievous gale that tosses me,
for I am swimming in a sea that teems with boys.

158

The goddess, Queen of Passions, gave me to you, Theocles.
Soft-sandaled Love threw me, a stranger in a strange land,
naked on the ground, and placed the sharp bit in my mouth.
I long to find a friendship without subjugation.
But you reject the man who loves you. Not time
nor tokens of our shared affection softens you.
Have mercy, lord, have mercy! Fate made you divine.
You have the power over me of life and death.

159

The cable of my life, Myiscus, is attached to you.
In you resides the breath remaining in my soul.
For by your eyes, boy, that speak even to the deaf,
and by your radiant brow I swear that if your eyes
are clouded over, I have seen the winter, but if
your gaze is tender, the sweet spring blossoms.

160 Anonymous

Bravely I will bear excruciating pain, endure
the cruelty of confinement by these fetters.
Nicander, I am not a novice in the wounds of love,
but I have tasted passion many times.
Nemesis, the harshest of the gods, and
Adrateia, repay with vengeance his malevolence.

161 Asclepiades (Poems 161–163)

As if she were a tender boy, Dorcion, who enjoys young men,
knows how to cast the lure of Vulgar Aphrodite, knows how
to kindle passion with her eyes . . . she wears a petasus,
her chlamys offers glimpses of her naked thigh.

162

My love is not cruel, nor does he have a bow.
A tiny child, he returns to Aphrodite carrying
a golden tablet. From this he lisps the love-charms
used by Philocrates to win the soul of Antigenes.

163

Love has learned what beauties mix the best:
not emerald with gold (which neither sparkles nor
is its equal), not ivory with ebony
(not white with black),
but Cleander with Eubiotus,
two buds of Friendship and Persuasion.

164 Meleager (Poems 164–165)

Mingling wine with sugared honey sweetens,
and when two boys who love are fair, that sweetens love,
just as Alexis now adores soft-haired Cleobulus.
The two of them are the immortal honeywine of Aphrodite.

165

Cleobulus: a snow-white blossom. Sopolis: there next to him,
is honey-colored. They are two flower-bearers of Aphrodite.
From this comes my desire for the boys. The Loves
declare they wove me out of black and white.

166 Asclepiades

Let this remnant of my soul, however small,
for god's sake, let this part at least have rest.
Or else do not shoot arrows but strike me with thunderbolts,
reduce me utterly to ashes and to cinders.
Yes, Loves, hurl them! Exhausted as I am with sadness,
I beg of you, if you will give me anything, this favor.

167 Meleager

The wind is icy, but sweet-weeping Love, Myiscus,
brings me to you on the winds of revelry.
Desire is a storm wind tossing me about. Receive me,
a sailor on the sea of Aphrodite, to your harbor.

168 Posidippus

Pour in two cupfuls (one of Nanno, one of Lyde), then pour one
of their beloved friend Mimnermus, and one of wise Antimachus.
Mix in a cup of me, and with the sixth, say,
Heliodorus, "for anyone who ever loved."
The seventh is of Hesiod, the eighth of Homer,
the ninth is of the Muses, and the tenth of Memory.
Aphrodite, now I drink this bowl filled to the brim.
Whether drunk or sober, the Loves are not unpleasant.

169 Dioscorides (Poems 169–171)

I fled from your oppression, Theodorus, but when I said,
"I have escaped the clutches of my fiercest demon,"
at once a fiercer demon caught me. Serving Aristocrates
in countless ways, I am waiting for my third enslaver.

170

Libation, Frankincense, Powers mingling in the bowl
who rule my love, I summon you as witnesses, solemn Powers.
Athenaeus, the boy with honey-colored skin, invoked you.

171

West wind, gentlest wind of all, return to me, as you
received him, the handsome traveler Euphragoras,
before more than a few months have elapsed. A brief
time, to a lover, seems a thousand years.

172 *Evenus*

If hating is pain, and loving is pain, of these
two evils I would choose the wound of noble grief.

173 *Philodemus*

Demo and Thermion are killing me: the one a courtesan,
the other one a girl who has no knowledge yet of Aphrodite.
The one I touch, the other I may not. On your name, Aphrodite,
I don't, I swear, know which of them that I desire more.
I will declare it is the virgin Demo: I do not wish
what is available, but I want anything that's being guarded.

174 *Fronto*

How long will you resist me, dearest Cyrus? What are you doing?
Do you not pity your Cambyses? Tell me. Do not become
a Medos, for in a whisker you'll be Sakas,
and hairs will transform you into Astyages.

175 *Strato (Poems 175–229)*

Either don't distrust your slave boys with your friends,
or don't provide effeminate cupbearers. Who is impervious
to love? Who does not like to ogle pretty boys?
That's what men do. If you don't like it, Diophon,
go off some place where sex and drunkenness are absent.
Once there, invite Tiresias and Tantalus to drink with you:
one looks at nothing while the other only looks.

176

Why so gloomy? Why, Menippus, does your tunic reach down to
your ankles? You used to hike it to your thighs.
Why walk right past me, silent, with that downcast look?
I know what you are hiding: I told you they would sprout.

177

Last evening, when we said good night, Moeris embraced me.
(I don't know if it really happened or I dreamed it.)
I can recall the rest precisely,
what he said to me, and what he asked.
But if he kissed me too, I just don't know. If so,
how can my feet be on the ground after my apotheosis?

178

I caught fire when Theudis shone among the other boys
the way the sun eclipses all the other stars.
I am still on fire, even though the sun is going down.
Though setting, he is still the sun.

179

Zeus, I swore to you that I would never say (not even to
myself) what Theudis told me I could have.
But my soul, which simply can't be trusted,
soaring high in joy cannot keep this secret.
Please forgive me, I will say it: he said yes!
Zeus father, what's the use of good news no one knows?

180

I'm so hot. Boy, please stop waving in the air
that napkin made of finest linen.
The wine you served ignited other sparks within me,
and you're just fanning them into a fire.

181

The myth is incorrect, Theocles, that calls the Graces good
and says that three of them live in Orchomenus.
For fifty graces dance around your countenance—
archers, thieves of other people's souls.

182

Now you give superfluous kisses, now that the fire of love
is out, and I don't even think of you as a friend.
For I remember your recalcitrance. Still, Daphnis,
late though it is, you can change your mind.

183

How can I enjoy the kisses, Heliodorus, if you
do not return them, pressing eager lips to mine?
Instead you offer lips shut tight and motionless.
I do not need you for such kisses. I could
get them from a statue that I have at home.

184

No need to use deception to seduce Menedemus.
Just signal with your eyebrows: he'll say, "Lead the way."
He won't delay: he outstrips the one who guides him.
He flows faster than an irrigation ditch—and a river.

185

These pompous boys, the ones with tunics edged
in purple, the ones that we can't reach.
They're just like ripening figs on craggy peaks.
The crows and vultures get to eat them.

186

How long will you keep up this arrogance of yours,
with not so much, dear Mentor, as "hello" for me,
as if you will stay young forever, always dance
the Pyrrhic step? Think of the future.
You'll grow a beard, the last and worst of evils.
And then you'll learn what it means to do without.

187

How will you teach the boy to sing, Dionysius,
when you are so unskilled at changing registers?
You pass too quickly from the high notes to the low,
from a limp note to a rigid one.
No slander meant. Just work at it. Strike both
and to the jealous just say Lambda and Alpha.
　　　[Sense obscure.]

188

If by kissing you I harm you, and you think it harassment,
then kiss me in return. Make that my punishment.

189

Who covered your entire head with roses? If a lover,
what a lucky fellow. If your father, he too has eyes.

190

Blessed the one who painted you, and blessed the wax
that knew how to be conquered by your beauty.
I wish I could become a crawling wood-worm.
Then I would climb up here and eat the wood.

191

Weren't you a boy just yesterday? We never dreamed your beard
was coming. How did the damned thing sprout
and cover up with hair what used to be so pretty?
A miracle! Troilus yesterday, today you're Priam.

192

Neither long hair nor excessive curls that smack
of Art, not Nature, give me pleasure.
I like a dirt-smudged boy straight from the playground,

the way the sheen of oil enhances fleshtones.
My passion prefers the unadorned. A deceptive
beauty bears the stamp of female Aphrodite.

193

You fail to understand what the Nemeses of Smyrna
are telling you, Artemidorus: "Nothing beyond proper measure."
But you are always showing off. The disdain and the cruelty
that bellow from your mouth would shame a comic actor.
Remember this, you little prig. You too will fall in love
and you will act the part of the girl who was excluded.

194

If Zeus still carried boys from earth to heaven
to serve him cups of honeyed nectar, some time ago
an eagle would have borne my beautiful Agrippa on his wings
to be the servant of the immortal gods.
I swear by you, Zeus (father of the world), if you see him
you will at once find Ganymede inadequate.

195

The flowers, fecund glory of the springtime,
in the breeze-kissed fields are not as plentiful
as are the noble boys whom you will see—all fashioned,
Dionysius, by Aphrodite and the Graces.
Conspicuous among them blooms Milesius,
like a rose that glistens with sweet-scented petals.
Perhaps he does not know, just as the flower's loveliness
is killed by heat, so is his beauty killed by hair.

196

You have sparkling eyes, divine Lycinus; or rather,
lord and master, you have eyes that shoot out flames.
I cannot, even for a moment, look you in the face,
so dazzling is the lightning from your eyes.

197

"Know the proper moment," one of the seven sages said,
Philippus. All things are more alluring in their prime.
A cucumber, seen in the garden patch, is prized;
but when it ripens we feed it to the swine.

198

I am a friend of youth. I will not, as a judge of beauty,
declare one boy the best. Each has his charms.

199

I am quite drunk enough. My mind and tongue
have loosened their restraints.
The lamp burns with a double flame, and by my count
(though I keep recounting) all the guests are twins.
Not only am I smitten by the boy who serves the wine,
but (with bad timing) I keep looking for the Water-bearer too.
　　　[The "Water-bearer" is a reference to the constellation Aquarius.]

200

I hate boys who resist my hugs and kisses, shout
belligerent objections, lash out with their fists.
Then too I am not much taken with a boy too pliant
once he is in my arms or too enthusiastic.
I like a boy midway between the two extremes: who knows
both how to give, and not to give himself.

201

If Cleonicus does not arrive right now,
I will never let him in my house by . . . I won't swear.
For if a dream he had dissuaded him and he appears
tomorrow, all is not lost because one day was lost.

202

Winged Love bore me through the air when I saw
your letter, Damis, announcing your arrival.
I soared from Smyrna all the way to Sardis. If Zetes
or Calais had raced with me, they would have lost.

203

You kiss me when I don't want kisses,
and don't want kisses when I give them.
When I'm gone you are inclined,
when I approach you, you decline.

204

You might say "gold for bronze" now. Playing "give and take"
are handsome Sosiades and Diocles the shaggy.
Who would compare a bramble with a rose or figs with toadstools?
Who would compare a lamb, smooth as curdled milk, with oxen?
What did you give? What did you receive from him?
Diomede gave gifts like this to Glaucus.
        [See Homer, Iliad, VI, 234ff.]

205

My neighbor's gentle little boy arouses me no little bit.
He laughs (far from naively) to signal his complicity.
But he's no more than twelve years old. The unripe grape
is left unguarded. When it ripens, look for garrisons.

206

"If you agree, then grab him around the waist and take him down.
Straddle him and pushing forward, lock your arms around him."
"You're crazy, Diophantes. I could barely do those moves,
but wrestling with a boy is different. Stand fast
and firm and, Cyris, lift up when I close on you.
He should practice with another before practicing by himself."

207

Last night while Diocles was bathing, up came his lizard
from the tub, his Aphrodite emerging from the foam.
And if someone had shown it long ago to Paris,
he would have liked it better than the three divine contestants.

208

Lucky little scroll, I am not jealous. Some boy
while reading you might squeeze you, touch his chin with you,
or press you to his dainty lips, or even place you on
his tender thighs to roll you up, most blessedest of scrolls.
You will often rest there on his bosom, and when he puts
you on his chair, fearless you will dare caress his bottom.
You will hold conversations all alone with him.
I beg you, little scroll, put in a word for me quite often.

209

Don't lie there next to me so sullen and so passive.
Don't be such an ordinary little boy, Diphilus.
Put some lewdness in your kisses and your foreplay:
fondle, scratch, caress me, speak to me.

210

Count as three the possibilities for two men to perform
and have performed on them in bed. Do I say something strange?
Not really. One man is in the middle, servicing two others.
He delights the man behind him and is pleasured by the other.

211

If you knew nothing of what I am trying to persuade you,
your fear would make good sense: it might be terrible.
But if your master has made you a skilled practitioner in bed,
why then do you refuse to grant this favor to another?
For he just summons you to do your duty, then dismisses you
and, as your master, doesn't even speak with you.

But here the pleasure is quite different: mutual play
and conversation, everything requested, not commanded.

212

Poor me! Why are you crying once again and so forlorn,
my boy? Speak openly. Don't torture me. What do you want?
You're holding out your open palm to me? Oh damn!
Perhaps you want some payment. Where did you learn that?
A slice of cake or honeyed sesame or little nuts
to play with: these no longer please you?
No, now your mind is set on profit. I hope he dies,
whoever taught you this. What a fine boy he has spoiled!

213

You pressed your shapely loins against the wall.
Why, Cyris, do you tease the stone? It's impotent.

214

Submit and take the coin. You will cry out "I'm rich!"
Then as a monarch would, grant me a favor.

215

Now you are spring, soon summer. What next,
dear Cyris? Think: you too will be mere stubble.

216

Now you're up and, damn it, hard, when nothing's near.
But yesterday, when something was, you went quite limp.

217

Now you're rushing off to war, an unsophisticated and
a gentle boy. What are you doing? Change your mind!
Now who persuaded you to grasp a spear? Hoist a shield?

Hide that pretty head inside a helmet?
Lucky man, whoever he may be, the new Achilles who
will enjoy himself inside the tent with this Patroclus!

218

How long must I put up with this? You only laugh
and never talk. Tell me outright, Pasiphilus.
I plead: you laugh. I ask again: no answer.
I weep: you laugh. What's so funny, boorish little boy?

219

You want to be paid in addition, teachers? How ungrateful!
Is it so little that you get to look at boys?
Converse with them? Kiss them when you say hello?
This by itself is worth a bundle, isn't it?
If anyone has pretty boys, just send them over.
Let them kiss me for whatever salary they want.

220

You are not imprisoned for your theft of fire,
my maladvised Prometheus, but because you spoiled
the clay of Zeus. When you made men, you threw in hair.
So boys grow awful beards and bristly legs. For this
the bird of Zeus, who kidnapped Ganymede, gnaws at you.
For Zeus finds beards obnoxious too.

221

Ascend to holy heaven, eagle. Off with you!
And take the boy. Go, spread your wings and fly.
Climb, holding tender Ganymede. Don't drop him,
that server of the sweetest cups for Zeus.
Be careful not to gouge him with your crooked talons.
I don't want Zeus to be upset and hurt.

222

A wrestling coach once saw his chance with a young charge.
He forced him to his knees and mounted him
while he massaged his balls. Just then by chance
the master entered, lusting for the boy. The coach
flipped the boy upon his back and straddled him,
his hands around his throat. The master,
who was not unlearned in the art of wrestling, said,
"Stop what you're doing. You are strangling the boy."

223

His charming face, as he approaches, is enough for me.
I never turn around to look as he walks past.
Thus we admire the statue of a god or temples—
from the front, but not the chambers in the rear.

224

We walked along a noble path. Consider, Diphilus,
how this can be steadfast just as it was in the beginning.
Fate gave us both a fleeting gift: for you,
good looks, and love for me. Both are ephemeral.
For a brief while they join in harmony. If they do not
take care to guard each other, both take wing and disappear.

225

Never, when the sun is rising is it fitting that
the Bull and flaming Dog Star intersect;
and when fruit-harvesting Demeter is moist,
don't make the bushy bride of Heracles all wet.

226

My eyes tear-stained from weeping, I try all night
to rest my spirit kept awake by anguish
(caused by my friend's departure yesterday
when Theodorus left me all alone, went home

to Ephesus). If he does not come back here soon,
the solitude here in my bed will be too much for me to bear.

227

Though I want to look past the pretty boys I meet,
I've hardly passed them when I turn my head.

228

The seduction of a boy too young to understand
brings worse disgrace to the seducer. If a youth
submits to practices for which he is too old,
then he bears twice as great a shame. But, Moeris,
there is a circumstance when it not unseemly
for two people, as is our situation at the moment.

229

What a fine divinity she is, that Nemesis, whom we
appease (afraid of her behind us) by spitting in our lap.
You did not see her tracking you; no, you thought
you would always keep your momentary beauty.
Now it has disappeared. The hair-assing goddess has arrived,
and we, your former servants, pass you by.

230 Callimachus

If swarthy, handsome Theocritus dislikes me, hate him
four times over, Zeus; but if he loves me, love him.
Yes, celestial Zeus, I swear by fair-haired Ganymede,
that you once fell in love yourself. I'll say no more.

231 Strato

Euclides, who is in love, has lost his father. Lucky as always!
His father gave him everything he wanted.
Now he's an acquiescent corpse. But I still play in secret.
Damn! I have an evil fate and a father who will never die.

232 Scythinus

Now you're erect, you damned thing, and not just hanging there,
as if you plan to stay tumescent all the time.
But when Nemesanus was ready to submit to me,
to give me everything I wanted, you played dead.
Stand up, plead, and cry: all to no avail.
My hand will show you no mercy.

233 Fronto

Comic actor, you think that your prime is *The Treasure*.
You don't realize it is more evanescent than *The Phantom*.
Time will make you *The Outcast*, then *The Country Bumpkin*.
Then you will search out *The Lady with the Close-cropped Hair*.
    [The poet is citing titles of comedies by Menander.]

234 Strato (Poems 234–255)

If you glory in your beauty, know that the rose blooms too
but withers quickly and is thrown out on the dungheap.
Fate gives an equal length of time to blossoms and to beauty,
and jealous time wastes both away together.

235

If beauty ages, give me some before it goes away.
If it abides, why do you fear to give away what will abide?

236

A eunuch has good-looking servant boys. For what?
He causes them unholy injury. Just like the dog
with roses in his food-dish who madly barks away,
he neither makes use of or gives away the treasure.

237

Goodbye, you hypocrite! Goodbye, you vulgar boy,
who swore so recently that you never give yourself.

Now swear no more. I know (and you can't keep it from me),
I know exactly where, and how, with whom, and for how much.

238

When puppies frolic, unabashedly they give
each other mutual delight. For, taking turns,
they mount each other from behind,
and alternate the active and the passive role.
Neither claims more than his share. The pup
who gave now stands and gets it from behind.
This is wholly prefatory. As the saying goes,
an ass knows how to scratch another ass.

239

You ask for five. I'll give you ten . . . you will have twenty.
Is gold enough for you? It was enough for Danaë.

240

Now gray hair infiltrates my temples, and
my cock hangs limp between my legs.
My balls are useless. Onerous old age attacks me.
Poor me. I know how to fuck and can't.

241

You made a hook, and I'm the fish you caught.
Boy, reel me in. Don't run or I might get away.

242

Alcimus, you displayed the rosy finger of a lizard yesterday.
Today you have one that is a rosy arm.
    [For "lizard" as a slang term for penis, see poem 3.]

243

If fucking has destroyed me and even given me gout,
then, Zeus, turn me into a meat-hook.

244

If I see a white boy I'm enchanted. Honey-colored?
Then I'm on fire. If he's tawny, I just melt.

245

Every animal devoid of reason merely fucks. But we
who have intelligence excel the other animals in this:
we have discovered buggering. Whoever is controlled
by women, he is no better than the mindless beasts.

246

A pair of brothers love me. I don't know which of them
to choose to be my master, since I love them both.
One goes away, the other one approaches. The best of one
is his proximity; and of the other one, his absence.

247

Just as Idomeneus once brought Meriones from Crete
to Troy to serve him, Theodorus, I have
such a proficient friend in you. In some ways
Meriones was his servant but in others was his friend.
And you, all day, take care of mundane things,
but by Zeus in the nighttime let's try to be friends.

    [Meriones seems to be a slang term here for penis.]

248

Who can tell if his beloved is getting past his prime,
if he is with him every moment, never out of sight?
Who was pleasing yesterday today might be unpleasant.
And if today he pleases, what might happen to reverse that?

249

Ox-born bee, where did you see my little honey,
from where did you fly straight to his glass-smooth face?
Won't you stop your buzzing? Stop trying, bee, to touch
his unsullied skin with your flower-loving feet.
Away with you! Go to your honey-cohorts, wherever they may be,
before I bite you. I also have a sting—of love.

250

As I went out one evening, slightly tipsy, after dinner,
I was the wolf who found a lamb, my neighbor Aristodicus' son,
who stood right by the door. I hugged him and
I had great pleasure kissing him, and swore that I
would give him many gifts. And now what should I give him?
He does not deserve deceit or broken promises.

251

Up to now we gave each other kisses and conducted foreplay
face to face, for you were still a boy, my Diphilus.
Now I beseech you by those whom we left behind, who are
no longer with us; let all things happen in their proper time.

252

Door, I will set a torch to you. Drunk as I am, I'll burn
the one inside. Then I will flee at once, an exile,
and sail across the wine-dark Adriatic, and as I rove
I'll lurk by doors that open in the night.

253

Give me your right hand for a little while. Don't keep
me from the dancing (though the handsome boy made me
a laughingstock). If he had not, at just the worst
time possible, been lying by his father, he would not,
I swear it, he would not have seen me drunk without a reason.

254

From what temple has emerged this band of Loves
illuminating everything? Gentlemen, I am amazed.
Who of these are slaves and who are freemen? I can't say.
Is their lord a man? It cannot be. If so, he is
much grander than great Zeus, who only had his Ganymede,
although he was a mighty god. How many does this fellow have?

255

Solitary man! Does not the word itself
teach you by the two that, fused, create it?
It is "boy-love," Dionyius, and not "man-love."
Have you anything that you can say in answer?
I govern Pythian Games, and you Olympian. The ones whom
I reject and cull, these you get for your games.

256 Meleager (Poems 256–257)

Love wove for you a multiflowered garland, Aphrodite.
With his own hands he plucked the boy-buds.
In this he wove the scented lily Diodorus,
and wove in too the sweet white violet Asclepiades.
He fashioned into it Heraclitus, who blossomed like a rose
among the thorns, and Dion like a vine in bloom.
He threaded in the gold-haired saffron flower, Thero,
and added Uliades, a sprig of thyme;
for soft-haired Myiscus, he placed an ever-blooming olive shoot
plucked from the fertile groves of Aretas.
Sacred Tyre, most blessed of all islands, home of
the scented grove where bloom the boyish buds of Aphrodite.

257

I, the flourish that proclaims the final lap,
most faithful guardian of written pages,
declare the task of gathering the work of many poets
into one anthology has been completed. I announce
that Meleager wove this poetic garland

for Diocles, to make his name immortal.
Coiled just like a snake, I have been placed
beside the final lines of this learned compilation.

258 Strato

Perhaps someone who in the future reads these playful poems
will think that all these pangs of love were mine.
But I compose poems all the time for other men who are
in love with boys, since some god gave me this ability.

CLASSICAL LATIN LITERATURE

James J. Wilhelm

There are obviously many similarities between homosexuality in Greek and Roman cultures, as there are in their literatures. For example, the Roman pastoral tradition, as represented by Vergil, clearly descends from the writings of Theocritus and others. The heroic tradition of Vergil's *Aeneid* looks frankly back at Homer's epics. And the lyrics of writers such as Catullus continue the traditions of the Greek lyricists.

But culturally there are some important differences. Homosexuality was widely practiced in the Roman Empire in all classes from the Emperors down to the slaves, but the class system created a different feeling in the poetry. The Greeks had emphasized a mentor relationship between an older man and a boy that had roots in their military system and then in their educational system, as can be seen in the Platonic dialogues in the relationships between Socrates and his followers. This kind of intellectual union is not as apparent with the Romans, where the love relationships are far more passionate than pedagogical or intellectual. Catullus, for example, does not seem to be the least bit interested in Juventius's mind, although his poems to older men (which are possibly just expressions of deep friendship) involve aesthetic pursuits.

The widespread presence of slaves also created a marked difference between the two cultures, as can be seen in numerous poems by Martial. The Romans did not seem to consider it the least bit wrong to seize love by force in a manner that most Greeks would have considered reprehensible. Note Poem 56 by Catullus and Martial's IV, 48 and V, 46. Often these relationships were frankly sado-masochistic.

The area in which the Romans excelled was satire. They were able to see both the good and the bad side of all sexual behavior, and were quick to point out the flaws and laugh at the ridiculous, without drawing unnecessary distinctions.

Relief depicting ball players. National Archaeological Museum, Athens, Greece. (Courtesy Foto Marburg/Art Resource, New York)

5. THE LYRIC

CATULLUS, HORACE, AND TIBULLUS

CATULLUS (ca. 84–54 B.C.)

Gaius Valerius Catullus is considered by many to have been Rome's most sophisticated lyric poet. His poems to the woman Lesbia are his most famous productions; they express a heterosexual love that is passionate and stormy, ending in separation. She was in reality the aristocratic Clodia, wife of Metellus Celer, who was the governor of Cisalpine Gaul in 62 B.C.

Born in Verona Catullus soon emigrated to Rome, where he mingled freely with the finest and basest of that metropolis' residents. Some of his poems are addressed to scoundrels and thieves, as can be seen in some of the selections which are addressed to rivals for the love of the boy Juventius.

Although the sequence to Juventius forms a distinct entity, it is often omitted from standard anthologies or seldom mentioned by critics. Yet the love expressed here is every bit as passionate as that expressed to Lesbia. It is clear that Catullus was bisexual, as were many Romans—especially those of the upper class.

The selections begin with a marriage hymn written for Manlius Torquatus and Vinia Aurunculeia. This is extraordinary because it contains a Fescennine Joke Song, which is supposedly addressed to the boy-lover of the groom, who is urged to depart the scene. It seems almost incredible to those living in a Christian era that such a song would be sung at such an occasion, but the Romans had a humorous vision of life.

Catullus's bitter words to Julius Caesar (Nos. 57 and 29) reveal a side of the great general that is seldom noticed. The fact that Julius's catamitic past was not invented by our poet can be seen in the portrait of Julius created by the historian Suetonius.

The numbers given to these poems follow the standard numbering process given to Catullus's poems since the Renaissance. In my translating, I employed the perdurable edition of E.T. Merrill (Harvard University Press, 1893, with many later printings), as well as the more recent editions of Kenneth Quinn and C.J. Fordyce.

61 *Marriage Hymn in Honor of Manlius Torquatus and Vinia Aurunculeia*
(INVOCATION TO HYMEN HYMENAEUS, LORD OF NUPTIALS,
BY THE LEADER OF THE CHORUS)
You who haunt the Hill
Of Helicon, son of Urania;
You who carry the tender maiden
Away to her man, Hymen Hymenaeus,
O Hymen, Lord of Nuptials!

Circle your forehead with flowers
Of sweet-smelling marjoram;
Gather your veil, hurry with joy,
Run here in clay-colored sandals
On your snowy feet!

Roused on this day of rejoicing,
Come and sing us wedding songs
With your bell-like voice;
Let your feet strike the sod, your hands
Shake the marriage torch,

For Manlius is marrying Vinia,
Who looks like Venus on Mount Ida
When she stepped before the Trojan judge—
An honorable maiden who will marry
Under auspicious signs,

Who is as shiny as the Asian myrtle
Blooming on flowery boughs
Which spirits of the woodland
Nurture as playthings
With drops of dew. . . .

(Fescennine Joke Song Addressed to the Groom's
Imagined Boy Friend)
Now a ribald Fescennine verse
Refuses to stay mute:
Let the lover-boy, hearing
That his man has jilted him,
Look at the wasteland of his love.
Give the smaller boys some nuts!

Give the boys chestnuts, you lazy
Little lover-boy. Too many years now
You've played with your master's nuts.
Now you have to serve the Lord of Marriage.
Lover-boy, give up your nuts!

How you used to hate country matrons
Just yesterday, my hairless one!
But now a barber has to shave
Your cheeks. O poor, poor little
Lover-boy, give up your nuts!

Perfumed husband, people will talk
If you don't hold back from your
Little playmates. Hold back!
O Hymen Hymenaeus, io!
O Hymen Hymenaeus!

We know that you'll indulge only
In what's lawful, and a married man
Is not allowed such things.
O Hymen Hymenaeus, io!
O Hymen Hymenaeus!

(Joke-Song to the Bride)
Bride, be careful not to say no
To anything your husband desires,
Or he might find it elsewhere!
O Hymen Hymenaeus, io!
O Hymen Hymenaeus!

48

If I were allowed to kiss
            your honeyed eyes,
                    Juventius,
say three hundred thousand times—
I still wouldn't be satisfied
            until the harvest of my kissing
was thicker than a field of ripened corn.

99 A Promise (or a Threat)

I stole from you while you were playing, honeyed Juventius,
            A little kiss sweeter than the sweet nectar of the gods,
And yet I didn't get away unscathed; for more than an hour,
            I remember, I was stretched out tightly on a cross,
Trying to purge my honor to you; yet not a flood of tears
            Could soothe one little bit your savage rage.
After the kiss, your fingers almost rubbed away
            Your lips, which you bathed with water,
So that nothing contracted from my mouth would linger,
            As if it was the filthy spittle of a drooling whore;
And even then you couldn't stop from turning poor me over
            To that jailer Love, to be tortured in every way,
So that my little smooch would suddenly change from nectar
            And taste more bitter than bitter hellebore.
Since you dole out such dire penalties for my poor love,
            Never again will I steal from you a kiss.

81

Juventius, out of all these crowds of people,
Isn't there some handsome man to satisfy you
Who is better than that "patron" from dead-end Pesaro?
Why, he looks paler than any gilded statue!
O well, I guess you've fallen for him.
Yes, you're daring to take him instead of me—
And you don't even know the crime
That you're committing.

24

Little flower of the Juventius family—
More flowerlike than any boy who ever was
Or ever will be in the years to come—
I'd rather have you squander the gold of Midas
Than surrender your love to that man
Who doesn't have a slave or a money chest.
You say: "Sure. But he's handsome." He is.
Handsome. And his slave? And his money chest?
Do what you want. Ignore it. Dismiss it.
But he still doesn't have a slave or a money chest.

15

Aurelius, I'm handing over my lover
(and therefore myself) to you, and begging humbly:
if you've ever tried with all your heart
to keep something pure, something undefiled,
then for god's sake keep this little boy safe for me.
I don't mean from the masses—O no! I'm not afraid
of the men who walk up and down our main streets
all wrapped up in their private affairs.
No, I'm afraid of *you*—and that wicked rod
you use to punish good and bad boys alike.
Go where you want, do whatever you want to
outside the house—where an awful lot can be done.
Just leave this one boy alone. I think that's fair.
But if you turn evil and are seized by a lust
that drives you toward some disgraceful act—you sinner—
if you dare to wound ME in such a treacherous way—
then, man, poor you! What a fate lies before you!
Fettered, with rear door gaping, you'll be stuffed
fowl-style with chopped radishes and mullets.

21

Aurelius, father of all forced diets—
not only your own, but all that were
or are or will be in the years to come—
YOU want to plunder my boy.

And not on the sly: always with him,
giggling, groping, you'll do anything anywhere.
No good! I'll counter your bitchy onslaught
quicker than even you can ram it home.
But if you have your fill, I'll shut up.
What worries me now, my poor child, is this:
with Aurelius, you'll be reared in hunger and thirst.
So stop! Come back—while you're still pure.
Otherwise I have grave fears about your end.

26

Furius,
Your little house
Isn't threatened by the south wind
        or the west wind
        or the bitter north wind
        or the east—
Just by fifteen thousand dollars.
But that's the cruelest blow of all.

23

Furius, you have no slave, no coffer,
no bedbug, no spider, no kitchen fire—
though you do indeed have a father and a stepmom
whose teeth are strong enough to bite through flint.
It's going great for you with your dad
and your dad's little wooden wife.
No wonder. You're all enjoying good health
and are always cooking up things together,
and you're afraid of practically nothing:
not fires or disastrous earthquakes
or evil thefts or treacherous poisonings
or any other life-threatening events.
No! you have bodies hard and tough as horn
(or like anything else that's hard and tough),
what with the sun and cold and your fasting.
Why shouldn't you be hale and hardy?
You issue no excess sweat or saliva

or mucus or hideous nose-runs.
No, and you can add something else that's clean:
your ass is purer than any salt-cellar,
since you never shit more than ten times a year.
And what comes out is harder than beans or pebbles,
so that if you rubbed it with your hands,
your fingers wouldn't be besmirched a bit.
Ah, you have lots of blessings, Furius.
Don't ignore them or consider them small.
As for that hundred bucks you're always begging for—
forget it! You have blessings enough.

16

Screw you both! I'll ram you deep,
Fairy Aurelius and Furius the Fag,
Thinking that I was far from decent
By penning little verses that you called "soft."
Well, a moral poet ought to be "pure in soul"
Himself, but that's not the case with his verse,
Which can show a little savor and salt,
Even if it's tender and not fully proper
And capable of exciting a prurient interest—
Not in boys, I insist, but in hairy men
Who can scarcely lug around their heavy cocks.
Because you read about my "thousands of kisses"
Do you think I don't quite measure up as a man?
Screw you both! I'll ram you deep!

To Foes and Fools

57

Fairies of a feather flock together:
        Mamurra and that lecher Caesar.
                Why not?
Their wings bear similar stains
That will not be washed away.
Julia is Roman.
        Miss Mamurra hails from Formiae.
They lie like two sick twins

On a single couch, working on master-pieces.
And they try very hard to stay friendly rivals
In their adulterous prey on young chicks!
Fairies of a feather flock together.

29 *Petition to Caesar (with a Parting Whiplash for Pompey the Great)*
Who can survey it and stand it,
Unless he's a pervert, glutton, or gangster:
Mamurra's getting what long-haired Gaul
Once owned—and far-flung Britain.
Degenerate father, do you see it? Stand it?
O so arrogant now, will he really, loaded,
Strut through every man's bedroom
Like Venus' dove or a decadent Adonis?
Degenerate father, do you see it? Stand it?
Then *you're* a pervert, glutton, or gangster.
Is this the sum total, One and Only Emperor?
Is this why you went to that western island,
So this screwed-up man we now call Dick
Could gobble up twenty or thirty grand?
Is this your kind of generosity? Left-handed?
Hasn't he squandered, burned up enough already?
First he ran through his father's goods;
Second, the spoils of Asia; third, of Spain.
(How well the gold-bearing Tagus River knows that!)
And now Britain and Gaul are all a-tremble.
Why do you pamper this pest? What can he do
Except devour more sweet-smelling patrimonies?
Is it for him that you and your rich son-in-law
Pompey are allowing everything won to drift away?

112 *On a Political Candidate*
You're everyone's man, Naso,
even though nobody goes downtown with you.
But you'll go down with anyone,
         you old fag.

74

Gellius heard that his uncle used to rave
　　If anyone mentioned having sex or had some,
And so, to protect himself, Gellius seduced the wife
　　Of that uncle, thereby turning him into the God of Silence.
Then Gellius did whatever he pleased. Yes, he could even
　　Screw his uncle, and the uncle wouldn't say a word.

80

How can I explain, Gellius, why those rosy lips
　　Of yours are whiter than the winter snow
In the morning when you leave your house or later in the day
　　When an afternoon hour shakes you from a soft siesta?
I don't know the cause for sure; but—do they whisper
　　That you feast on the fruit of fairies?
Yes, indeed! Poor little Victor's worn-out rod
　　Proclaims it—and your lips, stained by his fresh cream.

25 To Thallus the Thief

Fairy Thallus, softer than a rabbit's fur
　　or a duck's underfeathers
　　or the lobe of an ear
　　or an old man's lazy cock
　　or a spider's web
and yet—Thallus, wilder than any raging storm
when a rich hostess and her guests aren't looking!
Send me back that coat that you stole from me
and that Spanish napkin and those Bithynian tablets.
Fool, pretending that they belonged to your grandfather!
Unglue them from your fingers and send them back.
　　OTHERWISE, your downy back and delicate pinkies
　　will be branded like a slave's with a burning lash,
　　and you'll learn how to squiggle and to squirm
　　like a skiff caught at sea in a wild, raging squall.

98

Smelly Vettius, one can say about you (if about anyone)
        what one says about blowhards and fools:
that tongue of yours, if it gets a chance,
        will lick anyone's boots or bottom.
If you want to be totally rid of us all, Vettius,
        just open your mouth, and what you want you'll get.

33

O most successful of all the bathhouse thieves,
Father Vibennius and your fairy son
        (The father's most famous for his rapacious hand
        while the son's well-known for his greedy rear),
Why don't you both go off into exile,
Away to some damnable shore,
Now that the father's rapes are known to all,
And son, your hairy bottom can't be peddled for a dime?

56

O Cato, an absurdly funny thing just happened,
Something worth your hearing about and laughing!
Cato, if you love your Catullus, laugh!
It's a very amusing, too too funny thing.
I just caught this little kid
Heaving it into a girl. And by Venus I swear,
Instead of using a paddle, to the same timing
I whipped him half-dead with my rod.

POEMS TO CLOSE FRIENDS

9 To Veranius

Veranius, who means more to me
Than three hundred thousand other men,
Have you really come home to your family fire,
To your warm-hearted brother and elderly mother?
        You have!
O god, what wonderful news!
I have to make sure you're safe, have to

Hear all about Spain, its cities, its history,
Its people—in the way that only you can tell.
I'll put my arm around your shoulders
And kiss your happy lips and eyes.
Out of all the men in this world who are happy,
Who could possibly be happier than I?

13 To Fabullus

Fabullus, you're going to have a fabulous meal
At my house soon, gods willing!
With splendid girls and wine and wit and lots of laughter—
If you bring them with you.
    I repeat:
You'll have a fabulous meal, my dear friend,
If you bring all these with you.
Your Catullus' wallet is full of nothing but cobwebs.
All he can give you is his undiluted love—
    O yes!
And something even sweeter and more elegant:
Some perfume that Venus and Cupid gave his girl.
Once you smell it, Fabullus, you'll say:
    Gods! Make me all nose!

50 To Licinius

Yesterday, Licinius, in our spare time
we had a lot of fun among my notebooks
as we agreed to compose some subtleties.
Each of us wrote some love poems,
toying with this or that rhythm
in a pleasant exchange of jokes and wine.
I went away so kindled
by your genius, Licinius, and your wit
that no food could nourish my poor body
and sleep couldn't drape my eyes with peace.
No! I tossed with full frenzy upon my bed,
uncontrollably, eager to see the dawn,
anxious to be back with you, talk to you,
until finally my limbs, tired from their toil,

collapsed half-dead on that worn-out bed.
        And so, my dear friend,
I wrote you this little poem
so that you could survey my grief.
But don't be proud! And I beg you, my gem,
don't disdain my prayer for another performance,
or Nemesis might demand some payment from you.
She's a vicious goddess.
Don't ever cross *her* up!

38 To Cornificius
Your Catullus is sick, Cornificius.
God yes, I'm sick and in pain,
And I'm getting worse by the day and hour.
Where's that word of good cheer?
Such a simple little thing.
        I'm furious!
Is this how you treat my love for you?
        O,
Let me hear just one little word,
        and make it sadder
Than all those poems of sad old Simonides.

HORACE (65–8 B.C.)

Quintus Horatius Flaccus was born in Venusia, but lived much of his life in Rome, although he constantly sings of the beauty of country life. Most of his *Odes* are addressed to women, but the two which follow are both written for a young man named Ligurinus. Horace also wrote *Satires, Epodes,* and *Epistles* on themes that include politics, religion, and national greatness.

Odes *IV, 1*
O Venus, are you stirring up some new embroilments
        Once again? Spare me, I beg you, I beg you.
I'm no longer the man I was when I allowed
        Cinara to rule me. So stop,
Savage mother of sweet affairs, stop
        Bending me now hardened after fifty years

To your soft commands; yes, go away to where
  The flattering prayers of the young are calling you.
It's far more propitious for you to float
  On your resplendent swan's wings to the home   10
Of Paulus Maximus if you're looking for
  The right kind of heart to burn,
For he is noble and upstanding and never silent
  In defending his many troubled clients—
A young man with a score of talents
  Who will carry the standard of your forces far.
And when, feeling mighty in conquest
  He chuckles at the gifts of a generous rival,
He'll erect a marble statue in your honor
  With a roof of cedar by the Alban lakes.   20
There you'll inhale copious amounts of incense
  And you'll revel in the music that is made
By a Berecyntian flute, which is blended
  With the sound of strings with pipes not lacking.
There twice a day a troop of boys
  And tender maidens will hymn your deity
As they strike the soil with their radiant feet
  In a triple dance done in the Salian style.
But me—neither a woman nor a young man
  Nor the hope of one who believes in kindred spirits 30
Nor a long drinking bout delights me,
  Nor wearing a garland of flowers around my head.
But why, Ligurinus, why
  Does a tear now and then roll down my cheeks?
Why does my once eloquent tongue
  Fail me as I fall into awkward silence?
In my dreams at night I hold you sometimes
  Captive, and sometimes I chase after you
As you bolt away over the grassy Field
  Of Mars and swift-running streams, O you hard-heart!

IV, 10

O Ligurinus, who are still cruel and potent with the gifts of Venus,
When an unwanted stubble appears on your proud face
And the hair that now cascades over your shoulders begins to fall,

And your skin, which is now the color of pink roses,
Begins to change on your bristly face,
You'll cry out "Alas" every time you look into a mirror,
"This mind that I have today, why didn't I have it as a boy?
And why don't my cheeks regain their healthy vigor?"

TIBULLUS (50–17 B.C.)

Very little is known about the life of Albius Tibullus. His poems come down
in four books, but only the first two are by him. In the first book he hymns
two lovers: the woman Delia and the young man Marathus. Book II consists of poems to another woman, Nemesis, while Book III has six short
poems written by one of the few Roman poetesses, Sulpicia, as well as some
poems about her. My translations are based on the Loeb Library text
(Harvard University Press, 1976).

I, 4 Ode to Priapus, the Phallic God

"My Priapus—may your shady roof protect you,
    And may neither the sun nor the snow harm you—
Tell me what shrewdness of yours attracts pretty boys. Surely
    You don't have any shiny beard or well-combed hair.
You stand naked through all of winter's blasts,
    Naked through the scorching days of the Dog-Star."
I said this; and then replied to me the rustic child of Bacchus,
    The god who is armed with curving scythe:
"O run away from trusting yourself to the tender bands of boys,
    Since they'll always supply you with a just cause for love.   10
This one delights you by the firm way he reins in his horse;
    That one forces through the water with his snow-white breast;
This one captivates you by his strong audacity; and that one
    By the virginlike modesty that shows on his cheeks.
If at first he may refuse you, don't be disheartened;
    Little by little he will yield his neck to your yoke.
A long period of time has taught lions to listen to man;
    After a long time soft water has eaten through rocks;
It takes a year for grapes to ripen on the open hillsides;
    It takes a year to cover the stars in their certain round.   20
So don't be afraid to make pledges. The winds carry
    The worthless lies of lovers over lands and broad seas.

Great thanks are owed to Jove; our Father denied the validity
    Of any oath that a foolish lover swore in his passion.
Diana with her arrows allows you with impunity to affirm
    Your case, as does Minerva with her hair.
But you're wrong if you delay. Time passes by
    So swiftly! Days don't linger and they never come back.
How swiftly the earth loses its summer colors,
    And how swiftly the tall poplar loses its lovely leaves!   30
How the horse who once broke out of the stall at Elis
    Now lies unnoticed as fated by weak old age!
I have seen young men mourning the foolish days they lost
    As the later years were now pressing upon them.
O you cruel gods! The snake renews itself by shedding its skin,
    But the Fates never granted any man a reprieve.
To Bacchus and Phoebus alone is youth eternal;
    both gods are graced by their uncut tresses.
You, give way to anything that your boy happens
    To dare, because love wins the most by being obsequious.   40
Don't refuse to accompany him however far the route may stretch,
    Even if the Dog-Star bakes the soil with a thirsty drought;
Even when a storm threatens oncoming rain, a rainbow
    Will border the heavens with colorful hues.
If he wants to skim over the sky-blue waves in a light boat,
    You yourself pilot the bark with an oar in your hand.
Don't be afraid to submit to hard labor or
    To chafe your hands by undertaking unusual tasks.
And if he should want to enclose a valley in an ambush,
    Then, just to please him, lug out the nets on your shoulders.   50
If he wants to fight with weapons, then try with your limp hand,
    And let yourself be unguarded so that he can win.
After this, he'll be kind to you; then you can steal a belovéd
    Kiss; he will struggle—but let you steal it.
Yes at first he'll struggle, but later he'll supply it for the asking
    And finally after that, he'll want to cling to your neck.
Ah, but now alas! this age of ours deals in such miserable trades!
    Now our tender boys have grown used to expecting gifts.
Whoever you are who introduced love for sale, I hope
    That some damned stone will weigh down your bones!   60
Young men, you should love the Muses and learnéd poets!
    You should never let golden gifts overcome the Muses!

Poetry immortalized the purple locks of Nisus; without poetry,
    No ivory would have glistened on Pelops' shoulder.
The man the Muses sing of will live as long as Earth bears trees,
    And the heavens have stars and rivers running water.
And whoever disregards the Muses, whoever sells love,
    Let him follow the chariot of Ops of Ida
And wander like a bum through three hundred towns
    And cut off his vile member the Phrygian way.   70
Venus herself wants a proper place for her delights; she even
    Looks with favor on humble complaints and bitter tears."
These things the god issued from his throat for me to sing to Titius,
    But the wife of Titius forbids him to remember them.
Well, let him obey his own rules; but you should honor me as your teacher
    If any shrewd kid has bilked you with his clever craft.
We all have our own glory; you jilted lovers should consult
    With me; my door is open for each and all.
The time will come when I, who convey the teachings of Venus, grown old,
    Will be carried home by a flock of attentive youngsters.   80
O but alas! how my love for Marathus tortures me on and on!
    My arts are all useless; my craftiness has crumbled.
Mercy on me, boy, I beg you! Don't turn me into a vile piece
    Of gossip who is laughed at as my knowledge turns all vain!

I, 8 Words to the Cold Girl Pholoe About Marathus
. . . Alas, too late do we call back love and youth   41
    When white-haired old age has bleached our agéd heads.
Then we desire beauty; then the color of our hair is dyed
    So that we can hide our years with a nut's dark stain.
Then we strain to pull out the hoary hairs by their roots
    And to bring back a youngish face with the old one gone.
But while your age is still in its springtime, see to it
    That it doesn't slip away on tardy feet.
And don't torment poor Marathus. Where's the glory in triumphing
    Over a boy; be tough, my girl, against those worn-out old men!   50
Again I say: pity the tender one; he has no dangerous drive;
    It's only excessive lust that stains his flesh.
How often his poor unhappiness heaps complaints on those
    Who are absent, and how he bathes everything with his tears!
He says: "Why do you ignore me? I could have fooled your guards!

Some god can help the lovesick to cheat their way.
I know all about undercover love, how to breathe very lightly,
    And how to steal a kiss without making a sound.
Even in the still of night I can sneak up, and without making
    A noise, I can secretly unlock a door.   60
But what good are skills if some savage girl spurns her poor lover
    And runs away from that couch of love?
Then when she makes a promise, but suddenly turns traitor,
    I have to sweat out the night with many discomforts.
I am always picturing her coming when anything rustles;
    I always think I hear the sound of her feet."
Stop crying, my boy. She will not be broken,
    And your eyes will just be swollen with tears.
I warn you, Pholoe, the gods don't like indifference,
    And it's no good to offer incense to their sacred fires.   70
This very Marathus once used to laugh at the sad fates of lovers,
    Not realizing that the god of vengeance lurked behind him.
And it's often said that he laughed at the tears of the grieving
    And detained a lover by faking delays;
Now he despises all piety; now he dislikes every door
    That is turned against him with a harsh bolt.
But punishment remains for you, girl, unless you drop your pride.
      How you're going to wish your prayers could call back this day!

I, 9 To Marathus

Why, if you were about to destroy my pitiful love, did you offer me
    Vows through the gods which you would then secretly break?
O you poor boy! if anyone at first conceals his perjuries,
    Later on, Punishment will sneak up on soundless feet.
Gods, show him mercy! It is right that for one time the beautiful
    Should be allowed with impunity to offend your divinity.
Seeking gain, the farmer links his bulls to the able plow
    And pushes forward with the tough work of the land.
Seeking gain, the bobbing ships are pushed forward by winds
    Through the obedient waters by the fixed, certain stars.   10
My boy was been won over with gifts. But may god turn this
    Filthy lucre into mere ashes and flowing water.
Soon he will pay the penalty to me as dust disfigures
    His beauty and his hair is blown wildly by the winds.

His face will be burned by the sun along with his hair,
    And a long journey will wear out his weakened soles.
Many a time I warned him: "Don't sully yourself with gold!
    Very often a host of evils lies under gold.
If anyone violates love after being captivated by money,
    Venus is always very bitter and harsh.   20
Instead of that, let flames burn my head and go after my body
    With a sword and lash my back with a twisted ferze.
And don't hope to hide your sins while you are plotting them.
    God knows, and he forbids hidden trickery.
God himself one placed drink in front of a silent servant
    So that he would freely pour out words with strong wine.
God himself ordered a voice to sound that was quelled in sleep,
    And he made it unwillingly describe deeds meant to be covered.
I used to say this to you. Now I'm ashamed that I cried as I spoke
    And that I threw myself down in front of your tender feet.   30
At that time you swore that for no heap of glittering gold
    Or for any jewels would you sell out your faith—
Not even if Campania's territory was offered as the price
    Or the lands of Falernum that the wine-god tends.
By these words you could take away my faith that the stars
    Shine in the sky and that rivers rush down to the sea.
Yes, and you even cried. I, who had no education in deception,
    Full of belief, used to wipe dry your moistened cheeks.
Ah, what would I have done if you hadn't loved a girl?
    I pray she may be casual as she follows your example.   40
O how often, so that no one would be aware of your love,
    I accompanied you like a comrade with a candle in my hand!
Often she came to you unexpectedly as a gift from me
    And lurked in a veil behind a closed door.
Poor me, that began my undoing—since I foolishly trusted love.
    Yes, I should have been more wary of your traps.
But no, with a thunderstruck mind, I was hymning your praises.
    Yet now I'm ashamed of myself and the Muses.
Now I want Vulcan to burn those songs in a holocaust
    And some river to flush them away in a rapid flow.   50
And you—go far away with that figure you want to sell
    So that you can return with your hands loaded with loot.
And you, that john who dares to corrupt my boy with your "gifts"—
    I hope your wife freely dupes you with her countless affairs,

And when she has left a secret session with her young stud
      I hope she lies next to you—screwed out with a blanket between!
Let there always be the footprints of strangers next to your bed
      And your house always gaping open to the horny.
And don't let anyone say that her nymphomanic sister drinks
      More cups of wine or wears out more machos.   60
People will say that she stretches out her revels with wine
      Till the chariot of Lucifer summons forth the morning.
They will say that no one knows better how to eat up the night
      Or to arrange a more tasty menu for sex.
Your wife knows it all—yet you, you big fool, aren't the least aware
      When she moves her body in an exotic way.
Think it's for you that she dolls up her hair
      And runs the fine-tooth comb through her thin strands?
Is it your handsome face that makes her cover her arms with bracelets
      And appear all decked out in the latest Tyrian fashion?   70
No—it's for some handsome stud that she wants to look lovely,
      For whom she dishonors all your house and your holdings.
And she doesn't do this to be vicious; no, the pretty thing just wants
      To be free of your foul gout and your senile embraces.
And yet it's with *you* that my own boy has slept! I'd rather believe
      He joined himself in love with some wild beast!
Boy, did you dare to sell caresses belonging to me to someone else?
      Did you crazily pass on kisses to others that belonged to me?
Then you're going to cry when another boy enslaves me
      And reigns as sovereign in the place where you once reigned.   80
Then your chastisement will delight me and I'll offer Venus
      For her kindness a golden palm noting my good fortune:
TIBULLUS, WHO WAS FREED FROM LYING LOVE, OFFERS THIS
      TO YOU AND PRAYS THAT YOU ALWAYS SHOW HIM A HAPPY MIND.

6. VERGIL

Eclogue II

Publius Vergilius Maro (70–19 B.C.) is usually considered the greatest Roman writer, and certainly Rome's greatest writer of epic. He is best known for his *Aeneid,* a twelve-book story of the founding of Rome by the Trojan Aeneas. But he is also well-known for his other writings, such as the *Georgics,* four long poems on agricultural subjects, and the *Eclogues,* ten shorter poems on pastoral themes.

The *Eclogues* usually consist of dialogues between shepherds on subjects ranging from love to their occupation. The famous homosexual one selected here owes a great deal to the *Idylls* of the Greek Theocritus. It is the lament of an unrequited lover, Corydon, for the boy Alexis, and was imitated often (usually with a shift to heterosexual characters) in later generations.

The language of pastoral is highly artificial (both Vergil and Theocritus were city people, with Vergil living most of his life in Rome after moving there from Mantua), even though the settings are rustic and humble. Yet there is a charm of the sophisticated over the simple that accounts for the popularity of the genre: civilized (or over-civilized) people harkening back to the paradisal gardens of the past. Many of the words are difficult to define accurately; I have relied heavily on the suggestions of H. Rushton Fairclough in his revised edition of the Loeb Classical Library: *Virgil,* Vol. I (Harvard University Press, 1965).

It is not known whether Vergil was gay himself, but this *Eclogue* made it easy for later generations to proclaim him so. In any case his sexuality did not interfere with his reputation or career, and when he died at the age of 51 in Brindisi, on returning from Greece, he was already hailed as the founder of his nation's literature. His tombstone in Naples says:

Mantua Gave Me Birth; Calabria Took It Away; Parthenope
Now Holds Me; I Sang of Pastures, Farms, Leaders.

Most of the names in this poem (Amaryllis, Damoetas, Amyntas, and
Corydon itself) are standard names in pastoral literature.

The shepherd Corydon was yearning for handsome Alexis,
The plaything of his master, and he did not know what to hope for.
He just went day after day among the dense beech-trees,
With their shady tops. There all alone with his empty desire,
He would vent these ingenuous words to the mountains and trees:
    "O cruel Alexis, don't you care anything for my songs?
Have you no pity for me? You will force me finally to death.
Just now the cattle are striving for the shadows and coolness,
Just now the bushes are concealing lizards of green,
And Thestylis shreds for the reapers worn out by the savage heat   10
A savory salad composed of garlic and wild thyme.
But as I retrace your footprints, the groves resound
Under the blazing sun with the cicada's shrill song and mine.
Wasn't it better to suffer Amaryllis' sullen sulkings
And loathing scorn? Or to put up with Menalcas,
Though he was dark, and you are shining white?
O beautiful boy, don't put too much faith in your coloring!
The white privet-flower falls down; dark blueberries are plucked.
    "You look down on me, Alexis; you don't ask what I am—
How rich I might be in cattle, how flowing in snowy-white milk.   20
I have a thousand she-lambs which roam in Sicily's mountains;
I never lack fresh milk—not in the heat of summer, not in the cold.
I sing the way Amphion of Dirce always used to sing when
He was calling his cattle back from the Attic hills.
And I'm not one bit ugly. I just recently saw myself in the water,
When the winds were standing quiet over the sea; and with you as judge,
I should never fear lovely Daphnis—if images do not lie.
    "O, if only you wanted to share my poor rustic quarters,
To live in my humble house and to shoot the deer
And to drive on the flocks of goats with an hibiscus switch!   30
You could imitate Pan by singing with me in the forest.
It was Pan who first instructed men to put reeds together
With wax; Pan cares for the sheep and the sheep's masters;
And you won't be sorry if you chafe your lip on a reed.

What did Amyntas stop short of in order to learn this art?
I have a pipe put together from seven uneven hemlock stalks,
Which was given to me at one time by Damoetas, and he said
To me as he was dying: "It has you now as its second keeper."
So spoke Damoetas, while stupid Amyntas stood by jealous.
But even more, I have two roebucks that I stumbled on   40
In a guarded valley, and their coats are spotted with white;
They suck a sheep's udder twice a day. I've saved them for you.
For a long time now Thestylis has been begging to get them—
And she will, since my gifts seem so paltry to you.

     "Come here, you beautiful boy! For you the nymphs
Carry baskets overflowing with lilies; for you a shiny naiad,
Picking pallid violets and the heads of poppies,
Mixes the narcissus with the perfumed scent of fennel;
Then, interweaving these with cassia and other sweet-smelling herbs,
She blends together the tender hyacinth with the yellow marigold.   50
I myself shall gather some quinces white with tender fuzz
And some chestnuts, which my Amaryllis once treasured;
I shall add waxen plums; this fruit shall also be honored;
And I shall pluck you too, my laurels, and the myrtle nearby,
Because when placed together, you blend a delicate perfume.

     "O, you're a hick, Corydon! Alexis despises your offerings;
And even if you do contend, Iolla is not going to give up.
Alas, alas, what have I foolishly searched for? I have let
The south wind wither my flowers and boars muddy my springs!
O, madman, who am I running from? The gods once lived in forests,   60
As well as Paris of Troy. Let Athena live in the fortresses
That she founded, but me—let me above all enjoy the woods!
The savage lioness pursues the wolf and the wolf the goat,
And the lascivious goat goes after the flowering clover,
Just as I go after you, my Corydon—each drawn by his own desire.
Look now! The bulls are drawing home the plow suspended
On their yokes, and the setting sun doubles the growing shade,
But love still burns me, for who sets a limit for love?
O, Corydon, Corydon, what madness has seized you?
The vine on your leaf-filled elm is only half-cut.   70
Why don't you at least do something else, where you have a need:
Why not weave together some willow twigs with some pliable reeds?
You'll find another Alexis, even if this one scorns you."

7. OVID

Publius Ovidius Naso (43 B.C.–A.D. 18) is known as one of the most charismatic sensibilities of world literature, rivaling Chaucer and Boccaccio in this respect. He was born in the Italian town of Sulmona but died in dreary exile on the Black Sea at Tomi in modern Rumania, where he was apparently sent because his sometimes licentious works and behavior assaulted the sensibilities of Augustus Caesar and his prudish wife Livia; Augustus gave the poet's immorality as the cause of his banishment, but Ovid himself suggested that there was another deeper personal reason.

Ovid is well known for his very heterosexual *Art of Love* and *Amores* (Love Poems). The only important gay passages in his work relate to his telling of myth, and even these comprise only a small part of the corpus. This chapter brings together the highlights of Book X of his *Metamorphoses,* a long opus that sought to relate the change-of-shape myths in Greco-Roman mythology. Very few of these myths were homosexual, but Ovid ferrets some out.

Actually the most famous gay myth concerns the translation of the beautiful boy Ganymede into heaven as the cupbearer of Jove. This myth had an effect even on Arabic poetry, where the cupbearer figure conspicuously returns. One is surprised that Ovid's telling is so brief until one realizes that Ganymede never really changed shape; he remained a beautiful boy in heaven. Hyacinth, by contrast, the lover of Apollo (the most notoriously gay of the gods), became a flower.

Some anthologists classify the Iphis and Ianthe story as lesbian. This tells of a girl who is born to a peasant father who refuses to rear a female. His wife thwarts him, however, by dressing her daughter, Iphis, as a boy. Everything proceeds well for thirteen years, but the time arrives for a marriage, and the father couples her with the girl Ianthe. Thanks to the goddess Isis, to whom the wife has prayed, Iphis is magically transformed into a boy. The tale includes some lines that express lesbian passion: "Iphis was in love, but was despairing of fruition, and this only increased / The flames within her; a girl was in love with a girl" (Book IX, 724–25), but any passion is erased by countering lines such as: "I wish I weren't a woman!" She yearns for heterosexual fulfillment, and Isis grants it.

I have used as my text that of Frank Justus Miller published in the Loeb Library (Harvard University Press, 1951).

Note: The story of Orpheus opens with a recounting of how the poet's wife, Eurydice, died, and the poet won the great privilege of being able to take her out of the Underworld, provided that he did not look back at her. Unfortunately Orpheus did this and, therefore, was forced to give her up. This caused the depression that led him to turn (temporarily) gay.

Book X, 64ff. The Story of Orpheus

Orpheus was stunned by the double death of his wife. . . .	65
The guard of the River Styx drove him back as he begged in vain	73

For a second crossing. For seven days he sat on the bank,
Squalidly clad without any taste of bread.
His food consisted of anguish, sorrow, and tears.
Complaining that the gods of Hell were cruel, he removed
Himself to high Rhodope and Haemus, buffeted by winds.
Three times Titan Sun rounded out the year and returned
To watery Pisces, but Orpheus refused any contact

With female Love—either because things had gone badly,   80
Or he had pledged to his wife—though many women passionately
Wanted to join with the bard and were grieved by being repulsed.
Even further, he was the founder for the Thracians of the custom
Of transferring love to tender boys, and of enjoying the brief spring
Of their youth and of plucking their primal flowers.

[Orpheus removes himself to a hill full of trees]

The Story of Cyparissus (Cypress)

In the midst of these trees was a cypress with its cones—
Now a tree, but once a boy beloved by the god Apollo,
Who strings up the lyre and also strings up the bow.
Now there was an enormous stag which was sacred
To the nymphs holding the Carthacan fields, whose broad antlers   110

Offered deep shade to its own mighty head.
His horns were glittering with gold, and a jeweled collar
Dangled down on his shoulders from his smooth, round neck.
On his forehead a silver stud with small thongs had hung
From his early days, and around his concave temples
And down from his ears hung gleaming pearls;
He knew no fear, and putting aside any natural shyness,
He usually haunted the homes of men and often extended
His neck for petting even by the hands of strangers.
But above all others, Cyparissus, you prime beauty   120
Of the Cean people, was he prized by you; it was you
Who led him to fresh pastures, to crystal streams;
It was you who wove garlands of various flowers for his horns;
You, now here and now there, sitting on his back like a true
Horseman, you guided his tender mouth with your purple reins.

      It was summer, and mid-day, when the bent claws
Of the shore-dwelling Crab were burning with the sun's heat
And the stag, worn-out, laid his body down on the grass
And was drinking in the coolness of that shady place.
Him the boy Cyparissus unknowingly pierced with his sharp javelin   130
And, as he saw the stag dying from this bitter blow,
He wanted to die himself. O, what great solaces
Apollo offered! He admonished him to more moderately
Take perspective! Nevertheless the boy groaned and begged
For this supreme gift from the gods: that he could mourn for all time.
And then as his blood was waning from his racking sobs,
His limbs began to turn into a greenish color, and his hair,
Which formerly fell over his snow-white forehead,
Became a bristling crest, and assuming rigidity,
His now slender top gazed upward toward the starry sky.   140
The bereaving god groaned and said: "You shall be mourned by me,
And you shall mourn others and always be with the sorrowing."

The Brief Story of Ganymede

A tree-filled grove Orpheus had created, where he sat in the middle
Of his enclave of wild beasts and his parliament of birds.
And often he tried some chords by striking them with his thumb,
And when he felt that the various notes were harmonized, though
With a different pitch, he raised up his voice in this song:

"From Jove—for all things obey the power of Jove—my parent Muse,
Inspire my song! I have often sung before about the power
Of Jove; I sang with a heavier lyre about the Giants   150
And the victorious thunderbolts scattered over the Phlegraean fields.
Now I have to sing on a lighter lyre: let us intone the names of boys
Beloved by the forces above, and girls who were seized
By illicit lust and who paid the penalty for their crimes.
The King of the Gods once burned in his love of Ganymede,
The Phrygian, and Jove suddenly found that he preferred to be
Something different from before. And yet he would not condescend
To assume any bird-shape except that which carries his bolts.
Without any delay, splitting the air with his deceptive wings,
He carried off the Trojan boy, who now, despite Queen Juno,   160
Takes care of the cups and mixes the nectar for Jove."

The Story of Hyacinth and Apollo

"You too, Hyacinth of Amyclae, Apollo would have placed up above
If only dread Fate had given him time for the raising.
Still in some way, you are eternal, for however many times
Spring drives away the winter, and Aries follows watery Pisces,
That often you spring up and flower on the green turf.
My father adored you above all the rest. Delphi, which is set
In the middle of the earth, was lacking its lord
While Apollo was frequenting River Eurotas and unfortified Sparta,
And was honoring neither his cithara nor his bow.   170
Unmindful of these, he did not refuse to carry some nets
Nor hold back the dogs nor go as companion among the rough ridges
Of mountains in order to feed his long-held desires.
And now as the Sun was midway between the coming
And going night, about an equal distance from both,
Apollo and Hyacinth strip and gleam with the oil of rich olive
As they initiate a contest involving the broad discus.
Apollo sent the well-balanced disk first flying through the air
And split the opposing clouds with its heavy weight.
After a long time, the disk came falling back to its home turf,   180
Revealing the thrower's artistry joined with his strength.
Right away the Spartan boy, imprudently and driven by his desire
To carry off the game, rushed out toward the discus,
But, my Hyacinth, the hard-packed earth sent it reeling back upward

Straight into your face. Both the god and the boy grew pale,
And the god picked up the limbs that lay collapsed,
And he now tried to warm you, now tried to stop your bleeding,
Now tried to slow down your fleeing soul by applying herbs.
His art was no good. The wound was incurable.
Just as if anyone should break off violets or rigid poppies   190
In a garden or lilies standing erect with their yellow tongues,
And, withering, their heads should suddenly droop down overcome,
And they cannot stand up, but start to study the ground—
So too Hyacinth's dying face slumped down and, as vigor departed,
The neck, unable to sustain its weight, fell back upon his shoulders.
       "You have fallen, my Spartan boy, robbed of the prime of your youth,"
Said Apollo, "and in your wound I see the charge of my guilt.
You are the cause of my sorrow, my crime; my right hand
Is inscribed with your murder; I am the author of your downfall.
And yet, where is my guilt—unless playing with you can be called   200
A blame, unless loving you can be called a blame?
If only I could surrender my life for you, who deserve it, or
Share it with you! But since we are prevented from this by Fate's law,
You will always be with me, you will cling to my remembering lips.
Your name will be celebrated by the lyre plucked by my hand
And by my songs! As a new flower, you will answer my grief.
There will come a time when the great heroic Ajax will join
Himself to your flower and will be identified by its blades."
       While Apollo was uttering such things with honest lips,
You should see the blood that poured on the ground marking the grass,   210
And yet—it stopped being blood, and a flower sprang up, brighter
Than Tyrian purple, taking the shape of a lily, except that this
Flower had a dark purplish hue, and the lily is silver-white.
This did not satisfy Apollo, who, after all, created this honor;
He himself inscribed his cries on the blades, for the flower carried
This inscription: AI! AI!; these words of lamentation were engraved there.
And Sparta was not ashamed of having reared Hyacinthus; honor to him
Endures to this day, for they annually celebrate the Hyacinthine Rites
Like their ancestors with a very special celebration. . . .

Book XI, 1ff. The Death of Orpheus
Meanwhile the bard of Thrace controlled the trees with such songs
And the breasts of beasts and the stones, which obeyed him;

But look! some crazy young Ciconian women, their breasts covered
With hides of wild beasts, from the top of a hill suddenly spy
Orpheus, adjusting his songs to his vibrating strings.
One of these, with her hair floating out on the gentle breezes,
Shouted: "Look there! There's the man who bad-mouths us!" and hurls
Her spear at the singing mouth of the bard of Apollo,
But that, covered with leaves, made a mark but no wound.
A stone was another's weapon, which, hurled through the air,   10
Was overcome by the harmony of voice and lyre, and fell
And lay at the poet's feet like a suppliant begging forgiveness
For its crazed attempt. And still the reckless warfare
Increased as all measure vanished and insane Fury ruled.
All of these weapons would have been quelled by his music,
But a great outcry and Berecyntian flutes with fractious horns
And drums and breast-beats and the howls of Bacchants
Drowned out the sound of the zither until finally some stones
Grew red with the blood of the poet, who could not be heard. . . .

  The grieving birds mourned for you, Orpheus, as did   44
The packs of wild beasts, the rough-hewn rocks, and the trees,
Who so often listened to your songs; the trees now were shedding
Their leaves like women tearing their hair; and they say that
The rivers swelled with their own tears, and the naiads and dryads
In their dark funereal garments wore disheveled hair.
His members lay widely strewn; his head, River Hebrus,   50
You received with his lyre, and, miraculously as they floated
In midstream, the lyre poured out something sad, while the tongue
Inanimate muttered something sad while the banks sadly replied.
And then, borne out to the sea, they left their native river
And reached the shore of Methymna on the island of Lesbos.
Here a fierce serpent went after the head on those foreign shores
And attacked its locks, which were still wet from the spray.
Finally Apollo appeared, driving away the snake, which was ready
To bite the head, and he froze into stone the open jaws
Of the serpent, hardening that wide-reaching, gaping yawn.   60

  Orpheus' shade went under the earth, and seeing the places
Already viewed, he knew them all, and, coursing the fields of the blessed,
He finds Eurydice, and he embraces her in his loving arms.
Here then the two of them walk together side by side.
Now Orpheus follows her as she leads, and now he walks
In front of his Eurydice, able at last to look back on his belovéd.

8. SATIRE

MARTIAL, JUVENAL, AND PETRONIUS

MARCUS VALERIUS MARTIALIS (ca. A.D. 40–104)

Martial was born and died in Bilbilis, Spain, but lived the most important years of his life in Rome, whose foibles he exploited to the full in his *Epigrams*. His gallery of subjects ranges throughout Roman society, since no type eluded his scrutiny. Unlike Juvenal and many other satirists who are bitter, Martial maintains a good-humored equilibrium as he scans his cast of rascals and rogues. He writes in many meters, including the elegiac, which was usually used for love poetry. Many of his poems are short, pithy epigrams, with a sting at the end. He also wrote a few poems extolling life in the country, but the center of his world was Rome.

It is important to note that Martial's attitude toward homosexuality is not consistently negative, probably because, as he indicates in his poems, he himself freely indulged in gay sex. Some of his poems are sensitive, such as those written to dead boys (I, 88; VI, 28; VI, 68), and a few can be called love poems (see, for example, Nos. III, 65; IV, 7; VI, 34; and XI, 26). In this respect he is like Catullus, and he frequently has echoes of that earlier poet in his work.

I have used as my text that of D.R. Shackleton Bailey in the Loeb Classical Library, 3 vols. (Harvard University Press, 1993).

Book I, Poem 6

While the eagle was carrying Ganymede through the heavenly sky,
　　His burden clung to those talons that didn't want to hurt;
Now a new prey is softening Emperor Domitian's bold lions
　　And dallies like a bunny in their gaping mouths.
Which miracle to you is greater? The creators of both are supreme:
　　Our Caesar on the one hand, Jove on the other.

I, 9

You want to look like a pretty boy, Cotta, and act like a big man;
But a pretty boy, Cotta, is almost always petty.

I, 23

You only invite friends you pick up from the baths, Cotta;
Only men from the steam baths make up your guest list.
Cotta, I used to wonder why you never invite me—
Till I realized that in the nude I'm not up to scratch.

I, 24

You see that guy with the long, uncut hair, Decianus?
The one you're afraid of because of his glowering scowl?
The one who gabs about the Curii and other great heroes of the past?
Well, don't be afraid of that butch front. Yesterday he was a bride.

I, 31

Encolpus, the pet boy of his master, the centurion,
Is going to offer all the locks of his hair to you, Apollo,
When the centurion brings home his well-deserved
Promotion to chief. Cut off that long hair, Apollo,
As soon as possible before any stubble can darken his soft cheeks
And while those flowing tresses still grace his milky shoulders;
Yes, so that master and houseboy can enjoy your gifts a long time,
Make him shaven now fast, but a real man very late.

I, 58

The slavemonger wanted me to pay a hundred thousand for the boy;
I laughed, but Apollo forced me to pay the price.
As a result, my pecker is all worn out and blames me to himself,
While Apollo is praised at my expense.
I hear that Apollo's cock once earned him a good two million;
Give me that, and I'll rise again to the heights!

I, 77

Charinus is wonderfully healthy, and yet he's pale.
Charinus drinks with control, and yet he's pale.
Charinus has fine digestion, and yet he's pale.
Charinus takes the sun, and yet he's pale.
Charinus rouges his cheeks, and yet he's pale.
Charinus licks every slit, and never blushes.

I, 88 On the Dead Alcimus

Alcimus, who was taken from your master in your rising years
    And are covered by the light earth of Labicum,
Take from me not a ponderous marble sarcophagus,
    Whose vain artistry perishes into dust,
But this slender boxtree and the dark shadows of vines
    And some green grass that is wet with my tears.
Take them, dear boy, as monuments of my grief.
    May this honor to you last through all time.
And when the Fate Lachesis decides to snip off my final years,
    I order that my ashes should lie nowhere but here.

I, 90 To a Butch Lesbian

Since I never saw you, Bassa, linked close to men,
    And no gossip ever assigned you a boyfriend,
But a flock of your own sex was always performing its duties
    Around you, without the presence of a grown man—
I confess that I thought you a holy virgin like Lucretia.
    And yet, O Bassa! what an unholy fucker you've been!
You dare to put two cunts together, and your awesome
    Clit lies and pretends it's part of a man!
You've created a monster to match the Sphinx's riddle:
    Without any men, you still manage to commit adultery.

I, 92

Often Cestos complains to me with tearful eyes
    That he is prodded by your finger, Mamurianus.
Well, you don't have to use a finger. Use everything you've got,
    If Cestos is all that you need, Mamurianus.

But if you need a fireplace and a mattress for a bare bed,
    Or a broken cup such as Chione and Antiope had,
  Or if a faded, weather-worn cloak dangles over your loins
    Or a French cape hangs only half-way over your buttocks,
And if you feed only on the steam from a dirty kitchen,
    And you lap up filthy water on all fours like a dog,
It isn't your ass that I'll prod—though it's not really an ass,
    Since you haven't shat lately; I'll prod your last remaining eye.
No, I'm not jealous of you, and don't accuse me of being evil.
    In short, bugger away, Mamurianus; at least *that* way you'll be full.

I, 94

You sang poorly, Aegle, as long as you were *properly* fucked.
    Now you sing well—but I wouldn't kiss you anywhere.

I, 96

If it doesn't bother or annoy you, my lame-ending verse,
I ask you to utter a few words in the ear
Of Maternus, so that only he can hear them.
He is a lover of very conservative cloaks
(Preferring only northern wool and severe gray),
And he thinks that anyone who wears pink is not a man,
And believes that violet-colored clothes are for queens;
Let him praise what's primitive, and let him always wear
Conservative colors—but his morals are shady green.
He'll ask you: why do I suspect that he's a fairy?
Well, we bathe together, and his eyes never look up;
He's always devouring the private parts of butch fags
And studies their cocks with anxious lips.
You ask who he is? Ah, his name just escaped me. . . . *[See line 3]*

II, 61

When your cheeks were still sprouting with uncertain fuzz,
    Your improper tongue was already licking men's loins.
Now that your hateful head has earned the loathing even of
    Grave-robbers and the scorn of miserable hangmen,

You're finding another use for your tongue: seized by excessive ill will,
    You loosen its bark against any name mentioned to you.
It's better for you to let that evil tongue keep sucking genitals,
    Because while you're sucking, it can't spew out its filth.

II, 62

The fact that you're shaving your chest and your thighs
    And your arms and are thinning your pubic hair, Labienus—
All this shows everyone you're getting ready for your girl-friend.
    But for whom are you shaving your butt?

III, 39

Lycoris has only one eye, Faustinus, and it's set on a cupbearer
    Like Ganymede. How well those one-eyed can see!

III, 65

A tender girl's sweet breath after biting an apple,
    The sweet scent of saffron that comes from Corycia,
The smell of a vine white with the first spring blossoms,
    The odor of grass that is freshly grazed by sheep;
The perfume of myrtle and Arabic spices and amber,
    Of a fire whitened by frankincense from the East,
Of the earth just sprinkled with a light summer shower,
    Of a crown just worn by a head redolent with nard—
With all these, cruel little Diadumenus, your kisses are fragrant.
    Why don't you give them to me completely without holding back?

III, 71

I can see, Naevolus, that the boy's cock is as sore as your ass is;
    I'm no prophet, but I know very well what you're up to.

III, 73

You're always sleeping with well-hung boys, my Phoebus,
But what stands up for them doesn't stand up for you.
Phoebus, I ask you: what am I to make of all this?

I wanted to think that you were too soft to fuck,
But gossip says you're quite capable of taking it.

III, 80

You don't whine about anyone, Apicius, or bad-mouth them;
  But gossip says you have a wicked little tongue.

III, 81

What are you doing with a female chasm, Baeticus the Eunuch?
  Your tongue was made to lick the middles of men.
Why was your prick cut off by a Samian shard, Baeticus,
  If a pussy pleases you so much?
Your head should be cut away; for although you're a Gallus down under,
  You beat Cybele's castration, for in your mouth you're still a man.
   ["Gallus" can mean "a rooster, a Gaul, or a castrated priest of Cybele."]

III, 98

Are you asking me, Sabellus, how small your asshole is?
  Well, small enough to let anyone in.

IV, 7

Tell me, young Hyllus, why you're denying me today what you gave yesterday.
  Why are you so harsh, who was once so compliant?
Now you whine about your beard and your years and your body hair.
  Can one night be long enough to turn you into an old man?
Why are you making fun of me? You who were a boy yesterday, Hyllus,
  Tell me: how can you overnight become a man?

IV, 42

If anyone perhaps should grant me what I ask for, Flaccus,
  In the way of a boy, listen and I will tell you.
First of all I want a boy born on the banks of the Nile River:
  No other place schools boys better in naughtiness.
Let him be blonder than snow, for in dark Lower Egypt
  Nothing is more beautiful because of its rareness.

Let his eyes contend with the stars and his soft locks
    Cascade over his shoulders—I don't like them curly.
Let his forehead be narrow and his small nose a bit aquiline,
    And his lips rivals with the roses of Paestum.
Let him force me when I'm unwilling and deny me when I'm passionate,
    But let him be more generous when doing it than his master!
Let him not fear other boys and keep girls at a distance,
    And be a man to everyone else, but a boy to me.
You say: "Now I know who you mean; no doubt; I agree:
    Such a boy was my own Amazonicus."

IV, 48

You adore being impaled, Papylus, and yet afterwards you cry.
    Why, since you like the act, do you later whine so?
Are you ashamed of off-color sex? Or do you cry instead,
    Papylus, because the impaling is over?

V, 46

I only desire kisses that I have snatched from you struggling,
    And your anger delights me more than your face itself;
That's why I often strike you, Diadumenus—so I have to beg you harder.
    But the outcome is this: you don't shrink from me—or love me.

V, 55 *On a Painting of Jupiter and Ganymede*

Tell me, Queen Eagle, who's in your claws? "The Thunderer."
    Why isn't he carrying any bolts? "He's in love."
And who is he burning for? "A boy." Why are you looking
    At Jove with a watering mouth? "It's Ganymede I'm eyeing."

VI, 16 *To a Statue of Priapus*

You who with your penis frighten straights and fairies with your sickle,
    Watch over these few acres of reserved ground,
So that no seasoned burglar can enter your orchard—
    Only a boy or a beautiful girl with long, flowing hair!

VI, 28 *For Glaucias, the Dead Freedman of Melior*

That well-known freedman of Melior,
Who died and left all of Rome grieving,
That brief delight of his loving patron,
Glaucias, now lies under this marble
In a tomb just off the Flaminian Way.
He was chaste in his morals, fully controlled,
Swift in his wit, blessed in his charm.
Having lived through only twice six autumns,
He was just going to add another year.
Traveler, if you weep for him, may you never weep again!

VI, 33

Have you ever seen anyone more miserable than that faggot Sabellus,
       Dear Matho—and yet once no one was more contented than he?
Robberies, exiles, deaths of slaves, fires, and funerals have all left him
       Unaffected—but now the poor fool's fucking women.

VI, 34

Give me lots of kisses, Diadumenus. "How many?"
       You're asking me to count the ocean's waves
And the seashells that lie scattered on the Aegean shores,
       And the bees that buzz around on Mount Hymettus,
And all the voices and hands that sound in a packed theater
       Whenever the people see the Emperor's face.
I don't want all those that Lesbia gave, when asked, to her
       Lively Catullus. He desires little who is old enough to count.

VI, 37

From his ass, which is cut all the way to his navel,
Charinus doesn't have very much left,
And yet he scratches all the way up to his button.
O what scabies the poor thing suffers from!
He doesn't have a ring—and yet he's a big queen.

VI, 50

When he was courting decent friends, poor old Telesinus
  Wandered around looking squalid in a tattered toga;
But now that he's begun to service nasty faggots,
  Unrivaled, he buys silverware, tables, and estates.
Do you want to be rich, Bithynicus? Follow his lead.
  Pure kisses will get you little—or even nothing.

VI, 68 *For the Dead Eutychos*

Bemoan your crime, yes bemoan it over all the Lucrine Lake,
  You nymphs, and let even Thetis hear your lamentations
For the boy who was carried under the waves at Baiae,
  That Eutychos, who was your sweet double, Castricus.
He was a partner in your pursuits, a warm consolation,
  A great love; he was the Alexis of our Vergil.
Did some lusting nymph see him naked under the crystal waves
  And offer him like Hylas back to Hercules?
Or did some goddess, won over by the embraces of a soft husband,
  Now abandon your girlish Hermaphroditus?
In any case, whatever was the cause of this sudden rape,
  May the earth and the sea, I pray, be kindly to you!

VII, 67 *On a Tough Lesbian*

The lesbian Philaenis buggers around with boys,
And, more savage in her lechery than any husband,
In one day penetrates eleven young girls.
And, trussed up, she even competes in handball
And turns gold on wrestlers' sand, and flings around
Effortlessly weights heavy even for muscle-queens;
And, all besmirched from the stinking floor of the gym,
She takes a flogging from her oiled-up masseur.
She doesn't dine or recline for dinner
Until she has vomited up seven unmixed glasses of wine,
To which she thinks that she can return
After wolfing down sixteen entrées.
After all this when she starts to feel sexy,
She doesn't blow any man (no, that's not manly!),
But she completely devours the privates of girls.

May the gods keep you in your current state of mind,
Philaenis: always consider it manly to lick a cunt.

VII, 70

O Philaenis, dike of all dikes,
You rightly call a girl-friend the girl you fuck around with.

IX, 21

Artemidorus has a young slave-boy, but sold his land;
    Calliodorus now owns the land but lost the slave.
Tell me, Auctus: which of the two got the better deal?
    Artemidorus plows his love; Calliodorus his land.

IX, 25

Every time we look at your Hyllus pouring us wine,
    You look at us with a jaundiced eye, Afer.
What, I ask you, what crime is it to gaze at a tender servant?
    We gaze at the sun and stars and temples and gods.
Should I turn away my look as if some stony Gorgon was offering
    Me a cup or was scanning my eyes and my face?
Hercules was tough, yet he was allowed to feast his eyes on Hylas.
    Mercury was allowed to play around with Ganymede.
If you don't want your guests to eye up your shapely servants,
    Then you should only invite Phineus and Oedipus—the blind!

IX, 33

If you're ever in a bath, Flaccus, and your hear some applause,
Then you'll know that Maro's enormous rod is on display.

IX, 69

After you fuck, Polycharmus, you always take a shit.
Tell me: what do you do after *you're* the one who's fucked?

X, 65

Since you're always bragging that you're a citizen
Of Corinth, Charmenion—and no one denies it—
Why are you always calling me "brother"? I hail from
The land of Iberians and Celts and the River Tagus.
Do you think that we even look alike?
You wander around looking sleek with your curly hair,
While mine is wildly unruly in the Spanish style.
Every day a depilator makes your body smooth,
While I sport hair on my thighs and cheeks.
Your mouth is lisping and your tongue is faltering,
But I speak deeply from my guts;
We're more different than a dove from an eagle
Or a timid doe from a raging lion.
And so, Charmenion, stop calling me "brother"—
Or else I'll start calling you "sister."

X, 98

When a serving-boy softer than soft Ganymede
Adds some Caecuban wine to my cup,
And not your daughter nor wife nor mother
Nor sister reclining there is any the wiser,
Do you want me to stare instead at your lamps
Or your citrus-wood antiques or Indian tusks?
So that I won't have to recline there under your suspect eyes,
Then select for me from that herd on your run-down ranch
Some servant close-cropped, rough, crude, and stunted,
The son of some goat-smelling swineherd.
This sickness will get you, Publius. You can't have
High morals and gorgeous serving-boys at the same time.

XI, 26

My welcome refuge, Telesphorus, my tender care,
　　　Who surpasses all other boys who have ever lain on my breast—
Give me kisses, my boy, wet with the taste of vintage Falernian;
　　　Give me that cup that you've just made smaller with your lips.
If, besides this, you add the highest pleasures of Venus,
　　　I'll deny that Jupiter was ever better off with Ganymede.

XI, 28

That madman Nasica attacked Hylas, Dr. Euctus' boy,
    And browned him. Well . . . maybe . . . you have to consider him sane.

XI, 43

You, my wife, assail me with angry words, having caught me
    With a boy, noting that you also have an ass.
Well, Juno said the very same things to over-sexed Jupiter,
    But he nevertheless went on sleeping with the grown Ganymede.
Laying down his bow, Hercules also made Hylas bend over,
    And don't you think his wife Megara didn't have buttocks too?
Daphne, always fleeing, tormented Apollo; but the boy Oebalius
    Soon found a way of putting out those flames.
Briseis slept with Achilles, though against her will,
    But he found a more amenable bedmate in buddy Patroclus.
So stop applying masculine names to your body,
    And be glad, woman, that you are blessed with *two* holes.

XI, 63

You eye me, Philomusus, when we are bathing together
And you're always asking me why I have so many
Heavy-hung, smooth-cheeked young men around me.
I will answer you directly, since you ask:
Philomusus, they drive away nosy meddlers.

XII, 42

Bearded Callistratus became a bride to tough old Afer,
    And they even followed the rites of virgin and spouse.
The wedding torches burned, a veil covered his face,
    And a hymn to the god of marriage wasn't absent.
They even announced a dowry. Now listen, Rome: don't you
    Think this is enough? What do you want next—a birth?

XII, 75

Polytimus is always running after girls;
Hymnus only unwillingly admits he's a boy;

Secundus has buttocks a yard wide;

Dindymus tries very hard not to act like a queen;

Amphion could easily have been born a girl.

Avitus, I prefer all of their whims and tantrums

And bitchy complaints to anyone who'd give me

A marriage dowry of several million.

XII, 86

You have thirty boyfriends and the same number of girls, and

     Your poor cock can't rise to the occasion. What are you going to do?

DECIMUS JUNIUS JUVENALIS (ca. A.D. 60–131)

Juvenal was born at Aquinus, the native town of St. Thomas Aquinas, and lived a life that included the miseries of poverty and exile. As a result his 16 satires vent a ferocious scorn against the world, and homosexuals did not escape his rage. However, they often come off better than their heterosexual counterparts.

     Juvenal is perhaps best known for his statement of "the vanity of human wishes," a topic that appealed to the Age of Reason, especially sensibilities such as Voltaire, Samuel Johnson, Dryden, and Swift. Although much of his work seems petty or extreme in its misanthropy, he remains one of the primary fathers of satire.

     I have used as my text the edition of G.G. Ramsay contained in the Loeb Classical Library (Harvard University Press, 1918 et seq.).

Satire II, 159–170 A View of Contemporary Rome

Alas, we are reduced to this miserable pit! We have moved our weapons

Beyond the shores of Ireland and taken the Orkneys captive,   160

As well as the Britons with their shortened nights.

But the things that are done by the people of our victorious city

Would not be done by those that we conquered. And yet a certain

Armenian named Zalaces, who is more sissified than any of our own

Young men, is said to have offered himself to a lustful tribune.

See what foreign trade entails! He came here as a hostage,

But his type become *Menschen*. If you give them a long enough stay,

They'll never fail to find some lover here.

They'll throw away their pants, their knives, their reins and whips,
And they'll carry back to Artaxata the low morals of our youth.   170
          [The poem ends here.]

Satire V, 49–66 On Behavior at a Banquet

If Milord's belly is boiling over with food and wine,
A concoction more frigid than Thrace's frosts will be sent for.   50
Was I complaining just now that a lower grade of wine was put before you?
You're even drinking a lower grade of water. An African lackey
Will hand it to you—or the bony hand of some dinge from Morocco,
The kind you wouldn't want to bump into alone about midnight
As you're riding past the ghostly tombs up the steep Latin Way.
The Flower of Asia is serving Your Host, a kid purchased at greater price
Than the whole fortune of that aggressive Tullus or Ancus,
And, I'm not lying! one that makes the holdings of all the old kings of Rome
Seem nothing. That's the story, and when you feel thirsty, just
Look at your dusky Ganymede. That other kid bought for so many   60
Millions can't pour a pauper a decent drink; ah, but his beauty,
His youth make him arrogant. When will he come and wait on you?
When, if you ask for something hot or cold, will he deign to serve you?
Indeed, he disdains to wait on a broken-down hanger-on, resenting
That you ask for anything, and you recline while he has to stand.
The greatest part of our houses are full of such uppity slaves.
          [The poem continues to line 173.]

Satire IX, 27ff. The Confessions of a Bisexual Hustler

[The hustler Naevolus is talking to Juvenal:]
"A lot of men have profited from my kind of life—but me,
I've gotten nothing of value: sometimes a greasy cloak,
A gift to cover my toga, coarse and poorly dyed
And badly put together by some weaver up in France—   30
Or some silver trinket of second-class worth.
Fate rules all men—even those parts of us that
The toga hides. And if the stars abandon you,
The size of your humungous cock won't help you,
Not even if old Virrus with his slobbering lips sees you naked
And constantly sends you a lot of bland love letters
Tempting you in mock Greek: 'Men are excited by—queens.'

Who is a worse monster than some horny, stingy old auntie?
'I gave you this and then I gave you that, and you took much more!'
So he computes—and wiggles. Put away your calculator; bring on   40
The boys with their tablets; tote up your 5,000
For everything done—and then figure out the worth of *my* work!
Is it easy or right to drive an upright prick up
Someone's innards and to encounter yesterday's dinner there?
That slave who has plowed the fields is better off than plowing
His master, who says: 'You used to consider yourself a tender boy,
And pretty and worthy of handling the wine-ladle in heaven.'
And I: 'When will *you*, who are not prepared to pay for your sick vices,
Ever show any kindness toward a humble follower or servant?' . . . .

      [Naevolus continues speaking with Juvenal:]
What do you recommend now, with so much time gone by   125
And all my hopes dashed? The brief spans of our short, unhappy
Lives are rushing on swiftly like a fast-blooming flower
To their ends; while we are drinking and calling for garlands
And unguents and girls, old age is creeping up on us undetected.

JUVENAL:

Don't be afraid; you're never going to be without some gay friend   130
As long as the hills of Rome are standing; from everywhere
They'll rush here in their carriages and aboard ships—
All those johns who scratch their heads as a sign. And you have
Another better hope—you can always use love drugs.

NAEVOLUS:

Give your advice to the lucky; my own Fates
Are pleased if I can just use my cock to fill my belly.
O little gods of my household, which I always
Supplicate with a little frankincense or corn
Or with a little garland, when can I make certain
That I can keep my old age safe from a beggar's crutch   140
And a mat? All I need is the interest off 20,000 sesterces
Well-invested, as well as a few vessels of plain silver
(But the kind that old Fabricius the Censor would have
Noted down), and a couple of big bucks from Bulgaria
Who could put my litter on their necks so that I
Could be carried in style to the howling Circus.
I would also like a bent-over engraver and someone else

To dash off quick portraits. That would be enough
For a poor fellow like me. This is a piddling prayer,
But I don't even have hope for this because whenever I call   150
To Fortune, she always jams her ears with wax lifted
From the same ship that carried Ulysses past the Sirens.

GAIUS PETRONIUS CALLED THE ARBITER (d. A.D. 66)

The satiric novelist who wrote the *Satyricon* is probably the same person
who is described so eloquently by the historian Tacitus as a famous hedo-
nistic member of the court of Nero; his taste was so excellent that he was
called the Arbiter or judge of all things aesthetic. In his *Annals* 16.18, Tacitus
describes him as an "extravagant sensualist" who turned the night into day.
But his success aroused jealousy, and he was accused on a trumped-up charge
of conspiring against the Emperor. Refusing to grovel he cut his veins in his
bath and, surrounded by friends, listened to their "gay songs and light verse"
until he died.

   Very incomplete, the novel relates the picaresque wanderings of its
hero, Encolpius, who has been made homosexual apparently because he
violated the rites of a deity. He picks up with a pretty young man named
Giton, and they share numerous adventures. My translation is based on
the Loeb Library edition by Michael Heseltine (Harvard University Press,
rpt. 1951). An excellent translation is that of J.P. Sullivan (Penguin, 1977).

*[1] Section 23. Encolpius and Giton are staying in a house presided over
by a woman named Quartilla*

   Then in came a fairy, the most disgusting kind of all, but clearly he
was worthy of that house. He groaned as he cracked his knuckles and
then poured out a song like this:

   Come here, come here, quickly, you little queens with your bracelets!
   Run fast, get set, fly here on your fairy feet!
   With your soft thighs and agile butts and wandering hands;
   Come on, you tender kids and agéd fags and fat *castrati!*

Having polished off his song, he slavered me with the dirtiest of kisses. Then
he leaped on my bed, even though I was pushing him away as violently as
I could. . . .

[2] Section 79. Encolpius and Giton are spending the night in an inn, along with a supposed friend named Ascyltus, who is lusting for the boy

> O gods and goddesses, what a night we had!
> How soft was our bed! Hotly we clung together
> As we poured out our wandering souls through our lips
> Here and there! O goodbye all cares of mortal man!
> —But in this way I began to die.

Yes, I congratulated myself on my luck too soon. Because when I was overcome by the wine and took my drunken hands away from my love, Ascyltus, that inventor of all destruction, stole away my boy in the middle of the night and took him over to his bed. . . .

[3] Section 109. Encolpius and Giton fall in with a fraudulent poet named Eumolpus; they are joined by a wealthy prostitute named Tryphaena, who takes them aboard a ship

Then Eumolpus, who was drowned in his wine, started to throw around some words against bald men and branded criminals, and after he'd exhausted his frigid wit, he returned to his poetry and started to compose a Song on Hair:

> Hair, which is the essence of beautiful form, has fallen,
>> And bitter winter has carried away the tresses of spring.
> Now the temples having lost their shade are saddened,
>> And broad space shines where the hairs have been rubbed
>> away.
> O deceiving nature of the gods! The joys that you gave us
>> In our early days are the first ones you snatch away.
>> Poor fool, just now you were radiant with your locks,
>> And you were more beautiful than Phoebus or his sister.
>> But now your head is smoother than polished bronze
>> Or a rounded mushroom cap after the rain;
>> You flee, you're afraid of girls who will laugh at you.
>> Now you believe that death will come all the sooner;
>> Yes, for a part of your head has already died.

He wanted to go on with this lousy stuff, when the maid of Tryphaena took Giton down below on the ship and took out some of her mistress's curly wigs to place on the boy's head.

Medieval Latin Literature

Thomas Stehling and James J. Wilhelm

With the triumph and spread of Christianity one might have expected all homosexual literature to cease. The Early Church Fathers were clearly very hard on the subject, as they were to any sexuality outside the bond of marriage. And yet, as John Boswell showed in *Christianity, Social Tolerance, and Homosexuality* (University of Chicago, 1980), there was often a gap between the letter of the law and actual social practice.

In fact it may seem strange to some that the majority of men who wrote homosexual verse were clergymen, but this phenomenon occurred in numerous other societies, such as Japan. Sometimes the gap between love and friendship is difficult to measure—and border-line cases are usually omitted here. But there are still enough poems, and historical documents, to show that homosexuality was very much alive in this period. The very fact that men were segregated into monasteries and women into nunneries no doubt promoted this development.

There is very little surviving lesbian poetry in the Middle Ages. The two selections included here (pp. 174–176) are among the very few that can be found. It is clear that the women were repressed far more deeply than were the men.

Many of the translations in this section are taken from Thomas Stehling's *Medieval Latin Poems of Male Love and Friendship,* which I edited for the Garland Library of Medieval Literature in 1984, and have re-edited here.

AUSONIUS (ca. A.D. 310–ca. 394)

A successful politician under the Roman Emperor Gratian, Ausonius retired to his native Bordeaux in 383. He was married one time, and when his wife died, he never married again. He had a deep friendship with his favorite student, Paulinus of Nola, whose poetry follows. His epigrams imitate those found in the *Greek Anthology*. My translations are based on Stehling, Nos. 1, 3, and 4.

[1] *On Three Lecherous Men*

"There are three men in one bed. Two are taking something shameful,
    And two are giving it." "Well, that should make four."
"No, you're wrong. The two on the ends are guilty of just one crime,
    While the one in the middle is having it two ways."

[2] *To a Boy*

While nature was wondering whether to make you male or female,
    You were made half-girl, my beautiful boy.

[3] *End of a Letter to Paulinus of Nola*

Come quickly, our glory, my greatest care,
Summoned by vows, by good omens, and by prayers.
Hurry while you are still a youth and while my old age,
To please you, preserves its strength undrained.
Will this message ever strike my ears:
"Look! Your Paulinus is here! He's already left the snowy
Towns of Spain; he's already reached the fields of Tarbella,

Already approaches the houses of Hebromagus; now he enters
His brother's nearby estates, now glides down the river's current,
And now he's in sight. Just now his prow turns on the stream.
And after coming through the crowded entrance of his own port,
He goes past the whole crowd of people who have come to meet him,
And, passing by his own door now, he knocks on yours."
Can we believe this, or do those who love create dreams for themselves?

PAULINUS OF NOLA (ca. A.D. 353–431)

Like his teacher-friend Ausonius, Paulinus hailed from Bordeaux, where he
served as a consul to Rome. He married early, but became a devout ascetic,
living first in a monastery in Spain near Barcelona (where he wrote this let-
ter to Ausonius) and later in Italy, where he became Bishop of Nola in 409.
It could be argued that this poem expresses *amicitia* rather than *amor*, but
the passionate expression cannot be denied. Stehling's translation; No. 5.

The End of a Letter to Ausonius

You and me: for all time which is given
And destined for mortal men,
For as long as I am held in this confining, limping body,
No matter how far I am separated from you in the world,
You will be neither distant from me nor far from my eyes:
I will hold you, intermingled in my very sinews.
I will see you in my heart and with a loving spirit embrace you;
You will be with me everywhere.
And when released from this bodily prison
I fly from earth
To the spot in heaven where our universal Father places me,
There too I will keep you in my spirit;
Nor will the end which frees me from my body
Release me from your love.
For the mind, once it has survived loss of limbs,
Continues to grow out of its heavenly root,
And therefore must keep both its understanding and affections
Along with its life.
And just as it experiences no death, it will experience no loss of memory
But remain forever alive, forever mindful.
Farewell, my illustrious master!

ENNODIUS (ca. 473–521)

Born in Arles, France, Ennodius married, but then entered a religious life, becoming a teacher and moving to Italy, where he became Bishop of Pavia in 512 or 513. His epigrams imitate Martial. Translations are by Stehling, Nos. 7, 9, 10.

[1]

Your face is masculine, your gestures feminine, but your thighs are both:
You resolve an opposition in nature by negating the difference.
You are a rabbit and trample the neck of a great lion.

    [Rabbits were associated with lust and gayness.]

[2]

Look at this monster created by promiscuous rule—
Of common gender, or, rather, of all genders.

[3]

There is a constant deception at play in his double sex:
He's a woman when passive, but when active in lust, he's a man.

LUXORIUS (EARLY SIXTH CENTURY)

Little is known about Luxorius except that he was a Christian who lived in Carthage and imitated Martial. See Morris Rosenblum, *Luxorius* (Columbia University Press, 1961). Translations are by Stehling, Nos. 11–14.

[1] *To an Effeminate Lawyer*

Model of castrated men,
Utter disgrace of nature,
A Paris to be used as a woman,
An object of filthy lust:
Since you are so eloquent with your mouth,
Why do you promote useless causes
Or corrupt dealings?
And why handle mostly cases that should be lost?
I know: as I see it,

You want good stuff entrusted
Not to your mouth, I think, but to your asshole.

[2] *To a Hermaphroditic Girl*
Double-membered monster of the female sex
Whom unnatural desire makes a man,
With your raging cunt why don't you like to be fucked?
Why does this impossible desire make a fool out of you?
The cunt, with which you should submit and act, you don't use.
When you yield the part which proves
You are a woman, then you may be a girl.

[3] *To a Passive Homosexual Who Rewards His Seducers*
Riches, great feasts, and so many gifts,
The wealth of your grandfather, great grandfather, and all your ancestors
        left you:
Though you squander these things, giving them to all your "husbands," Becca,
The man you want to give them to still takes more.
I don't know what wretched thing you're hiding, Becca: if you were
Offering good pieces of meat, you should have sold them for a goodly sum.

[4] *To an Effeminate Charioteer Who Never Wins*
You go ahead, Vico, but you never come out ahead.
Unmanned by this wretched practice, you let your guard down
On the flank you should have protected.
If you ever want to win in your chariot,
You'll have to get your seducer in the rear.

POEMS FROM *THE LATIN ANTHOLOGY* (EARLY SIXTH CENTURY)
This collection, made in North Africa, includes many earlier poems. An older
edition by Franz Buecheler and Alexander Riese has been superseded by
Shackleton Bailey (Stuttgart: Teubner, 1982). Translations are by Stehling
from his Nos. 15, 17, 20 to 23, and 25.

[1] On Hylas and Hercules

Hylas the waterboy is abducted: the nymphs' joys increase.
The wrath of Hercules swells: Hylas the waterboy is abducted.

[2] On Orestes and Pylades

Love kindles quarrels so that it can burn the lovers more deliciously.
To crown their faithfulness, love kindles quarrels.

[3] On Hyacinth

While he, as chance would have it, is playing, Hyacinth
Runs up to life's edge, splitting his temples with a discus.
Apollo could not steal his lover back from fate,
But the dead boy's blood replenishes the flowering fields.

[4] Again on Hyacinth

Circling back, the discus shattered the player's temples
And beautiful Hyacinth died a cruel death.
But a great dispensation gives comfort for the boy taken by death:
For all time Apollo's love rises up again in a flower.

[5] On Martius, a Passive Homosexual

What good is it that your name is taken from the name of Mars,
When it is Venus who itches in your notorious ass?
It would have been a better fate had you been named Cypridos [Venus],
And nature had given you Mars's members.
Now lacking both, you are a tale of unknown sex:
Though you're not a woman, you still cannot be a man.

[6] To a Beloved Boy

Why are you so wild, Cyparus? Why do you press now on the tame
Young bull's back? Why force a tender horse to run?
While he is starry-eyed and young, and still knows nothing of love,
Let him go; he will be forced to take it when he's older.

[7] On a Dead Friend

Crispus has been taken from me, friends.
If a price could be paid for him,
I would freely give up half of my years.
My best part has now left me:
Crispus, my fortress, my desire,
My heart and delight. My mind now will see
That nothing gives pleasure without him.
Badly wasted and feeble, I live on,
Though more than half of me has passed away.

ALCUIN (ca. 735–804)

Born in England and for a time the master of the cathedral school at York, Alcuin was summoned by Emperor Charlemagne to his court in Aachen to perform literary and educational tasks. He later directed the Abbey of St. Martin at Tours, where he ascribed bird-names and epithets from Classical pastorals to his students. The Lament was written, as E.S. Duckett has claimed in her *Alcuin, Friend of Charlemagne* (1951, pp. 153–54), to a young man with the nickname of Cuckoo, who left his abbey. My translation is from my *Medieval Song,* No. 24. The original poem is much longer.

The Debate Poem is a familiar medieval genre, and Winter and Spring are common participants. Spring represents the positive side of life. Once again the Cuckoo figures as a character. My translation is from my *Medieval Song,* pp. 61 ff.; the original is longer. The third poem is from Stehling, No. 26.

[1] Lament for a Lost Cuckoo

Alas, my cuckoo, who always used to sing for me,
    What curséd hour has snatched you away?
O, o! my cuckoo, where, in what place did I leave you?
    To me that was a most unfortunate day.
Every manner of man everywhere is lamenting you,
    For the cuckoo is lost; yes, that cuckoo—mine.
O, don't let him be lost! Let him come in the springtime
    And coming let him sing for me happy songs.
Who knows if he'll come? I'm afraid he has drowned,
    Swirled in a whirlpool, dashed by the waves.   10
O God! if that Wine-God has drenched him in liquid,
    Who gathers young men in his deadly whirls!

If he lives, let him come, let him run to our warm nest;
    Let no crow grasp him with clutching claw.
O, my cuckoo, who grabbed you away from your father's home?
    He stole you, he stole you; now will you ever come back?
If you care for my songs, cuckoo, then come quickly.
    Come quickly, I beg! O yes, quickly come!
Don't delay, little cuckoo; I beg you: come running.
    Your belovéd Daphnis wants to possess you again.   20
The springtime has come; cuckoo, arise from your slumber.
    Look! old father Menalcas wants you here.
The bulls are now grazing around in our pastures;
    Only the cuckoo is absent; who pastures him?
O God! not that Bacchus, that impious Wine-God,
    Who's quick to turn every heart into evil.
Weep for the cuckoo. Yes, all men go weeping.
    He left us rejoicing. I fear he'll come back in tears. . . .
Alas, he has fled, he has fled; my lament now grows bitter.   30
    It's all I have left; my gentle cuckoo is gone.
Let me send my songs after him, songs of bereavement,
    For singing might carry my fledgling home.
O, I pray you: be happy wherever you wander;
    Remember me, cuckoo, and forever—farewell!

[2] Debate Between Winter and Spring

SPRING: I want my cuckoo to come, my most beloved bird;
Above all others he was always a welcomed guest
Up on my rooftop, singing through reddish bill.

WINTER: Let no cuckoo come! Let him sleep in dark, dark caves,
For he's always bringing hunger wherever he goes.

SPRING: I want my cuckoo to come with the happy blossoms;
Let him drive away cold, this long-time friend of the Sun.
Phoebus adores the cuckoo when the days are long and serene.

WINTER: Let no cuckoo come! He creates all kinds of toil;
He promotes constant battles, he disrupts the blessed peace;   10
He's a great troublemaker, stirring both land and sea.

SPRING: Ah, slow old Winter, why are you hurling these charges?
You huddle in your shadowy den weighted down with torpor
After the banquets of Venus, after the cups of loose Bacchus.

WINTER: These are my riches, these my happy carousings;
Ah, sleep is sweet with a warm fire in your hearth.
But this your cuckoo can't know; he just serves the corrupt.

SPRING: Let the cuckoo come with flowers in his beak, ministering honey;
Let him build up his mansions and sail on a halcyon sea,
Engendering offspring and brightening happy fields.   20

WINTER: Ah, how I hate all these things you so delight in!
I like to count up my hoard that I treasure in chests,
And have a big meal, and then slip away in slumber.

SPRING: O heavy Winter, always ready to snooze, just tell me
Who would get you that hoard, would heap up that treasure
If Summer and I didn't work for you year after year?

WINTER: You're right. And because you kowtow to all my details,
You're my slaves; you'll do anything that I ask.
Yes, slaves to me, your lord in all of your toils!

SPRING: You our lord? Why, you're shabby, stingy, and proud!   30
You wouldn't be able to feed yourself for a single day
If the cuckoo didn't come and bring you his sweet alms.

Then Palemon spoke, rejoicing from his high throne,
And Daphnis too, and the flock of pious shepherds:
"That's enough, Winter. You talk too much; you're too harsh.
No, let the cuckoo come, sweet friend of the shepherds,
And let the gladdening seeds burst forth on our hills;
Let the cattle have pasture; let peace reign over the meadows
And branches green lift parasols for the weary;
Let the goats come to the barnyard with udders swollen with milk,   40
And the birds salute the Sun with their varying songs.
For all of these reasons, come now, my cuckoo, come!
You are now my sweet love, a most welcome guest for all.

All things await you—the earth and the water and sky.
Hail, my sweet honor; yes, for all of the ages, hail!

[3] To Arno of Salzburg

Love has penetrated my heart with its flame,
And is ever rekindled with new warmth.
Neither sea nor land, hills nor forest, nor even the Alps
Can stand in its way or hinder it
From always licking at your inmost parts, good father,
Or from bathing your heart, my beloved, with tears.
Sweet love, why do you inspire bitter tears,
Why do bitter draughts flow from devotion's honey?
If now your sweetness, world, is mixed with bitterness,
All prosperity will alternate rapidly with misfortune,   10
All joys will be changed to sad lamentation;
Nothing lasts; everything can perish.
Therefore, world, let us flee from you with all our hearts,
As you, ready even now to perish, flee from us.
Let us seek the delights and ever-enduring realms
Of heaven with our whole hearts, minds, and hands.
The blessed hall of heaven never separates friends;
A heart warmed by love always has with it loves.
Therefore, father, abduct me with your prayers, I beg you;
Then our love will never be estranged.   20
Look with joy and with a gladdening heart, I pray,
At these little offerings which great love sends you,
For our gentle Master praised the two copper coins
The needy widow put in the temple's treasury.
A holy love is better than any gift,
And so is firm faithfulness, which flourishes and endures.
May divine gifts follow you, dearest father,
And at the same time precede you. Always and everywhere: Farewell!

GOTTSCHALK (ca. 805–869)

Also called Godescalc, Gottschalk was an aristocratic Saxon whose father placed
him in a monastery when he was very young. He tried to get out, but was not
permitted. Later at Orbais, he wrote an inflammatory treatise in which he pro-
nounced pre-Calvinistic views of man's predestination, which were bitterly

attacked by John Scotus Erigena and others. He apparently died after long imprisonment, which this poem dramatizes; it was written to a young friend (who is called by numerous epithets for "boy") who had asked him for a song to lighten their despair. Translation is from my *Lyrics of the Middle Ages*, No. 1.

Why do you order, little laddie,
Why command me, little son,
Telling me to sing a sweet song
When I'm exiled far away
      Out at sea?
Why do you order me to sing?

Better for me, poor little young one,
To do some weeping, little boy-child;
I'm for descant, not for chanting
The kind of song that you demand,   10
      My sweet dear one.
Why do you order me to sing?

You know I'd rather, little lad,
Have you join me, brother of mine,
Weeping with a ready heart,
Sharing now my heavy mind
      In lamentations.
Why do you order me to sing?

Well you know, divine novitiate,
You know, heavenly protégé,   20
I have been here long in exile
Many a night and many a day
      Always suffering.
Why do you order me to sing? . . .

Yet since you desire it so strongly,
Finest companion for a man,
I shall sing to the Son and Father
And to the Spirit that always runs
      Out of them both.
This I *will* sing willingly.   30
Blessèd are thou, holy Master,

Father, Son, and Paraclete,
God of might, of majesty,
       Just Divinity,
This I *will* sing willingly.

WALAFRID STRABO (ca. 808–849)

A poor Swabian, Walafrid Strabo was educated at Reichenau, Germany, and later studied at Fulda with Rabanus Maurus, a student of Alcuin. He tutored Charles the Bald, son of Emperor Louis the Pious, and was later Abbot of Reichenau. He writes numerous poems to friends, who may not necessarily be lovers. These translations are by Stehling from his volume, Nos. 30 and 31.

[1] *To the Young Novitiate Liutger*

My dear, you come suddenly; suddenly, my dear, you depart.
I hear you, don't see you, yet inwardly I see, and inwardly
I embrace you even as you flee from me—in body but not in faith.
For just as I have been sure, as I am now, so will I always be
That I am cherished in your heart, you in mine. May passing time
Never persuade me or you of anything different.
If you can visit me, it will be enough to see my most welcomed one.
But at other times, write me; write me anything—I've known your sorrows,
And reflect on them with grief; grief is a possession of the whole world.
Those things you consider serene flee the most quickly into the clouds
And the sad shadows. Like a bird that hovers over the globe,
Now rising, now falling, so turns the wheel of the world.

[2] *To a Friend*

When the splendor of the unclouded moon shines from the sky,
Stand under the heavens and see with a wondering gaze
How the moon shines like a clear torch
And how with its single splendor it embraces loved ones
Divided in body but joined in spirit by love.
If one face cannot gaze on another loving one,
At least let this light be our pledge of love.
A faithful friend has sent you these little verses.
If on your side the bond of faith stands firm,
Now I bid you farewell; be happy forever!

NOTKER BALBULUS (ca. 840–912)

Born to a noble Swiss family, Notker Balbulus entered the famous musical Abbey of St. Gall, where he was a stammerer (hence the nickname "Balbulus"). He became famous as the developer of the sequence, a form of medieval chant set syllabically over a Latin text. The first selection here is not a sequence; it and the other were written to Salomo, Notker's favorite pupil. Translations are from Stehling, Nos. 32 and 33.

[1] To Salomo

How quickly I am cheated by my new-found friend—
    That is, if you still deserve the name of friend.
The lie you concealed so long has finally been detected by my cunning,
    For love has uncovered the heart of the matter:
You leave us so happily to visit your dear relatives
    Because that nun there seems even dearer to you.
Better remember, brother, a brother sharing the same mind and soul.
    Therefore return if you can—I suffocate in my fear for you.
If you don't come willingly, you'll be brought against your will,
Though vows fulfilled under duress are not well rewarded.   10
If you don't want to return, neither the banks of the raging Rhine
Nor the shore of Lake Potamicus groaning its sad tidings will obstruct me.
Neither the Iller's roar nor its steep waterfalls will discourage me;
I will run after you, hunt you down, bind you with cords,
A vigilant sentry, conquering both night and day.
I taught you, forgetting food and drink for myself;
I put aside everything for you to satisfy your requests.
But now I am spurned; someone else has your love.
If, however, it's that old man, stirred by his wicked hatreds,
Who has divided friend from friend with his raging heart,   20
Then I will mourn with equal sadness and sorrowing heart;
I will follow you and wet your pillow with my tears.
Whatever places you travel to, whatever fates befall you,
May God accompany you and fill you with His plenty.
Transcribe these remembrances of me into your steadfast heart;
Think always of what you read and turn over in your mind.

[2] *To Salomo*

O wicked loved one, once my beloved friend,
Why, I ask, don't you speak to me as before or even better?
In the past you gave me poems and speeches in prose;
This year you don't even want to join one word to another.

SALOMO (ca. 860–920) AND WALDO

Salomo and Waldo were two aristocratic brothers who were students of
Notker's at the monastery of St. Gall. Both served Emperor Charles the Fat
in France. For some interesting anecdotes about them and their master,
Notker, see the notes for Stehling, No. 34, pp. 146–47; his emended trans-
lation appears here.

To Notker Balbulus

O nourishing image of our belovéd master, why aren't you here?
O, what have you done? Why were you ever made known to us?
O, why do you come so seldom? Why do you notice us last?
Now we beg you, come! Give us your teaching more often,
So that the Lord will want to add for you his thanks a hundred times.
Our pens are calling you back; our parchments yearn to see you!

O ADMIRABILE VENERIS IDOLUM (ca. 900)

This poem, often considered the first real love poem of the modern world,
was probably written by a man to a student who had run away to Italy (see
the River Adige in stanza 2). It is contained in a Verona manuscript that is
now in Rome (Vat. Lat. 3227). It is also in the *Cambridge Songs*. A melody
survives that can be heard in the RCA Victor *History of Music in Sound*,
LM 6015 (side 2). My translation is from *Lyrics of the Middle Ages*, No. 4.
For text, see Erich Auerbach, *European Literature and the Latin Middle Ages*
(1953), 114, in his section called "Sodomy."

O admirable image of Venus,
Of whose material nothing is frivolous:
May the Ruler protect thee who set stars and poles
And fashioned the waters and made the earth whole;
May the cunning of thievery never come near to thee,
And Clotho, who bears the distaff, look on thee tenderly.

"Please save this young man" without hypocrisy
I cry out to Lachesis, sister of Atropos,
With fervent heart, not to cut him away.
May you have Neptune and the lady-nymph Thetis
As guides as you sail on the River Adige.
Where, I ask, are you fleeing, since I love you?
What shall I do when I in misery can't see you?

Hard-shelled matter created mankind
From Mother Earth's bones as stones were tossed down;
This one boy-child was born out of these,
Since he pays no attention to tears and to sighs.
As long as I'm desolate, my rival will be happy,
While I bellow like a hind whose young stag has run away.

GODFREY OF WINCHESTER (d. 1107)
Perhaps born in Cambrai, France, Godfrey was in Winchester by 1082,
where he served as Prior to St. Swithin's until his death. Translations are by
Stehling, Nos. 38, 39, and 43, which is heavily emended.

[1]
Whoever looks at you, Grosphus, sees two men in one:
    From behind, he sees a boy; from the front, a man.
If you play, you're a boy; give your rear, and it's all right,
    But you're holding up the game; turn around and you'll be free.

[2]
"Live, remarkable boy," sang Adonis with joy,
    And he still sings now: "Live, remarkable boy."
He's not and never has been silent about your love-name with me.
    No, trying to love you, he isn't silent and never has been.

[3]
That you pursue boys, love them, and are loved by them
    Is a worthless activity, not for a man; it's bird-hunting for a fool.

Did I say you love them? Yes, if hatred can manifest love,
  Or if deluding them with clever traps is called loving.
You teach sin, and yet you put curbs on sinning;
  Tatus, the season of sinning begins with you.
To join your sinning, your subjects always pay with a gift,
  And to get you to conceal the deed, they offer a second gift.
The fault is yours that their holdings and reputations suffer.
  It's your fault that they lose their esteem and good name.
Impalings must be added to impalings, and heavings to heavings;
  To succeed, keep on heaping one wounding after another.
To get the better of your subject, feed him just on scant oats;
  This way, he'll never be full, and you can overcome him again.
Already, dear friend, this strict diet has kept your colt in line,
  And my own has yielded entirely to a stronger stud.

MARBOD OF RENNES (ca. 1035–1123)

Marbod of Rennes was born in Angers, France, where he became the master of the cathedral school around 1067. In 1096 he became the Bishop of Rennes, though he died in his native Angers. He was the teacher of Baudri, whose work follows. Translations are by Stehling, Nos. 45 and 48.

[1] *To an Absent Friend*

If you cherish anything in the city you love and don't want to lose,
And if you cherish it chastely, you shouldn't care about the court.
Cut short all delay; hour by hour your loss is increasing,
A loss all the greater since it can never be made up.
Put off everything that makes you stay in Chalonnes;
You're losing more here than you're gaining there.
For what is as valuable as a boy who plays fairly with his lover?
He's playing fairly now, but with delay, he'll turn bad
Because, in fact, he's being tempted with many enticements.
And if a boy's tempted, you have to be afraid that he'll be netted.
And so, come back fast if you want to hold on to what you love.
Give up the castle *[castellum]* if you want to retain your pup *[catellum]*.

[2] *Against Homosexual Coupling*

There are a hundred thousand sins invented by the Devil,
And with them he drags this world to punishment's abyss,
Where those who are imprisoned die by being unable to die—
Indeed, they would rather die because no death equals their pain.
There that wretch rages, roasted by a perennial flame:

Brow, eyes, nostrils, neck, ears,
Mouth, throat, and breasts become fodder for flames.
Back, sides, and belly blaze without any relief;
Guilty hips and an accomplice cock never grow cool.
O how sad is that man who is handed over to those flames!
How gloomy he looks, now that he has become food for snakes;
He can scarcely stand the terrible stench hour after hour.
He is beaten on all sides with the lashes of his savage torturer.
And although the vengeance of Hell is hard on everyone,
There are, nonetheless, degrees of punishment.
As sins are weighed, so are they punished:
Greater pain for greater sins, and lesser for lesser.
Therefore copulation performed by members of the same sex,
A crime less serious than none, is punished above all others.
So, anyone fearing punishment who has not yielded reins to sin
Should not yield them now, and he who's committed it should draw back.
O wicked sin! Just as if a billy goat was lusting after a kid
When female goats were around; the world's grief clings to him!
Less serious than none, it is punished more severely than all.

BAUDRI OF BOURGUEIL (1046–1130)

Born in Meung-sur-Loire, France, Baudri of Bourgueil studied under Marbod
at the cathedral school in Angers, and in 1089 was made Abbot of Bourgueil-
en-Vallée and later Archbishop of Dol in Brittany. His copious works have
been edited by Karlheinz von Hilbert (1979) and can be found in part in
Boswell, pp. 244–47. These translations are selected from Stehling, Nos. 51,
52, 56, 60, 61, 64.

[1] To Avitus on Alexander
The name of Alexander and his image stick to you as closely
    As a fingernail to the flesh, or as a bloodsucker to skin.
The name of Alexander grows inside you every hour,
    Just as much as a mushroom grows during a thundershower.
The name of Alexander is so constantly in you
    That it could become the better part of your soul.
The name of Alexander—if anyone trickles it into your ear,
    You smile, you jump, and fearlessly tremble.

If anyone wants to calm your anger,
>Let him say "Alexander," and your anger quickly subsides.

You are completely, instantly distracted from any undertaking
>If someone makes you remember your Alexander.

No reward, no death, no money
>Could make you forget him.

Therefore, if I can, I'll be humble and obliging toward him
>To oblige you by obliging him.

There are two Alexanders my sermon refers to:
>The younger one now has an existence; the other departs.

If anyone asked what Alexander I mean,
>The young one is contained in this satire I'm writing.

Time and age harden the cheeks of the other one;
>Another beard is snatching the boy away from himself.

And you to whom my letter is particularly directed,
>Even your name comes from the Latin for "grandfather."

[2] One of Several Eulogies of the Dead Alexander of Tours

Though death has brought countless tears to the world,
>She now brings even greater weepings,

Because Alexander, the special glory of young men,
>Stricken by an untimely illness, has perished.

A mere adolescent, he had not completed twenty years
>When this beautiful rose withered away from what it was.

He was a canon at Tours, a young man of outstanding talent.
>But what was once a rosy blossom is now mere clay and ashes.

[3] To a Certain Walter

May an exchange of letters always unite us while we are apart,
>And may this letter now bring me into your presence.

Let my letter now greet you, repeat my greetings,
>And repeat them a third time to please you even more.

Lately I received some sweet poetry from my Walter,
>Which, since you wrote it, was touched by your hand.

I received it with the honor it deserves
>And immediately called you to mind with my love.

Now my poem gladly returns your visit,
>And I pray that you will cherish me with your love.

If you wish to take up lodging with me,
  I will divide my heart and my breast with you,
I will share with you anything that can be shared;
  If you command it, I will share my very soul.
You will be lodged completely within my breast
  And will continue as the greater part of my soul.
Meanwhile I will humbly pray for some good fortune
  Until our talks together can reinvigorate us.
Different clothes—if you aren't aware—would bring this about:
  The name of a monk would make this last forever.
In order for you to enjoy our true love,
  This new life would alter your access to me—
Whether a love of God recommends religion to you
  Or a fear of punishment—or both.
In case you decide to come to us in this guise,
  I have ordered some of our men to escort you.
And if gossip has whispered that I am about to visit you,
  This is in doubt; it might be true, or it might not be.
But now therefore, rush over. "Delaying harms the ready."
  Think about tomorrow—do what you have to do today.

[4] To John, Who Wanted to Leave Him

You prepare for a return to revisit your homeland
And see your family; yes, you prepare your return.
You prepare this return because duty requires it,
And yet I wish that the gods would turn you away from duty.
O let the work which keeps me here keep you here too.
By going away, you leave me now with nothing but tears,
And like mine your face is streaked with them.
But still, let what should nourish friends nourish us:
Before long a happy day will follow this sad one.
Let us always hope, and in hope repeat this:
The gracious gods will grant us better times.

[5] To a Friend When John Did Not Return

I wonder, and cannot stop wondering
Why my friend, that John, has not returned quickly,
Since he pledged me over and over that he would return.

Either the boy is sick or, out of his mind, has been stolen.
He is really out of his mind if he's forgotten me;
If he drank three draughts from the River Lethe,
Then he's plain fickle; every young man is fickle.
I can say this much: he has not been delayed without cause.
One is never safe; he can't now hurry enough.
But, John, in case you're rushing back to this soul who
Longs for you, at least I'll do this: I'll continue to wait,
And as I watch, I'll make Fear my new companion.

[6] To Vitalis

O, my song, send some greetings to our Vitalis.
    Tell him what is appropriate and what will please him.
Endear me to him; I want to oblige him,
    This boy that my heart caresses and embraces.
More than all others, he alone has stayed in my heart.
    More than all others, he alone touched me deep inside.
If you want to know what singles him out, it is:
    Manners, nobility, good looks, dignity, honesty,
Shrewd simplicity along with a simple shrewdness.
    Another thing is his beauty, and a beauty diverse:
He is as cunning as a snake, humble as a cooing dove,
    And because of these both, he conquers time.
Beyond this, so much eloquence has inspired this boy
    That Cicero could scarcely equal our Vitalis.
If he wanted to learn the lyre or develop a singing voice,
    Or both, he could become a second Orpheus.
And so, Vitalis will never be parted from me
    Until some bitter day takes his healthy soul from me.
Even then if I'm able to beg favor for me or for him,
    The breaths of us both will become a single spirit.
In the meantime, let us embrace with our radiant love,
    And may the souls of both become ever brighter.
And let no one deny us the name of a holy love.

HILDEBERT OF LAVARDIN (ca. 1055–1133)

Born in Lavardin in northwest France, Hildebert was educated in Le Mans, where he became the bishop in 1096. In 1125 he became Archbishop of Tours. Translations are by Stehling, Nos. 65, 67 and 69.

[1] On the Wickedness of the Age

[Hildebert enumerates the many sins of his period and then says:]

... People sleep together in any combination, with no rules.   33

Venus can scarcely set her weapons in motion to increase the race.

More common than any other lewdness is the plague of sodomy.

Men pay what they owe their spouses to other men.

Countless Ganymedes tend countless hearths,

And Juno grieves to have lost the duty she used to claim.

Both boys and men, pimps and old men defile themselves

With this vice and no class escapes it.   40

All of you who turn nature's honor to this practice

And neglect legitimate love for the forbidden,

Shouldn't you remember the lesson of Sodom's example—

To beware this sin and shun it lest you perish in brimstone?

You Who rule all things, through Whom law's power stands firm,

May the hearth of a man pleased by this game become his Hell,

Or, sparing him, but avoiding what displeases You,

Fill these hearts, emptied of their own concerns, with Yours,

And, with things turned around, let the flesh, which now dominates

The power of mind, become the master of itself!   50

[2] On Ganymede

Eyes, neck, cheeks, waves of blond hair,

These features of Ganymede lit a blazing fire in Jove.

Wanting to allow himself a few liberties with this lad,

The god decreed all things shall be permitted with boys.

Forgetting his guardianship of the heavens and the gods' mutterings,

And his wounded wife's tongue, and unmindful even of himself,

He snatched the Trojan boy away to the heavens, a star to the stars,

And then at last believed that he was a god.

And so that the boy-concubine would be available to touch and sight,

Ganymede gave Jove kisses by night and wine by day.

[3] Apollo on the Death of Hyacinth

As god, as doctor, as lover, trying in vain

To rescind the funeral rites of Hyacinth, Apollo speaks:

"Spare this boy, gods, if we cannot both die;

I would rather follow him than survive as a god.
If you forbid this, let a part of us survive,
While another part falls. I forgive my being less than a god.
Each of us will joyfully tolerate losing a part of himself;
While one part descends to the shades, the other rises to heaven."

PETER ABELARD (1079–1142)

One of the most famous medieval philosophers, Abelard was born in Brittany but educated in France, where he distinguished himself in the intellectual life of Paris. He was author of *Sic et Non (Yes and No)*, a book of philosophical dialectic that showed the essential relativity of things, using a strictly logical procedure which opened the way for science and later philosophy. By his own testimony, he used his fame as a teacher and his good looks to seduce Eloise, the niece of a canon at Notre Dame whose name was Fulbert. When Fulbert learned of the affair, he hired men to enter Abelard's quarters one night and to castrate him. According to a letter by Eloise to Abelard he wrote love songs to her (see F.J.E. Raby, *Secular Latin Poetry*, II, 324–25, although none can be authoritatively attributed to him). However, his hymn *O quanta qualia sunt illa Sabbata* (see Wilhelm, *Lyrics of the Middle Ages*, No. 12) was written at her request to be sung at Saturday vespers in the Abbey of the Paraclete, which Abelard built but handed over to Eloise to direct as abbess. Abelard's teachings were condemned in 1141 through Bernard of Clairvaux, whom he had attacked, and he spent his last years under the protection of the monasteries of Cluny, dying at Chalons-sur-Saône in 1142. This selection is based on the famous biblical friendship of Jonathan and David; see 2 Samuel 1:26 and 1 Samuel 31. Many see the Jonathan-David relationship as nonsexual, like Orestes-Pylades and Achilles-Patroclus. A melody for this piece can be found in Dronke, *Poetic Individuality*, pp. 203–209.

David's Lament for Jonathan
Comfort for sorrows,
Relief from distress,
Such is my lute for me.

And as my sorrow now is greater
And mourning more just,
My lute is the more necessary.

The great massacre of my people,
The king's death and his son's,
The enemies' victory,

Leaders' desolation   10
And people's desperation
Fill everything with grief.

Amalech grows in strength
While Israel flees;
Faithless Philistines
Exult
While Judea torments itself
With wailing.

A faithless people
Taunts the faithful;   20
A people intent
On highest honors
Is now scorned by everyone
And divided.

"The king their god granted as leader
Lies conquered.
Such is the choice
Of their god;
Such is the anointing
Of their great prophet!"   30

So the mockers say:
"See how the god they twitter about
Has betrayed them;
Their god
Has been overthrown by many gods
And fallen."

O Saul, strongest of kings,
O unconquered strength of Jonathan,
He who could not conquer you
Is allowed to kill you.   40

And if he had not been anointed
With the Lord's oil,
He is murdered in battle
By the sword of a wicked hand.

Jonathan, more than a brother to me,
One in spirit with me,
What sins, what crimes
Have sundered our hearts?

O mountains of Gilboa, may you be
Without dew and rain,   50
And may the first fruits of your fields
Offer no relief to your people.

Woe, woe to you, earth,
Wet with the slaughter of kings,
Where a wicked hand has dashed
Even you, my Jonathan,

Where the Lord's anointed,
The anointed of glorious Israel,
Are lost with their own people
In wretched death.   60

For you, my Jonathan,
I must weep more than for all the others.
Mixed in all my joys
There will always be a tear for you.

O daughters of Sion, raise
A lament for Saul;
The rich red of his generous gift
Adorns you.

Alas, why did I agree
To the wretched advice   70
That I should not defend you
In battle?

Stabbed like you,
I should have died happily,
For love can do nothing
Greater than this,
And to outlive you
Is to die at every moment:
Half a soul is not
Enough for life.   80

I should have
Paid friendship's single
Obligation then,
At the time of greatest need;
As sharer of victory
Or companion in ruin,
I should have either rescued you
Or fallen with you,
Ending for you the life
You so often saved.   90
Then death would have joined us
Even more than it parted us.

Instead, having achieved
This ill-omened victory,
I have seen how empty,
How brief its joys are!
How quickly came that
Hard-hearted messenger,
The messenger whom, after speaking out
The pride of his own soul,   100
Death adds to the number of men
Whose death he announced.
Thus sorrow's messenger
Becomes sorrow's companion.

I give my lute peace,
And wish I could do so
For my mourning and weeping.

My hands are hurt with wringing,
My voice is hoarse with lamenting;
Even my spirit fails.   110

HILARY THE ENGLISHMAN (EARLY TWELFTH CENTURY)
Hilary the Englishman was apparently born in England, but he studied un-
der Abelard in Paris and lived most of his life in France. His poems are
overtly homosexual. The first two selections are from Stehling Nos. 71 and
72; the third is from my *Lyrics of the Middle Ages,* No. 13.

[1] *To a Boy of Angers*
Beautiful boy, unparalleled boy,
I pray you to look kindly
At this letter sent by your suitor;
See, read, and follow what you have read.

I have thrown myself down at your knees,
With my own knees bent, my hands joined;
As one of your suitors,
I employ both tears and prayers.

Face to face with you, I am afraid to speak:
Speech fails me; I am seized by silence.   10
But now at last in a letter I confess my sickness,
And since I confess it, I deserve health.

Miserable enough, I could almost endure it
As long as I wanted to hide my love.
When I could conceal it no longer,
I finally held up my hands in defeat.

Sick, I demand a doctor,
Stretching out my hands like a beggar.
You alone have the only medicine;
Therefore, save me, your cleric.   20

Long held in this grim prison,
I have found no one who wishes to help me.

Since I cannot be freed with bribery,
I lead a life worse than death.

O my sadness, my ruin,
How I wish you wanted some money!
But it is better that you have decided
That such a bargaining is vicious.

Nonetheless, boy, it is certainly stupid
To show such a want of feeling,   30
. . . .
Who acts out of modesty to handsome men.

The heavy theme of chastity
Condemned beautiful Hippolytus;
And Joseph almost came to his death
When he opposed the passion of a queen.

[2] To an English Boy
Hail, handsome boy, you who seek no gain,
Who think that to be purchased by a gift is the highest vice,
In whom beauty and integrity choose their dwelling place,
Whose appearance captures the eyes of all who see.

Golden hair, beautiful face, and white neck,
Soft, sweet conversation—why praise things one by one?
You are completely handsome; there is no flaw in you—
Except this worthless decision to devote yourself to chastity.

When nature created you, it wavered for a moment,
Deciding whether to produce you as a girl or a male.
But while she fixed her mind on this choice,
Look! you came forth, a boy born for all to see.

Later, when she put her final touches on you,
She marveled that she could have made such a creature.
Yet it was true that nature had made one mistake:
Assembling so many good things, she made you mortal.

Any other mortal is worthless when compared to you,
Whom nature made as a unique son for herself.
You Beauty chooses as her very domicile;
Your dear flesh shines as radiantly as the lily.

Believe me, if the ancient times of Jove ever returned,
Ganymede would no longer be Jove's private servant;
But you—swept away on high—would offer Jupiter
Cups pleasing by day and draughts more pleasing by night.

You stand out, an object honored by young men and girls;
They sigh and long for you, knowing you are unique.
Those who call you an Angle truly make a mistake—or sin.
Let them reverse the vowel and call you "angel."

[3] To an English Boy
Beautiful boy, with the beauty of flowers,
My glittering jewel, I would like you to know
That the radiance of your visage
Was for me a torch of love.

As soon as I saw you, immediately
Desire struck me—but with despair
For my Dido is now restraining me
And greatly do I fear her wrath.

O, how blesséd I would be
If, by finding someone else,
As is the custom these days,
I could slough off this current love!

But I'll succeed, I do believe,
And I'm yielding myself as your prey;
I'm the spoils, and you the spoiler,
And I gladly surrender to such a thief!

Even the ruler of the gods above
Was once a kidnaper of young men;

If he were here, he would surely snatch
Your beautiful figure to his heavenly bed.

In his great palace up on high,
You could render him double duty:
At night in bed, pouring drinks by day,
You could please completely our great Jove.

Bernard of Cluny (mid-twelfth century)

A monk of the Benedictine monastery at Cluny, about whom little is known,
Bernard was also called Bernard of Morlas or Morlaix. His best-known work
is *De contemptu mundi (Contempt of the World)*, a 3,000-line poem on the
evils of his time. The following has been excerpted; Stehling, No. 75.

From "The Contempt of the World," *Book 3*

Alas! wickedly public are the fire and heat of sodomites.
No one suppresses this sin or hides it or sighs that he is sinful.
Close your eyes to this beastly sin, all of you here;
Unholy rage rises where someone is aware of it or witnesses it.
Unnaturally, outrageously, he becomes she.
Juno and even Petronilla are abandoned.
Bemoan the world and everything in it, which are full of sin;
Men forget what is manly; O madness! O terror! how like hyenas!
Look how many are buried beneath this unnatural filth.
What category, what name does this abomination have?   10
The horror of this sin, alas! resounds even to the stars.
Act and outcry are naked; groan, O chastened mind!
Men become each other's helpers, this one with that one.
Your law, your voice, your providence, Christ, are half-dead.
Sodom's law spreads openly; countless Ganymedes arise, alas!
As long as he shows signs of the sin, this beast tends any hearth he pleases.
The choicest seats and all the bedrooms belong to Ganymede.
Juno has been deserted, and billy goats—O madness!—replace the female.
You demand to know the number of this flock. I'll quickly announce it,
Broadcast it, proclaim it at once like a tragic actor: 20
They're as plentiful as barley in a field, oysters at sea, sand on a shore,
Islands in the Adriatic, incense in India, or reeds along the Tiber.
Castles, outskirts of towns, and even our churches are overrun

By this filthy plague. O for shame! horrors overflow.
The lazy world dies; it desires the horrid and does even worse.
It feasts itself on sulphur; it looks like old Gomorrah.
O ultimate madness! There are now far too many hermaphrodites!
Husbands recite meaningless marriage vows.
Moderation is in mourning as unnatural sins persist;
This leprosy clings to the lesser and the worse. The law of nature
Is perishing, acknowledged customs ruined by this plague.   30

SERLO OF WILTON (ca. 1110–1181)

Born in England, Serlo of Wilton moved to Paris, where he taught until around 1171, when he became abbot of the Cistercian monastery of L'Aumône near Chartres. He wrote erotic verses in his youth. The Welsh writer Giraldus Cambrensis tells us in his *Speculum Ecclesiae* (II, 33) that when he met the elderly Serlo, he leaned forward and said, "Do you think it is possible that a beautiful youth such as you are could die?" Translations are by Stehling, Nos. 77 and 78.

[1] From a Parisian to Paris

From a man in Paris to Paris himself: happily I watched over your life,
And now unhappily I miss my little Ganymede.
All the crowds of beggars and bums, the flocks of whores,
And the mobs of camp-followers have little joy without you.
I, your Flora—drooping without you, thirsting without my flower—
My concern is that you should stay well, and even more—return.
Naevolus without his mate can't play games at night.
He says: "Hispo, come back! I've pledged myself to you!"
Without you I go begging; but if you tear yourself away from this buddy,
And come back to me, even late, I shall serve as host to the world!"

     *[Flora is commonly used as a name for a male homosexual;
Naevolus is a male prostitute from Juvenal's* Satire IX; *Hispo a gay queen
from* Satire II]

[2]

Serlo, he who wants to be yours offers you whatever is his,
But know this: don't be foolish if you want to be mine.
The man who wants something will always be poor. Don't be anxious

That you don't have what you want. What you see absent can be there.
Clotho orders without hesitation that what she doesn't know should be.
Look at her and the other Fates! Without any proof, we believe they exist.
And so I am crying because I see that you are less than happy.
But I also see that you don't care a bit for my sorrow.

WALTER OF CHÂTILLON (ca. 1135–AFTER 1184)

Born in France near Lille, Walter of Châtillon studied at Paris and at Rheims, and taught at Châtillon. Besides teaching he served on the staff of King Henry II of England and of Archbishop William of Rheims. He died at Amiens. Walter wrote an epic on Alexander the Great and numerous pastourelles and satires. Raby calls him a "scholar and man of letters who, although a profound humanist, loved the new rhythms and rimes, and turned them to his purpose while most of his friends clung to the classical forms in which they had exercised themselves in the schools" *(Secular Latin Poetry,* II, 190). These selections are from Stehling, Nos. 79 and 80. In No. 1 below, line 4 quotes the last line of Juvenal's Satire II; the selection is from a 30-stanza satire on the corruption of the world called "Fools with the prudent rush toward the crown." No. 40 is an excerpt from a 20-stanza satire on the corruption of the clergy whose first line is "The law of human fate is fallacious and changeable."

[1] Excerpt from "Stulti cum prudentibus currunt ad coronam"
When they are young, sons of the nobility
Are sent away to France to learn scholarship;
Corrupters of youth recruit them with coaxes and cash,
And so they bring their obscene habits back to Artaxata.

These are the practices of barbarians, Romans, and Greeks;
And the priesthood is just like the laity: the blind lead the blind.
Men make women of themselves, and stallions turn into mares;
You can see this change in everything from man to beast.

And since they aren't afraid of risking their souls,
Rulers turn this crime into common practice.
A new marriage god shamefully joins man to man;
Women have been driven off and no longer get inside the door.

[2] Excerpt from "Fallax est et mobilis lex humanae sortis"

Men with the white hair of old age abundant on their heads
Still nurture the flower of their youth in their loins;
Only dimly aware of the way of virtue,
They attack other men with their sharpened swords.

Among these we have known many to be Sodomites:
They don't accept goddesses, but take to the gods;
Yet no matter how many He finds guilty of this crime,
The One who dwells in heaven will always scorn them.

ALAN OF LILLE /ALANUS DE INSULIS (ca. 1128–ca. 1202)

A famous French philosopher known as "the Universal Doctor," Alan of Lille
was interested in Aristotelian developments, but his imagination was prima-
rily Neoplatonic, as is revealed from this praise of the goddess Natura, taken
from his *De Planctu Naturae (Plaint of Nature)*, translated by J.J. Sheridan
(Toronto, 1980), which was largely a complaint about human violations of
the role of Nature, especially through homosexuality. The hymn voices
homophobic feelings in the most negative way possible. This translation is
from my *Lyrics of the Middle Ages*, No. 18. Alan also wrote the encyclope-
dic *Anticlaudian*.

Hymn to Nature

O offspring of God and mother of all things,
Chain of world-being and stable bond,
Jewel for the earthbound, mirror for the fallen,
    Light-bearer of the world.

Peace, love, virtue, governing, power,
Order, law, the way and the end, light and source,
Life, glory, splendor, beauty, and form,
    Model for the world,

Who, controlling the earth with your reins,   10
Binds all things that are held here together
With a peaceful tie, for with a bond of peace
    You wed heaven and earth.

You, gathering the pure ideas of Mind,
Coin the individual species of things,
Clothing all matter with form and shaping the cloak
    Of form with your finger.

The heavens look with favor on you, and the air attends you,
While the land worships you, and water reveres you;
Considering you the mistress of the world, everything
    Pays you tribute.   20

You link each day to each night in its turn,
Providing the candle of the sun for the daytime
And at night stilling the clouds with the clear mirror
    Of the moon.

You gild the poles with their various stars,
Making the realm of the atmosphere bright and fair,
Filling the heavens with your jeweled stars
    And your armies of constellations.

Proteus-like you change the face of the sky
By adding new shapes, donating both breath   30
And bodies to our region of the air,
    Binding everything with your laws.

At your nod, the world grows young again;
The forest waves its leafy head of hair,
And the land grows proud as it put on
    Its tunic of flowers.

You release and repress the threats of the sea,
Truncating the furious rushing of its storm,
So that the force of the waters can never succeed
    In burying our land.   40

11. ANONYMOUS POEMS
FROM LATER MANUSCRIPTS

FOUR POEMS FROM AN ELEVENTH-CENTURY GERMAN MANUSCRIPT
(ZURICH C. 58/275)

[Stehling 82] Invective Against a Snarling <u>Queen</u>
Listen, you scum of youth—what you say is venom;
What you do is filth; your heart is full of shit!
See for yourself who you are. Laugh at your faults, not mine,
Or rather weep at them and try to be improved.
You stay up all night and sleep all day,
Praising the lecherous and cursing the virtuous.
You sneer at men content with little, and love the rich,
Oppress the unfortunate, and extol the prosperous.
You look sadly on joy and look joyfully on sadness.
Stirred by a double wind, your mind in one minute
Wants what it didn't want and shuns what it once wanted.
After you've eaten, you swear you tasted nothing—and don't care
Who dies of hunger, since your belly is full.
You're broken by adversity and boast of your prosperity;
You ruin married women, and break promises made to whores.
You go to bed like an animal and don't hold back on your loins.
You prefer defiling yourself even to making money.
You'd rather lie about things than bring your ship to port.
You're dedicated to usury, and don't lack the crime of theft.
Friendly with playboys, you have a taste for expensive things.
You run after dinners, and lick over the left-over plates.
First you swill down the wine, and then you lap up the dregs,
And then you vomit and bring out the wine you've packed away.
Look at your filth! In what a supercilious way you criticize others!

[Stehling 84]
With his boyish beauty and laughter,
His happy look, sweet voice, witty talk, he won over
Those men his age that he chased and made them easily,
For with some similar kindling, a mutual fire would burn.

[Stehling 85] A Complaint About Gay Clergymen
This chorus of goats shouldn't be sitting on the right side,
Because God will want to put them on His left.
Either remove this smelly flock away from our quarters,
Or be informed that we're going to leave, dear Bishop!

[Stehling 86] About a Gay Bishop
The man who governs this diocese out-Ganymedes Ganymede.
Let it be heard why he excludes all married men from the clergy:
He himself finds no pleasure in a wife's service.
A prostitute is already disgusting, but a sodomite is viler;
A male prostitute is much worse than a female slut.
Copulation with a woman yields the harvest of children;
When a sodomite copulates, he only leaves behind pollution.

GRAFFITI ADDED TO A NINTH-CENTURY MANUSCRIPT
(LEIDEN, VOSSIANUS LAT. IN OCT. 88)
[Stehling 91] On Some Wicked French Cities
Chartres and Sens should be destroyed, where Adonis prostitutes himself
According to the laws of the whorehouse. The foul acts of sodomy
    are there.
Infected with the same evil, the noble and distinguished city of Paris
Rejoices that it, like Paris of old, is wed to a delicate master.
But you rage on worse than all these, my Orléans, who,
Carrying the prize for this crime, are approaching perdition.

[Stehling 92] More on Some Cities
Now Chartres and Paris are befouling themselves constantly
With the vice of Sodom, and in Sens the boy Paris becomes Io the cow.

[Stehling 93]

The men of Orléans are the best—if you happen to follow
The customs of men who go to bed with boys.

[Stehling 101]

He ought to die in shame, this man bound to a shameful love,
Who gives to a young man's thighs what he owes the mouth of the womb.
From now on, sweet friend, avoid the enemies from Gomorrah;
Burn such men at the stake, but remember this:
Two and three times each, these cities underwent destruction.
When you lie on your back, when you recline in the house of death,
You turn cocks into hens, and young boys into girls.

[Stehling 104]

The greedy woman has a vessel in three places, but guards each well.
And so the sin of Sodom is restored, a sin that many can imitate,
Since all that it takes are some tender, pretty boys.

[Stehling 105]

For some relief, the undiscriminating Venus embraces anything,
But the choosy Venus takes her delight in tender little Ganymede.

[Stehling 106]

I've heard it said that he's always playing the game of Venus,
But Venus herself is happy, because he only plays it with boys.

[Stehling 108]

When his face is laughing, his flesh shines, his thighs are
Delicate, his groin is tender, his heart gentle, and his beauty appealing.
His manners are polished, his shyness hidden, his spirit
Eager for any boyish mischief—and his body's ready
To take on any kind of sport. This young man surpasses
Any kind of treasure. Nothing in the world is more blesséd than he.

[Stehling 109]

You will find many who say that wickedness with boys
Should be cursed, but they do not shrink from the deeds.

[Stehling 110]

Many, to hide what they love and freely do,
Curse with their words what they wallow in with their deeds.

[Stehling 111]

Any kind of Venus can be kindled, but her greatest heat
Comes from the sin of sodomy, as all who try it know.

TWO LESBIAN LOVE LETTERS FROM A GERMAN MANUSCRIPT
(1100S, 1200S; MUNICH CLM. 19411)

[Stehling 112] To C.—

To C.—, who is sweeter than honey and the honeycomb,
B.— sends all the love that one can send to love.
    O my unique and special one,
Why are you delaying so long in that far-off land?
Why do you want me to die, your one and only
Who loves you, as you know, with all her body and soul,
And who, like a hungry little bird,
Sighs for you at every hour and every moment?
For ever since I was cut off from you sweetest presence,
I have not wanted to hear or see anyone else but you;   10
Just as a turtledove, after she has lost her husband,
Remains forever sitting on its barren twig,
So I lament without end
Until I once more can enjoy your faithfulness.
I look around and do not find my lover,
Nor anyone to console me with a word.
While I very happily
Review in my mind the sweetness
Of your conversation and your appearance,
I am oppressed with terrible pain,   20
For I find nothing like them now.
What should I compare to your love?

It is sweeter than honey or the honeycomb.

And compared to it, the luster of gold and silver are worthless.

What else can I say? In you are all sweetness and value.

Thus my spirit always languishes in your absence.

You have none of the poison of treachery;

You are sweeter than milk and honey.

You are singled out from the thousands;

I love you more than all the others;   30

You alone are my love and my desire;

You are the sweet refreshment of my soul.

There is no pleasure for me

Without you.

Everything that was pleasant with you

Is wearisome now and dreary without you.

And so, I wish to say in all truth

That if I could pay my life for you, I would not hesitate

Because you are the only woman I have chosen with my heart.

Therefore, I always pray to God   40

That bitter death does not come to me

Before I enjoy the sight of you, so long desired and so dear.

Farewell.—

Have all my faith and love;

Accept what I have written and sent you

And my ever faithful spirit.

[Stehling 113] To G.—

To G.—, her unique rose,

A.— sends the bond of precious love.

     What strength have I that I may bear it,

That I may endure your absence?

Is my strength the strength of stones

That I can wait for your return?

I never cease from aching, night and day,

Like someone missing a hand and foot.

Without you anything happy or delightful

Seems like mud trod underfoot.   10

Instead of rejoicing I weep;

My spirit never seems joyful.

When I remember the kisses you gave me,

The way you refreshed my little breasts with sweet words,
I would like to die
Since I cannot see you.
What should I, most wretched, do?
Where should I, most poor, turn?
O, if my body had been committed to earth
Until your longed-for return,   20
Or if I could go on a journey like Habakkuk,   *[see Daniel 14:33–39]*
So that just once I could come to where
I saw the face of my lover,
Then I would not care if I died that very hour.
For there is no one who has been born in the world
Who is so lovable and dear,
No one who without feigning
Loves me with so deep a love.
Therefore, I ache without end
Until I am allowed to see you.   30
According to one wise man, the worst misery
Is to be far from someone one cannot live without.
As long as the world endures,
You will never be blotted out from my heart's care.
Why do I linger with so many words?
Come back, my sweet love!
Don't put off your journey any longer.
Know that I can no longer endure your absence.
Farewell—
Remember me.   40

[Stehling 114] A Debate Between Ganymede and Helen
This well-known poem, which exists in at least eight manuscripts, was
probably composed in southern France in the late 12th century.

The sun had entered Taurus, and spring, the mother of flowers,
Had stretched out her head adorned with blossoms.
Reclining under an olive tree, with grass providing me a bed;
I then took delight recalling the sweet things of love.   4

The spreading scent of flowers, the youthfulness of the time,
The soft-breathing breeze, the harmonies of the birds—

While these things soothed my spirit, slowly sleep stole upon me.
O, if only sleep had never been taken from my eyes! 8

For I seemed to see a Phrygian boy and a Spartan maid
Standing on the spring grass under a lovely pine:
Their demeanor was royal, their appearances fair,
Their brows vying with the lily, cheeks with the rose. 12

They seemed to sit together on the ground
And the ground seemed to smile up at their faces.
Rumor has it that gods had taken on these shapes:
Each of them marveled to find someone equally pretty. 16

These two, then, were discussing various things
And arguing back and forth about their looks.
As if bright Phoebe and Phoebus were to quarrel,
The impudent youth compared himself to the woman. 20

Already thirsting for a man and ripe for bed, she
Had already felt for a little while the prick of love.
The Phrygian inflamed her with his unrivaled beauty,
And her inner heat now showed itself in outward signs. 24

Where love plays host, modesty departs.
The maid no longer maintained a maiden's modesty,
But since he was not asked, she asked him, touched him,
And presented him with her breast, sweet mouth, and lap. 28

They were both stretched out on the green grass
And were just about to be blessed with copulation,
When the Trojan, not knowing his part in the famous rite,
Aligned himself with the woman, as if to be passive. 32

She saw his mistake, his vice, and was astonished.
She backed away from the Phrygian, cursed him,
Indicted nature, said that the gods were to blame
That a monster should be given such a beautiful face. 36

This incident made the two of them quarrel;
The more she praised women, the more he young boys.

They appointed Nature and Reason
As judges to settle the case. 40

Therefore, with no further delay, they both mounted horses.
The third dawn saw them still racing along
Until they were received at the world's eastern edge.
This is the house of Nature; here they bent their reins. 44

In Jove's palace, Mother Nature,
Pondering the secret generation of things
And clothing matter with many varied shapes,
Creates things according to fixed weights and measures. 48

Close by is her companion, Reason, under whose guidance
She makes things that have been born grow and sows the unborn.
They mingle the unequal sexes, and from this mingling
Springs a brood of diverse species. 52

There too, taller in stature, stands Providence,
Whom Nature's father bore out of pure intellect.
Neither past nor future things deceive her;
Every creature is always before her eyes. 56

"Look," she says, "I see two people coming,
Elegant and beautiful, astonishingly lovely.
I am amazed that the earth could have given birth to them;
Heaven itself could boast of these children. 60

"They bring a quarrel among them; I think that I hear them:
I recognize the argument, but I wish that I didn't.
Now you will see all the gods gathering here."
She had spoken, and they saw what she said happening. 64

Rumor awakens Jove and his offspring.
Helen attracts some, and Ganymede others.
The palace was open, and its seats unfilled,
But the gods filled the lofty house with their majesty. 68

Meanwhile the Trojan boy and Tyndareus' daughter
Are led in and are now approaching the palace's entrance.

They leave their horses and climb the gold stairs,
Enter the heavenly mansion, and immediately are seen.   72

Without warning, the boy is seeing entering
Like the morning star that always precedes the day.
He seems to disdain everything with his eyes,
Arrogantly refusing to cover his face or his manhood.   76

His golden hair looks like fleece
That has been dyed with pure Oriental saffron.
When it attempts to reach down to his eyebrows,
It curls and is flicked from his broad forehead.   80

His eyebrows are neatly separated;
His eyes beam sweetly with a lurking ray.
His mouth, as if it were asking, invites a kiss;
His whole face smiles, seducing the seducer.   84

Helen follows a little behind, blushing,
Still ignorant of men, still very modest,
Like Aphrodite arising out of an Aegean wave;
In looks, she is not inferior to the boy.   88

Some of her hair is flowing unfastened and free;
Some, to prevent tangles, is all pinned up.
It is parted right at the top of her forehead,
Which is slightly bowed, as if from respect.   92

Her eyebrows are firm, her eyes are playful;
Her nose protrudes beautifully, her lips colorfully alive.
Venus made her mouth savory with her own nectar;
A god polished her chin with his own hand.   96

To keep her flowing hair from hiding her beauty,
She pushes it away toward one ear and the other,
And then her face takes on the appearance of the dawn,
Which on its coming mixes rosiness with white.   100

Then you should see the gods everywhere restless;
Apollo grows hot and Mars is playing wantonly,

While Venus is yelping as if in someone's arms:
This noise she can't contain is a disgrace to hear. 104

Jupiter, without any shame, summons Ganymede,
While Nature has prepared a seat for the maiden.
She takes it hard that this boy has entered the palace;
She considers him neither her son nor her heir. 108

Silence descends. The boy has stood up.
Rising across from him, Helen has uncovered her face.
Confident of her cause, she enters the contest first;
The whole assembly have turned their eyes toward her. 112

"Alas!" says Helen, "I feel sorry for you:
You openly despise having sex with women.
Through you, the order of things is overturned and laws perish.
Since you don't procreate, why did your father engender you?" 116

Ganymede: "Let old men eager for children engender some sons;
Let tender young men sport freely in their lust.
The game we play was invented by the gods,
And it is still being played by the highest people." 120

Helen: "Your face, which is a beauty of beauties,
Will die along with the rest of you, since you're
Always ignorant of women; if by chance you do know them,
Your son will carry on his father's beauty." 124

G: "I don't want my face being duplicated;
I'd rather have it attract men with its uniqueness.
I hope your own face will sag down with age,
Since I believe that it makes me loved all the less." 128

H: "O how happy is that love between opposite sexes,
When a man caresses a woman in a mutual embrace!
He and she are drawn together by natural inclination;
Birds, beasts, and cattle are all happy in this bond." 132

G: "Men shouldn't be imitating either birds or cows!
Man has been given the power to reason.

Peasants, who can be called cattle—these are the ones
Who should stain themselves with women!"   136

H: "No love of a boy ever truly touches the heart,
But when one bed unites a man with a woman,
This is a bond that's productive, that follows the right order,
For between the sexes there is equal affection."   140

G: "Opposites always fight; the right way is like with like.
Man can be linked to man in an elegant conjunction.
If you don't know this, look at the gender of adjectives:
Grammar dictates that masculines go with masculines."   144

H: "When man's creator fashioned the human race,
He made sure to make the female more lovely than the male,
So that he would lure a man to a bond with a woman,
And never would a man love a man more than her."   148

G: "I might agree that it would be proper to love them
If their beauty corresponded with the honesty of their morals.
But the wives are always defiling the marriage bed,
And unmarried ones make cheap markets of themselves."   152

H: "Men should all blush! Mother Nature should grieve!
Men don't care a thing about Nature's binding.
Venus lets men join together in a sterile union;
Boys forget their sex and sell their thighs."   156

G: "We know that honorable men approve of this act,
For men who have ruled the world and held highest offices
And have passed judgment as censors on behavior and sin—
These don't shun the silky crotches of boys."   160

H: "Let's pass over those who are so madly inflamed as to
Do such things. You boys, reason in no way defends you!
A boy here isn't acting out of pure pleasure,
And so he sins and offends all the more gravely."   164

G: "The scent of money is good; nobody runs away from it.
Indeed, I have to confess that lucre lures us all.

A boy who wants to get ahead should never give up this game;
No, it carries them forward; it makes them rich."   168

H: "Even if we grant that boys shouldn't be blamed for this,
No rationalization can ever excuse older men.
I have to laugh when I see some old guy who won't give up;
This sport of boys is a sin for the gray-haired set."   172

G: "I don't excuse the old either; their age accuses them.
It's disgraceful that, when they see their bristles whitening,
They throw themselves into these games, grabbing the fun.
But these old guys don't cramp the style of us boys!"   176

H: "Tell me this, boy! When those boyish looks begin to change,
When some fuzz sprouts on the cheeks and the face gets wrinkled,
And there's bushy hair on the chest, and the belly's scraggly,
What does a cocky body-rubber think of himself then?"   180

G: "Little girl, tell me this: when a virgin's beauty is withered
And her lips are rough and her skin all dried up,
And her eyebrows bristly, and her eyes all runny,
Won't her lover, no matter how hot, droop over then?"   184

H: "I wish you could turn all smooth and hairless down there,
And that a woman's chamber would suddenly appear,
As nature turned you with full vengeance into a girl,
Since you've so nastily declared a war on her!"   188

G: "I'd like to be smooth and hairless in my crotch,
But please—no lady's chamber!
It so happens that I reject women because I hate them,
For what's the difference between a woman and a she-ass?"   192

H: "O if I wasn't held back by my delicate sense of shame,
I'd talk now without any rhetorical coloring.
But I'm ashamed to use any language that's foul;
Filthy words dwell badly in the mouths of maidens."   196

G: "We came here prepared to talk about filthy things;
This is not the place for anything respectable.

We should put shame and religion behind us,
And we shouldn't spare either the virgin or truth." 200

H: "I don't know where to turn, for if I don't answer
With the same filthy talk, they will say I've been beaten;
But if I should try to match your words,
It will have the savor of a slut's foul talk." 204

G: "Well, wander around and find some stranger to fool.
I know who you, on your back, opened your legs to.
Where was your dovelike innocence then?
Right away you changed from Thais to a simple Sabine." 208

H: "O you men who lie on top of other men,
Who monstrously un-man other men,
You shamefully pollute yourselves and boys at night,
And in the morning—I won't say it—there's shame on your sheets!"

G: "And you men who let concubines sleep in your beds,
And who love to get wet in their female slop,
When your Thais lies back and opens up to you,
You know what the bilge inside smells like!" 216

H: "The whore Thais smells like Thais because of her habits,
But a young girl smells sweeter than balsam;
On her lips there is honey, a honeycomb in her mouth;
Happy's the man who enjoys sharing the sleep of a virgin." 220

G: "When Jupiter lies in the middle of his bed
And turns first to Juno and then to me,
He tries the sport of boys—and prefers it to girls' games.
When he turns to Juno, he either argues or snores!" 224

H: "Your Venus is sterile and unfruitful
And very harmfully unjust to us women,
Since one man submits to another in shameful turn
As this monstrous Venus pretends she's a woman." 228

G: "It's not a monstrous thing to avoid a monster—
That gaping cave with its sticky bush around it,

That cavern whose smell is the end of everything,
That cavern too deep for any long staff or oar."   232

H: "Stop talking so roughly; stop talking so harshly!
Please speak more modestly, you impure boy!
If you don't care to show any respect to a maiden,
Then at least show respect for Nature and the gods!"   236

G: "If questions are cloaked in the trappings of fine words,
Then filth, dressed up, would be able to deceive us.
But I am not going to gild over dross;
It is right for words to be akin to their substance."   240

H: "Now I'll throw away my cloak of modesty,
And, since you force me, talk totally nude:
Since this filthy heresy has coupled with you,
And you squander Venus's liquid between male thighs,
Ha! if you don't know it, the loss of a man is there.
Yes, my words are harsh, but the matter's harsher still!"   246

When the boy hears about this unspeakable crime,
Amazement ties up his tongue; a blush suffuses his face;
Warm dew trickles down furtively from his eyes;
Lacking any rational answer, he does not defend himself.   250

He is silent. Reason rises up to speak,
And prudently handles the matter with a brief speech:
"There's no need for a judge, since the matter speaks for itself.
With the boy's permission I'll say: 'The boy is defeated.'"   254

He replies, "I have nothing to say to the contrary.
Now I recognize my crime; now I've learned what it is."
Apollo says: "I too, indeed, have come to my senses."
Jupiter says: "Now I'm burning for my dear Juno."   258

The age-old heresy is now put to flight by the gods;
A choir of virgins rejoices; Juno offers her thanks.
Reason celebrates with the children of Nature,
And with general approval a maiden is crowned.   262

The young man from Mount Ida wants the maiden as wife,
And every god who is present approves of the match.
A joyful Hymen joyously joins them;
The voice of bliss rings out; my sleep abandons me.   266

This vision came to me at the nodding of God;
Let Sodom blush and Gomorrah weep;
Let everyone guilty of this sin be converted.
God, if I ever do this, may you forget my name!   270

A Poem from the Carmina Burana

This famous collection of medieval Latin lyrics was assembled from about 1220 to 1230 at the Benediktbeuern Monastery in Bavaria, which supplies the name *Songs of Burana (Beuern)*. It is now in Munich, under the call number of Clm. 4660. The following poem (Stehling No. 115) was described by Dronke as "a deliberately obscure song of homosexual love" in his *Medieval Latin,* I, 300. In line 16, the poet says that he is substituting one sex for another in his poem, and calls his lover a "bearded Cypris," referring to her later as "she." In line 74, he urges his reader to unscramble his message by switching the genders back to their original standings. The names Philogenus, Erytreus, Aethon, and Lampas are the names of the horses that pull on the Sun.

Quocumque more motu
In whatever manner the seasons are turned in their motion,
I beat the same drum celebrating their temperate passage.
Whether Philogenus
Delays in the Underworld,
Or Erytreus
Can be seen blushing in the usual seeds of spring,
Whether glistening Aethon is filled again with summer light,
Or radiant Lampas is enriched with autumn's plenty,
My well-being is always destined to come from one divine power.

When I saw Pasithea for a moment,   10
She urged me on,
But after I had waited
Such a long time, Euryale at last sneered.
Let Euphrosyne, who grudges any restraint, be my sole patron.

Naked Dione has smiled sweetly on me through someone!
For she sang this song she promised with the genders switched.

Let this bearded Cypris
Rejoice in secret!
She has now been renewed
With the riper excitement of adults.   20
Once a virgin who used to counterfeit
The deportment of a woman,
She no longer pretends to be a maiden
Now that she is skilled in the ways of Venus.
Let her grow pale at a chaste word
And be cautious in her libations to Venus,
Lest her speaking about it burst out
Too plainly or too knowledgeably.
For once she was deflowered,
She showed no reluctance to repeat nature's mingling.   30

O Paris, be patron
Of love's struggle.
O Venus, enjoy
Adonis's embraces!
I offer myrtle and cry aloud
In Cythera's temple;
I show my shackles as witness
Of my condition.
Since I am not encumbered by the unchanging laurel,
I am not confined.   40
Hope encourages this difficult affair
As long as I enjoy my noble bedmate.
And this does not happen by chance,
For I have battled hard inside the latch of the virgin's gate.

I would grow pale unless this wonderfully beautiful girl
Tried me at my age;
I would droop unless, with my hope of love darkened by fear,
She pricked me on.
So marvelous an affair, if discovered, is lost and decrees my fate,
And so I have made my petitions.   50

For her, devoted kisses and delicious kisses on kisses
I have multiplied.

I drink the drink of life from her;
To me this honor is sweet.
She is refined enough for me,
Ready for many an age to come.
Just now at the right moment,
I confessed to her.
I eased my burden amazingly
While I embraced her.   60
Since I have desired
Joy's favor honorably,
Let this girl, who is wreathed
By her manners and appearance,
Who is adorned by her bloom
And her dowry of charm,
Let her caress me with signs of sweet love.

Remember these things; keep them in your heart,
That my Minerva,
Now prudent, now wanton,   70
In many shapes thus far, proclaims you in harmony;
In prose, verse, satire and rhythmic song,
She sings your praises through the world in a scholarly symphony.

If anyone switches back what I have turned around,
And as a lover understands the translation
With a heart free of disapproval,
And if he asks, hopes, and begs that my love for him endure,
I will pay him back in turn and never be a false traitor,
So that our trusting alliance may see its jubilee year.

A DEBATE BETWEEN GANYMEDE AND HEBE

This anonymous poem exists in a thirteenth-century manuscript that is now
in Munich (Clm. 17212). The poem features Ganymede, who has just been
carried off from Mt. Ida near Troy, and Hebe, the little girl who served as
cupbearer until he replaced him. Reference is made to other love affairs men-
tioned in Ovid's *Metamorphoses*. This emended translation is by Stehling

(No. 118), who thanks John Boswell and Ralph Hexter for providing him with a new text. The sense is difficult in lines 79–80.

[Stehling 118]

After the boy's abduction by the eagle, after his sweet wickedness,
Juno wept by herself in her bedroom for the cups snatched away from Hebe.
But Juno did not dare to vent her sorrow openly.
She encouraged Hebe to take up a quarrel and promised her favor.
She supplied her with rhetorical ploys beforehand
And taught her envious words to scorch the boy with.
The handmaiden learned her part from her mistress—
What kinds of speeches, what artistic gestures to make.
The court assembled to think over these sportive arguments.
In their midst, Hebe asks for silence, then opens her mouth.   10
Her face blushes, and its color colors her words.
She blushes to speak, and her blush promotes her own case.
        "Immortal race, image of the eternal father,
Nature's prize, Nature's first offspring,
Who bear down on the unjust with holy justice,
I beg justice for the just; I complain about a broken law.
While grace was favoring me, I was Jove's cupbearer,
Blessed by your decree and by his.
But a new guest has entered my domain, an unequaled enemy!
O, should I keep quiet? He's only a boy. But why? You know all this.   20
This Phrygian, this disgrace from Troy, has invaded the stars
And set up a Trojan camp in the heavens.
This rabbit excites the other rabbits by using his charm
And he wafts the scent of his gamy body into heaven.
You're a recent plunder, boy, and now you're plundering what's mine!
Having been raped yourself, have you come to rape the rights of goddesses?
But the Fates are preparing vengeance at your persuasion, Apollo.
Troy has fallen, and a woman will give it its deserved devastation.
Already this little punk has thrust himself into the vows of marriage;
Already earth and sky have been signed over to him as a dowry!   30
O native home! O seat of virtue, once innocent of lust!
A parvenu Trojan flute plays lewdly in your halls.
He makes little gestures with a turn of his side, shoulder, or foot,
While Virtue, pushed to the side, sits far off and weeps.
He shows off his face and curls his locks with a curling iron.

Evil sprouts everywhere with this Ganymede as its master.
In his face, he nurtures a thousand arguments for evil;
Now that he's calling the tune, let each of you gods be on guard—
As well as the thousands of deities of sea, land, and sky! A boy
Has been led to marriage among the stars—an impure boy, that one!   40
In the daytime our King calls for this Trojan nephew;
And indeed at night he wakes up this nephew from Troy.
I'm not mentioning what this cupbearer serves Jove by day;
I only ask this: who rolls the cupbearer over at night?
Now, gods, Nature is blushing; our benign mother
Asks you with her tears what punishment this crime deserves.
Juno, Athena, and all the goddesses request
That the verdict of you heaven-dwellers be swiftly reached."
    She had finished. A rumor snaked through the crowd; a tumult arose.
But the boy stood up, and his face commanded silence.   50
Night departed, and daytime followed. Just as you always, god of the Sun,
Overcome the Moon, so Ganymede's honor surpassed that of Hebe.
Atlas is happy to hold up the burden of this star,
And Pallas feels for this boy for whom any woman would sigh.
Apollo thinks of Hyacinth, Silvanus of Cyparissus [Cypress] ;
Venus recalls her Adonis, whose beauty is in this young man.
Mars almost seems to embrace him as he takes him in with his eyes.
And as he stares, he sighs for kisses from those tender lips.
Jove is silently possessed by his own joys, and believes
He is more godlike because grace has favored him with this boy.   60
Like a true descendant of Dardanus, the boy lifts his eyes from his feet,
Which seem to flash like twin suns out of the heavens.
His beauty itself pleads for pardon if he has committed any sin;
His face and his figure both plead the case for his lord.
Judgment returns, as if moved by a boyish wonder at the boy;
Words of grace flow out of his delicate mouth:
    "Here is my father Dardanus, here the whole line of his offspring;
And our race from Teucer is well known even among these stars.
What have I done? I did not storm the heavens, and Jove
Did not abduct me, but like a faithful friend showed me the way.   70
For he said to me, 'My table, which is the council of the gods,
The heavens, the Fates all welcome you to life above the upper air.'
So I came. This honor was given me, and I enjoy it. Should I be punished?
Was it so shameful that a 'shameful man' asked me to mix his nectar?
Or is it better that some foul old man with dirty hands

Or some little frump should act as servant at the table of Jove?
Let me be yours; let me serve anyone, as long as Jove stays the same.
Men now are sucking where once women wiggled their asses.
Those of our sex who stir up a furrow without using a plowshare
Squeeze the bellows together and forge lightning to open cracks.   80
Tell me—do you scan the heavens to see if the moon is favorable?
And do you blush every time the Red Sea is rough?
In her fox's den, Hebe's mother sits, making up new stories;
Every time she talks, the pen of her tongue cunningly invents nasty gossip.
Was it my fault that men liked to go hunting on Ida?
A woman faithless to herself knows nothing about good faith.
She eggs me on, provoking me with the gall of her talkative tongue.
Ah yes, a virtuous whore and a woman of peace are rarities now.
Either I'll enjoy your heaven with virtue as my guide, or else
Fate's course will make it necessary for me to commit a crime."   90

POEMS FROM MANUSCRIPTS OF THE THIRTEENTH AND FOURTEENTH CENTURIES
[Stehling 121]
A maiden loved Graecinus; Graecinus loved a boy,
But the boy was taken only with the maiden.
Graecinus handed her over to the boy, and the boy gave himself to Graecinus.
So, both man and boy enjoyed the fruits of their prayers.

[Stehling 123]
If anyone in this life chooses not to live as a sodomite,
Then he'd better get out of Chartres—unless he wants to become a woman.

[Stehling 125]
Whoever deprives the clergy of women, in whatever way,
Turns deacons and priests into sodomites;
The more there's sin and a furrow to be plowed is not plowed,
The more the use of women will be shamefully excluded.

[Stehling 127]
Be forgiving, boy, if by some chance an improper sound reaches your ears
Boldly demanding some unmentionable gift.

For you can remember that if he keeps the law,
Anyone may be chaste and long preserve his chastity,
But once blind love has shot his arrow
With its gilded tip and struck a tender wound into the heart,
Then modesty and shyness even in a holy heart
Fall to every evil. The heart grieves, alas, at its wishes, is amazed
At its fiery passions, and is finally forced
To submit and kneel before the tyrant god.
Therefore, take action, dear boy! Your looks, beauty,
And intelligence—which bear the fruit of every virtue and can resist
The Pierides' sacred labors and all of Pallas's arts—
These qualities always vex my heart with a tireless flame.
Help me, I pray, and cool this raging fire.

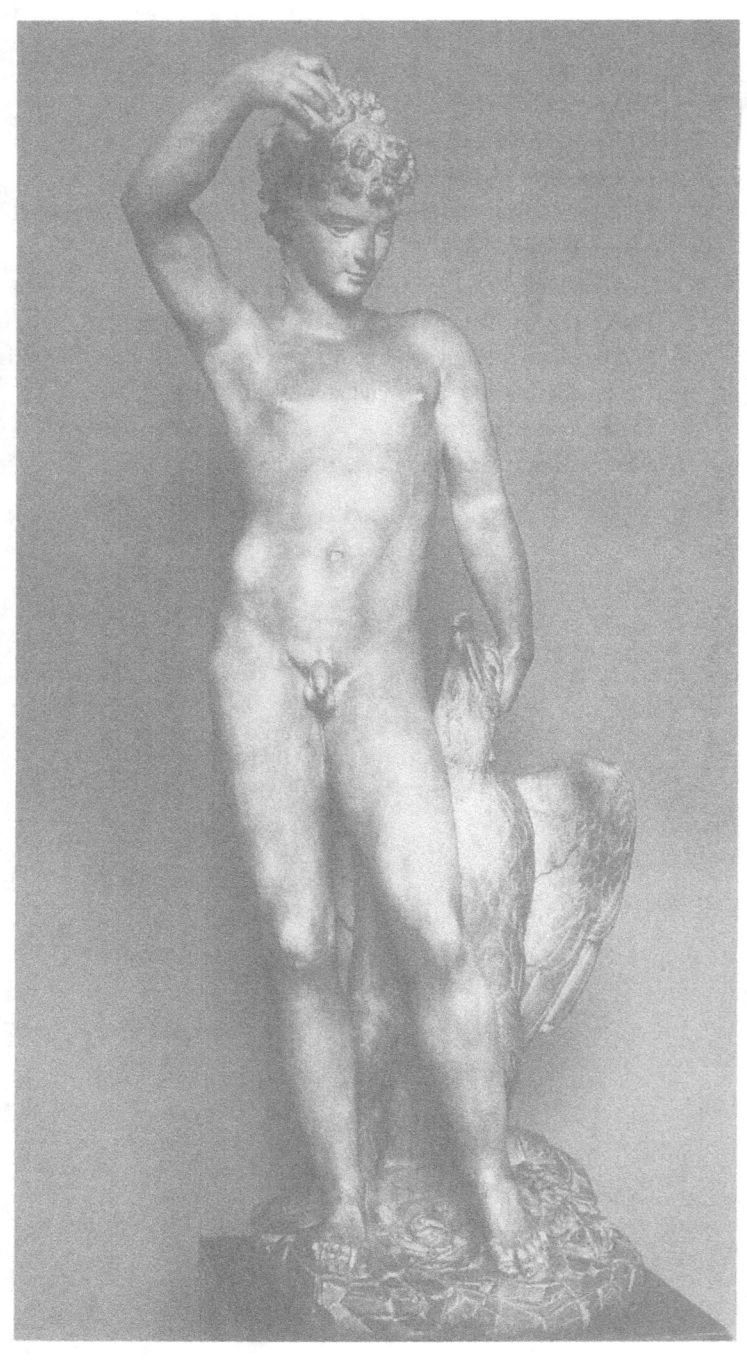

Ganymede with the Eagle *by Benvenuto Cellini. (Courtesy Alinari/Art Resource, New York)*

ARABIC POETRY

Arthur Wormhoudt

When the Arabic-speaking Moors of North Africa invaded the Iberian Peninsula under Tarik in 711, they ended the Romanized Visigothic Kingdom of Roderick and introduced Arabic as a new language. Soon the Umayyad dynasty was founded, and Córdoba became the capital of the Western Caliphate, which was distinguished for its mosques and palaces such as the Alhambra of Granada.

In 1086 the rugged Berbers of Morocco established a new dynasty of the Almoravids, but they were replaced in 1174 by the Almohads. Still, pressure from the Christian North was constant, and in 1212 at Navas de Tolosa, Alfonso VIII of Castile confined the Moors largely to Granada, which fell in 1492 to Ferdinand V of Castile and Isabella I, who laid the foundations for modern Spain.

The Arabs had a literary tradition from the time of Mohammed, their prophet, and it throve in their empire, which stretched eastward to Baghdad. Their poetry was noted for its quantitative meters (like Greek and Latin), varied rhyme schemes, and precise imagery, which is often quite different from that of the Christians. By the 900s, Hispano-Arabic poets were writing poems in classical Arabic called *muwashshahs*. These originally had short final refrains or envois called *kharjas (jarchas)*, which were often written in a more colloquial style and spoken by a girl. After the 1110s, poems called *zajals* were composed entirely in the colloquial Arabic of Spain, and other forms of poetry emerged.

Many scholars have tried to link Arabic poetry with the Provençal troubadours of southern France, especially in the cult of love often called "courtly love," but this link has never been established. The large corpus of homosexual poetry, for example, is totally removed from troubadour poetry, as the next chapter reveals, with its one possible sample. It is far more plausible to link the Neoplatonism of Ibn Ḥazm's *Dove's Neck-Ring* with

Dante and the Tuscan poets of Italy. And it is even more convincing to note ties between this poetry and that of the *Greek Anthology*, especially in the figure of the cupbearer.

Readers often wonder if the isolation of the Spanish Arabs from the east accounts for the large amount of homosexual verse, but that is not the case. Eastern poets such as Abū Nuwās are just as prolific in this vein, and often more obscene. Homosexuality far predated the advent of Islam, and even that often rigid religion was unable to stamp it out.

Most of the following translations were published by me along with the original Arabic, and can be obtained by writing to Arthur Wormhoudt Arabic Translation Series, Department of Foreign Languages, William Penn College, Oskaloosa, Iowa 52577; they are also available in major research libraries.

One may also consult A.R. Nykl, *Hispano-Arabic Poetry*, (Baltimore, 1946); James T. Monroe, *Hispano-Arabic Poetry: A Student Anthology* (Berkeley, 1974); G. Goodwin, *Islamic Spain* (San Francisco, 1990); A.R. Arberry, *Arabic Poetry: A Primer for Students* (Cambridge, Eng., 1965). See also the *divan* (*diwān*) or collection for an individual author; these are cited in the head-links for each poet.

EDITOR'S NOTE: These poems are opaque, difficult, and fraught with multiple meanings. Rather than overweigh them with copious, tentative footnotes, I have allowed Wormhoudt's translations to stand.

12. Medieval Spanish Selections

Ibn Darrāj al-Qaṣṭallī (958–1030)

Ibn Darrāj al-Qaṣṭallī, Abū ʿUmar Aḥmad ibn Muḥammad ibn ʿAsī ibn Aḥmad ibn Sulaimān. He was born in Spain, although his ancestry was North African Berber. He was a court poet to many rulers and died in Saragossa. He has been edited by numerous scholars, including E. Lévi-Provençal (Beirut, 1956) and Maḥmūd ʿAlī Makkī (Damascus, 1961).

I knew your jealous disgust,
    Which was clear even for a year of good times.
I had scarcely given you an odd look
    Or hung around meekly like a gold chain.
Then I smelled sweet clouds,
    As your breath wafted strongly to me.
A boring night was almost half gone
    When your dawn flared in a fight.
I was sweating with life's water—a face
    Rushing to him with the water of life.
Why if my thanks to you were clear
    Did you confirm a hostile pledge?
Time announced the morning
    With the call of faith and generosity.

Al-Sharīf al-Ṭalīq (961–1009)

Al-Sharīf al-Ṭaliq, Marwān ibn ʿAbd ar-Raḥmān ibn Marwān ibn ʿAbd ar-Raḥmān an-Nāṣir Abū ʿAbd al-Mālik. He was a descendant of the Umayyad caliphs and was imprisoned for years (possibly for killing his father over a girl). This poem consists of a description of a beloved, a drinking scene in a storm,

and a vaunt about his family. Some translators make the beloved female, but
the adjectives and the word for "lover," *habīb*, clearly indicate that love object
is masculine. For the opposing view, see E. Garcia Gómez (Madrid, 1942),
p. 38; see also Monroe, pp. 154ff.

A *branch* swaying on a sand dune,   [*usually a penis in Arabic poetry*]
    And my heart takes fire from him;
Beauty rises for us in his face—
    A moon that will never be waning.
Seducing with a fawn's bright eyes,
    His glance is an arrow aimed at my heart;
His smile is like a pearl necklace
    Plundered from his neck into his mouth.
The *lam* of the curls on his temples   [*letter "l"*]
    Flowed golden to enrich our silver plates.   10
Beauty was consummated in him,
    A branch that was just starting to leaf out.
His waist is so thin that I thought
    It was a lover due to its slenderness,
As if his buttocks had enslaved it,
    And so it became worried and tormented.
Slimness aimed at softness, the way
    My lover will remain to embrace me.
I wonder at how alike they are to us,
    Not wanting flight nor parting.   20

Many a cup adorned the wingéd darkness
    With a coat of light until the dawn's ray;
Many a night I drank to a *gazelle*,   [*common term for a lover-boy*]
    Who had a sleepy look that mine kept awake;
The cup hid from the eyes till I thought
    It feared from his stare what was fearful to me;
It shone in his hand's purity
    Like the sun's beams greeting the sky,
As if the cup in his fingers were
    A saffron narcissus rising among leaves;   30
It appeared like a sun, with his mouth a sunset,
    With his cupbearer hand resurrecting the sunrise.
When the cup went down to his mouth,
    It leaves compassion on his cheeks.

This shower in cloudy downpours is
     A friend to gardens singing and drinking,
As if earth were his dungeon, and
     The growth were a felon in prison.
The lightning honors its borders
     With a colored coat when it flashes,   40
As if its dark cloud were
     The black made into the pinto,
As if the wind as it blows
     Drives the magpies into the sky;
There are nights when wandering stars stray
     In confusion, not knowing their paths.
Lightning lights its lamp;
     The face of the darkness is dawning,
And thunder sings the bass part
     As the cups of clouds take root.   50
The sun comes to entice us
     And wrap with its rays the drowning,
As if the sun-reviving breath
     Were a bright, passionate beloved;
As if the rose shining in the dew
     Were a beloved's cheek with sweat,
The sun bursts with gilded saffron.
     I thought it hid its love for the rose,
The way two lovers embracing act,
     The one ashamed, and the other fleeing.   60
O those stars in the garden
     That climb from the beds on high
And look on the morning sun
     Like flower buds trapping eyes,
As if the dewdrops as they flow
     Stayed like quicksilver on the leaves.

What man is like me in bravery
     And bounty, word and deed and faith?
My eminence is myself; my jewel is
     My wit; my sword is speech encountered;   70
My tongue for one who inquires
     Is a serpent that no charmer can turn;

My hand is lucky for poor beggars,
>   Joining praise that was scattered.
My grandfather is Nāṣir li Dīn, who
>   Drove divisions far from partings,
Noblest of the noble in himself
>   And his kin; when they are high, I am highest:
The boast of ʿAbd ash-Shams is in me.
>   Their honor shines that was dulled.   80
I adorn their faded glory
>   With jewels, the bright jewels of my poems.

Ibn Shuhaid (992–1035)

Ibn Shuhaid, Abū ʿĀmir Aḥmad ibn Abī Marwān ʿAbd al-Mālik al-Ashjaʿī.
Born into an aristocratic family in Córdoba, he wrote a book describing his
experience with the souls of great poets of past Arabic literature. He was a
close friend of Ibn Ḥazm, whose work follows. For texts, see Wormhoudt
Arab Translation Series, No. 133 (1991); his *Diwān* ed. Charles Pellat
(Beirut, 1963).

He passed me in a herd of deer,
>   A smiling moon with lucky teeth;
They adorned his face with pearls,
>   While rounding his ass like a dune;
The winds of passion urged me as
>   The call of pleasure concealed me,
So I turned to give him greeting
>   But then arrogance cared not for me.
He said: "The slave! does he dare?
>   What makes him so sure of my anger?
O my dirty looks knock his block off;
>   No doubt about it, he's a smart aleck."
He turned his glance to hit me,
>   And I before him was in full flight.
If only you'd seen me sweet on him,
>   As I stroked him with loving passion,
You'd have thought he was brave and strong,
>   And I a tender menace in prophecy.

IBN ḤAZM (994–1064)

Ibn Ḥazm al Andalusī, Abū Muḥammad ʿAlī. Born in Córdoba, he was a distinguished politician who was persecuted for his opinions and died in Montijo. He wrote a book called *The Dove's Neck-Ring*, which comments on his own poems of Neoplatonic love. His poetry has been edited, among others, by L. Bercher (Algiers, 1949).

[1]

I love you with a love that won't soften,
    Though other men's love is only a mirage.
My milk for you is pure and fresh, and in
    My heart a picture carved and written.
If any other is in my mind, I'll clear
    Him out like a veil torn by both my hands.
My intent with him is only love.
    Nothing but that is desired from you.
When I have it, both earth and men
    Are just old camels lingering in the desert heat.

[2]

I like to talk when he is mentioned.
    He clings to me like the scent of amber.
If he speaks I don't hear others—
    Only the words of that terrific charmer.
Even if the Amir Muminin were here,
    I would not turn away on his account.
If I have to go I can't help but
    Turn back and walk as if I'm lame.
My eyes are on him as my body goes,
    The way a drowning man looks at the seashore.
I choke on water when he's absent,
    Like one who yawns amid dust and wind.
If you say: "You can't reach heaven,"
    I say: "Yes but I recognize the stairs."

[3]

Are you from the angel's world or the world of men?
    Tell me, because weakness makes me unable to understand.
I see a human shape, but when I start to consider,
    Suddenly the flesh becomes celestial.
Bléssed be The One who created the ways of being
    So that you have the nature of incandescent light.
I have no doubt that you are the breath
    That is given to us to join in likeness our souls.
We have no hint to attest to your making or to compare
    With anything else, except for your visible good looks.
If it were not for the eye's witness of your inner being,
    We could only talk about true, elevated Reason.

[4]

Men know that I am a man and a lover
    Who is saddened and crazy—and yet for whom?
When they stare at me, they are certain,
    But if they ask, they fall back on suppositions.
I am like a writing whose lines are clear,
    But if they try to interpret it, the sense is difficult.
I am like the sound of a dove cooing in an aik tree,
    Whose gurgling echoes in every tune.
Our ears are pleased by the melody,
    But its ideas are strange and inexplicable.
They say: "By Allah, give us the name of him
    Whose love has driven sweet sleep away from you!"
No such thing! Whatever they try, I will first lose
    All of my wits and face bloody fortunes.
Forever they will be stuck in doubts,
    Caught in broken thoughts and fragmented suspicions.

IBN ʿAMMĀR (1031–ca. 1084)

    Ibn ʿAmmār, Abū Bakr. Born near Silves, was a close friend of the Caliph al-
Muʿtamid in Seville. But eventually they quarreled and the Caliph killed him.

We are two friends; neither love
    Nor choice calls us to embracing;

We are separate in uniting,

    The way we were night and day.

    Ibn Khafāja, Abū Isḥāq Ibrāhīm ibn Abī al Fatḥ ibn 'Abdillāh. He was born near Valencia at Alcira, where he spent his entire life. The turbulent times made this retreat the safest option for him. He wrote a good deal of nature poetry, which has its roots in earlier Arabic poems describing desert camp-sites, where an abandoned lover laments his beloved, who has gone. When this scene is transferred to Spain, the desert blooms with flowers and trees. For texts, see Wormhoudt Arab Translation Series, No. 87 (1987).

[1]

A forehead nearly pale, soft, clear—

    He pours the mixture between us flowing;

Drowsy, he gets to every heart

    To crush every infatuated cruiser;

Staying on a buddy's breast,

    You reckon him to be fated as an equal friend.

I bend as he drinks—a memory;

    I see him both as a drunk and drinker.

Cool wine; between us you see

    The mixture on his cheek and a blush.

[2]

Long neck, jewels on perfumed

    Pecs like a love prelude to a poem;

He has a narrow waist, but his ass is

    Softly fertile, the belt is sterile;

He sucks in beauty's garden;

    His stance is a stem, his bud a smile;

He pours the way a dove sings at evening time;

    Well-aged wine bright with bubbles

He makes red but the glass is

    Crystal, and its fullness is flaming.

In a shaking flood whose foams are

    Blossoms, while its wave is a sand dune,

Events come from it, proof for us
    As wine and the beloved make us rejoice.
Eyelids seduce us like narcissus,
    And his smile is as cool as a camomile.
By Allah I'll drag out a skirt for a fucking,
    Gaining fresh life from this youth's hands.

[3]
No! by the sorrow that rages
    In him the affair splits.
I don't sleep except in tears
    That flow to melt me all alone.
Hot, I drew out sighs and
    What a fine comfort in sadness!
The eyelids won't close for you.
    No bedfellow, not even any side at all;
Loving I long for you
    Like some weirdo with buckets of tears.
I tell the south wind:
    At sunset embrace me in a blast.
Can't you heal me with a cool draft
    As I seek healing in your wind?

[4]
O like many a bright brow with
    Traces of a brand on both sides,
The eyes go ape in fear of him,
    And hearts at night love his wit;
Shirts are torn off for him at dawn;
    Veils are dewy in the twilit skies.
I hit the john with hot piss
    Like a mirage torn from his shirt.
Where breathing was in the wind,
    Stinking like the Euphrates' waters,
Many a smooth body went wading;
    A phantom like meteors splits the skies;
I knelt on both banks as he held
    Me in joy and youth and we drank delight;

I wept at his Tigris and he laughed
>In pleasure as a lover and the end to torment.

[5]

I saw a mole on his dimpled cheek,
>The heart of love in a denying fire;

I feared short of breath a kiss,
>But he gave it as a pledge of love;

He came to endow me with passion;
>He played the fool with a narrow waist.

[6]

True to us, he had a smooth page;
>His cheek now has ink flowing on it;

Darkly the youth is bereft
>As the cheek scatters black upon youth.

[7]

Bless its bouquet like his breath;
>I drank it from his hand in passion—

Smooth as if it was his saliva,
>Crimson as if it was his cheek.

[8]

One of many *nighthawks* poured for us   *[son of night; a black boy]*
>As the sun rose over his forehead

And stayed to blacken his color
>As the cup spread to his blushes,

As if a bag of charcoal
>Were burning in his furnace;

And passing the glass,
>He lit the coals with wine;

It laughed with bubbles
>As the water kissed his lips,

And it took hold of rubies
>That paled to yellow pearls

Until I bent the branch
  And the sun gilded the gold;
A twinkle returned the sun;
  For him languor was sickness;
The dark kohl-powder changed to mist,
  And his tears turned to pitch.

[9]

He came to pour out his winy saliva,
  Then revived me with his fine cheeks.
I took mind's idea from marigolds,
  Smelled in them the odor of daisies;
His face has a mole in the hollow of his cheeks
  Like crushed musk on a burning brand.

[10]

Slender, holding a heart,
  With hermaphroditic sides and look,
Eyes filled with glances
  Whose beauties make a bracelet—
When he gazes, when he moves,
  When he sings, when he hides,
He resembles a gazelle and a cloud
  And a dove and the moon of good luck.

[11]

Balls bearing a saffron smell,
  Fresh aloe logs breathe on coals—
I put off my patient coat of love
  But poise is good in this passion.
No wonder what the eye sees
  With the seed inside and the wine outside.

[12]

A great singer crooning a song
  Finds a long night and it's short;

The boy unveils for us a mark;
      The night's moon throws and wins;
I made love to him in wine and
      Bubbles, blushing cheek and stare—
The mixture a horse neighing brightly,
      Lightning a saddle torn in blood,
As if drink twists his side like
      Winds embracing a flowering branch,
Filling ears and eyes with beauty.
      I don't know: am I drinking or just staring?

[13]

O flash of sparkling cup and cloud,
      Pouring as it rides winds in its coming,
Say to those winning lips on the dunes:
      The slender one ties a belt around his waist;
O red branch, rise to part your hair
      Like a dove who is breaking its blooming bud.
Don't worry if I draw your figure at night.
      Won't you bear fruit for me in a kiss?

[14]

O many a day the cup urged him on!
      It flew away and our happy days were short;
I tripped at evening time upon his skirt,
      Taking a drunken step on the windy wave.
Flowers were spreading on every hill;
      The gold was flowing on them at sunset.

[15]

Dizzy from his saliva's wine,
      His sucking me and our drunkenness,
My eyes and his face were dripping
      As coals burned my heart and his cheeks.
Thin was my share of his delicacy.
      I don't know who had the witchcraft:

Both of us were healed by verses and lips:
>His lips and my words, my verses and his lips.

[16]
Sleepless—my friend slept afar,
>A stony heart gone, split in his love;
No worry—just a flashing cloud
>Rising over the hills to greet the dawn.
I see its light, but the sky is veiled
>As my eyes are drowned in tears for him;
He thinks of me as night bedews him,
>His sides beating as his smile flashes,
Dragging his robe in smoke at Gada
>With cool sweet spittle on his dark red lips.
So say to the cum: You are guided.
>When your side bends over, a snake rushes out.
The shot wad goes down to the bottom.
>As you watch his blade, you see armor.

[17]
O age of folly now gone, ended.
>Bless the time of youth departed.
I slept in the shade of desire,
>Gathering the fruit of content.
Then he went away; I thought of him
>As a faint star or a flickering flash.
He denied my wavering approach
>Until nearby he turned opposite
And passed unnoticed or looking bothered.
>I wanted some greeting or attention.
He only shone in the folly of the night
>Like a gray dawn to wrong my appearance.
He gave to my eye a guiding light
>And to my heart the fire of Hell.
My temples were white, while his were black.
>Would that I could see his night grow bright!

[18]

Slim with honey lips and spittle,
    With a smooth necklace, jewels, and butt—
I unsaddled my horse as flashes fluttered
    And a rainstorm favored my longing.
I offered sweet faith, words, and lips
    To his fine face—gems and *benefits*.   *[money]*

[19]

I looked on his cheeks for some signs
    Of hair, some finely written characters.
I said: I see a sun in eclipse;
    So rise up! let's offer a bit of prayer.

[20]

I wooed him as a lover; there was a clear sky—
    No denial of fear in those cheeks.
He stumbled on his robe ankle-high;
    On the sides were brocades—then his branch.
The mole on his cheek was bright,
    Like a star burning in the sunlight.
I wondered, with my eyes wet and my heart hot,
    What path would take them to Paradise.

[21]

Beauty inclines to its likeness;
    A mirror doubles in his embrace;
A shaft shot from them both bends
    To rise in honor from nobility;
He looks at it from the side,
    The way a fawn gazes at his shadow.

[22]

Waken to the joy of an honest friend
    As he rises to take off his worn pants.

He loosed the sparkling red cup.
>O, he gave it as a man's best gift.

Many a long night I played there,
>Making love openly, drinking compassion.

We didn't scatter any wordy pearls
>Until I kissed him; then we smiled a string.

Many a blaze of tears I showed
>Making a trip as I burned in heat.

You see how red his cheeks flame,
>And how black is the coal of his hair!

[23]

Silent I listened, not taking blame,
>With a longing heart neither sober nor loving.

My sickness suffers from his look.
>Empty of shadows filled by dark eyes,

I complain of thirst, wetness on cold stone;
>If I drink I'll be cured of him.

He who sleeps with a man is wakeful,
>With his heart tossing between grief and hope.

What wounds his ribs inflict on me, and
>What a bright blade is in ʿAlī's eyes!

O you who beat out Yūsuf for good looks,
>This fucker exceeds all others in comparison!

Take what you see and leave gossip alone.
>If the sun rises, do without these stars!

[24]

Bushes in his valley overwhelmed
>The wasteland of whiskers on his smooth cheeks.

The sun was near to hurrying
>Westward, gazing down with darkened eye,

As if its rays upon his blade
>Were a bit of blood on a smooth sword.

[25]

I forced him by love's law to meet me,
    And in our embrace I was an *alif* and *lam*. *[an "a" and "l," both phallic]*
We slept held tightly and hugging, the way
    They mingle cloud-water with wine.
My complaint to him was easy and small.
    I was awake with sorrow while he slept.
I avoided his name for fear of hatred
    Between us and feeling for his shame.
There is no joy except in the seeker's eyes
    To awaken him by reciting while he slept.
No poem before him ever brought me joy.
    The highest poetic honor is in generosity.

[26]

A cupbearer with thoroughbred eyes, peak
    In his form, runaway, lacking all patience—
You see youth's fire glowing in his cheeks,
    With blackish sideburns like smoke.
He pours like a new moon shining at evening,
    Like a scimitar curving for armored men.
Generous he hands out the wine—the best,
    Not mixed with cloud-water. A stallion foams;
Darkness spreads from a darkened cloud
    With a lightning whip and a cool bridle.
A sweet sun stained a garden throat
    As the dew fell like pearls upon him.
A tree grew with paradisal treasures
    With the light of his lip and the breath of his tongue.

IBN ḤAMDĪS (1058–1132)

Ibn Ḥamdīs, ʿAbd al-Jabbār ibn Abī Bakr ibn Muḥammad al-Azdī aṣ-Ṣiqīllī.
Born in Syracuse, he left Sicily after the Norman Conquest, going to Seville,
where he joined the court of al-Muʿtamid; when the Almoravid dynasty rose
he fled to Mahdiyya, dying in Bougie. This poem contains an extreme ex-
pression of a hedonistic vision of life. His *Dīwān* was edited by Iḥsān ʿAbbās
(Beirut, 1960).

Many a *saqī* poured cups for our friends   [cupbearer]
    Of yellow by a stream—a forbidden flow.
Every glass overflowed, as if it held
    The soul of the sun in the moon's body.
When a glass arrives in the hands of a drunken comrade,
    He takes it lovingly with his ten fingers.
He drinks in the drunkenness of grape clusters,
    Drowsing half-sober with unwitting eyes.
He sends it out on waves as he returns it
    To the hands of the *saqī* who offered it.
We modulated the wine-drinking to our ears
    With a melody that the birds sing unversified.
Our *saqī* was like water flowing without any hands;
    Our drink was fire shining without any coals.
He poured out happiness with many shares
    For us, as if we had poured out a sea,
As if the cities on the riverbanks contained
    Shiploads of wine that sailed over to us.
Life exists only in enjoying pleasure,
    Putting off *bridles* that adorn the cheeks.   [beards]

IBN ARFAᶜ RA'SUH

Ibn Arfaᶜ Ra'suh, Abū Bakr Muḥammad; his dates are not accurately known. He wrote poetry in the court of Toledo; this poem is a panegyric in praise of the court's ruler, who is named at the end. See Monroe, pp. 224–27.

The lute sings   With a rare warble
And the rills cut   The garden fields;
    The birds sing   On willow branches
    As happiness clasps   Lions on the plain.
    All are emirs,   Sultans in wine.
The talking strings   Are a clear enchantment
As the birds reply   From the myrtle stalks.
    Come, give me heat   As the garden expands;
    The rain-stars incline   In the sweet morning.
    Urging us to drink   Is a handsome gazelle
Like a soft penis   In a rosy cloak;
His embroidered sides,   Broken as he bends,

Arise to love; Drink to double glory,
Support of lands In the east and west,
An aid to believers, The offspring of Yaʿrub,
A great king Subduing sultans,
Ordering processions Like a lion of the plain,
A lord with a heart, Fiercer than a leopard,
And his fingers are Nobler than showers.
If the time frowns For a day or darkens,
He meets it smiling Like the garden's light.
His acts are stars For the world and religion.
The lover refuses To return a greeting,
But burns in his heart With excessive desire.
Thus sorrow sings A song of passion.
You pass but do not greet me, As if you were Caliph Ma'mūn,
The terror of armies, Yaḥya ibn Dhīn-Nūn.

IBN AL-ZAQQĀQ (ca. 1096–1134)

Ibn al-Zaqqāq, ʿAlī ibn ʿAṭiyya Abū l-Ḥasan al-Bulughghīnī al-Mursī. He
was a nephew of Ibn Khafāja and also wrote nature poetry. See his *Diwān*,
ed. ʿAfīfa Dairānī (Beirut, 1964).

[1]

Many a garden of peonies appears
        As perfumed winds are guided there.
I visited one when clouds had cooled it
        As flowers spread the red color of wine.
I asked: "Why so red?" He answered:
        "They stole a sailor's blushing *cheeks.*"   [buttocks]

[2]

O many a curving, slim body,
        If his absence nears life from afar,
Moans when absence favors it.
        Like a happy drunk, he will sing
When the arrow's head makes a hit.
        So say: "Stars were shot at Satan."

[3]

The fawn's eyes destroy me
    As if my illness were a coat;
A glance unsheathes a sword
    To kill me, but sheathes itself back in sleep.

[4]

O fawn living in Fas,
    Where is the sun of which you are the light?
The curls on your cheeks glow
    Where roses and myrtles grow;
Your tender body offers drink
    Like the swaying branch of a willow;
Your eyelids are enough wine for me.
    Your cheeks breathe your perfume.
Do your pour wine, and after that,
    Do you provide a cup for what it does?

[5]

His perfume fills love's breath,
    His favor the sand dune's stalk.
He passed us as he cruised by.
    His glance drew his eyelid's sword.
Wine flowed from his smile.
    I thought of *pus* in the scar nearby.   *[possibly from a social disease]*
He offered a kiss as a greeting.
    My mouth said: I want to be his hand.

[6]

O star shining among bright stars
    And flower blooming in dawn's glow,
At evening we embraced; yours was the gift.
    One day you offered me cups at evening.
I left my brothers' bridle restraint.
    Before me was a sweet-flowing liquor.
So be kind and return a goodness
    Now gone that still leaves a heart enamored.

[7]

The stream from my eyes spread
    Its waters like a mirror;
A youth swam in it;
    His glance was a fawn's glance,
I thought, when he showed himself
    Like a moon in its weary waning.
He stayed on as the mists hid him
    At times, and then suddenly he appeared.

[8]

O you who know my joy,
    Grant your favors openly.
I give you the pure soul
    From me and you, my lord.
My thought was refined,
    So linger in my thoughts.

[9]

I yearn for the Jew's faith but
    Fear the sword if I were Jewish.
I only fear the sword because I would
    Die of love and leave him alive.

IBN SAHL (ca. 1210–1251)

Ibn Sahl, Abū Isḥāq Ibrāhīm al-Isrāʾīlī al-Ishbīlī. He was a converted Jew who wrote famous love songs in Seville, as well as poems of praise for eminent men called *qasidas*. In his love poetry Ibn Sahl writes poems to boys named Mohammed, a Muslim, and Musa, a Jew. Ibn Sahl is believed to have drowned in the Guadalquivir River in 1251. See Wormhoudt Arab Translation Series, No. 57 (1981).

[1]

Return the stolen sleep to my eyes.
    Tell me about my heart, which is now so pitifully lost!

I knew when I rejoiced in the house of love
      That the dream in my eyes was an angry one.
I said: "O rage, silence better befits me!"
      Beauty is angry if I say things like "O rage!"
My revenge on Musa and his chastity
      Is not needed, for he is loosed when bound.
I am excused by my blood shed for him.
      I say: "I took shedding with a weary hand
One whom Allah made from the water of life,
      Whose remnants flowed over his cool teeth.
My soul delights in grief, is used to it.
      Does anyone know the cause of my sad soul?"
They said: "We thought you among the sane.
      Why are you straying?" I said: "Seek a cause in his look."
O absent one, my eyes wept for your going.
      Clouds since morning's sun was hidden poured down.
My thoughts met his sunny image in a mirror,
      And its reversal warmed my bosom into flames.
When you went away, I tried patience by probing elsewhere,
      But I found his wood neither soft nor hard.
Many a night I spent as the stars watched over me,
      Smitten by love, and I conquered it entirely
By wandering in night's sorrow; if the stars
      Could talk, they'd be amazed at my behavior.
I plundered ruby tears from sorrow
      As I saw that those bright pearls were looted.
Is an eye cured of you if you are its
      Vision? if night's desired darkness is taken from it?

[2]
This is parting, Musa; you were a guest
      And your nearness to the camp was not mine.
O garden, hope that my grass may wither with parting!
      O sun of beauty's horizon, now is my sunset near!
Before parting I had cut myself free from desire,
      Had kept my eyelids awake in the hope of my love.
But soon the raven croaked for our camel.
      O patience! if I made a trip to the east, he went west.

O solace in love, he left me wrongly
>	And without faith, and now, O sleep, be gone!
From this day I date my first bad luck from you,
>	And the end of time for my tormented heart.

[3]

I taste a love that is as bitter as a *colocynth,*	[bitter-apple, a gourd]
>	But I recall his red mouth, and it is sweet.
Every eye yearns for and loves his beauty.
>	As if all men's eyes for him had become hearts.
Musa—and not disbelief in Allah—kills me,
>	So how can Musa be a lover of my heart?

[4]

They blamed me when my love's source shone.
>	They said: "You came with passion to his door."
My cheeks ran with tears of love for
>	One whose cheeks thirsted for the water of youth.
Sweet words he spoke, as if his terms
>	Had the same speech as his honeyed saliva.
By Allah, O Musa, death is sweet, so strike!
>	Do not hold back the pain of the wound.
Harut leaves his magic in your look,	[the angel of death]
>	As if his torment struck my heart with you!
You heal my despair in your embrace
>	The way a doubtful letter is fixed in grammar.

[5]

Often I said to my lover: "Sleep safely."
>	He said to me out of pride: "*You* sleep!"
I continued to run after him, stuck
>	To his track humbly, but he didn't turn back.
Everybody blames his lover; then
>	When he sees my patience, he's amazed.
He likes to see you veiled from his eye;
>	Tears perplex the flooding in his censer;

When he sleeps with a ghost, he hunts,
    And his dirge and his lament drive you to waking.
Tears for you in daylight are an adversary,
    Waking along with words his guard.
When he wins, part of him is his enemy;
    If he's overcome, his doctor is his weakness.
If Satan's solace circles in my mind,
    A meteor of my passion attacks him there.
What are ornaments for me if he is naked?
    The moonlight's beauties are in his blemishes.
His chastity under the veil is looted,
    A plunderer between his suspect eyes.
Hard—what is between his ribs is harsh;
    Pliant—what is under his cloak is tender.
His face, softer than the wind's passing breath,
    Makes me envy his face and the movements
Of his cheeks; his thrust breaks piety's bond
    For me, and his parting takes away my chastity.
Modesty kindles like coals his two cheeks;
    His sweetness clings to his beauty spot.
The crimes of his glance are forgiven for his ills;
    He leaps, but his sins are not inscribed against him.
Musa is not kept from wading in the sea
    Of my tears as his guide, my slanderer, drowns.

[6]

O you to whose love I was guided, my
    White way in the path of lust was straight.
Your glances kindled love in my mind;
    Truly the blow of the flint produced flames.
The first look was not complete in you
    Until I knew your love was my disgrace.
You are the *Simak* of mankind, and often   *[constellation Pisces]*
    Your glance raised you to Simak's lights.
O lovely Musa, do not hide my solace from me.
    Lust appears and wisdom's efforts betray me.
I love him until my eyes keep awake
    For him and my wounds suffer in sickness.
O why did my eyes see his early parting?

Misfortune's measure lies in exhausted sleep.
The breast knows that the heart was my friend;
> The body knows that the soul is my own handshake.

[7]

Do not grieve for a sad condition.
> Your embrace tomorrow erases today's flight.
I know you broke the bond with me but
> Often I held the rope, wanting to touch your hands.
You repaid me with a rage for a happy state of mind,
> And offered a solitary state for good friendship.
You were not used to passionate quarrels.
> Difficulty for a man cannot become a habit.
I hid my heart's love for Musa in spite of my grief.
> And he seduced me with tears from wakeful eyes.
You are only a youth that grief conquered, but
> Your glance did the work of an Indian blade.
The Merciful One gave you a crown of beauty
> And bright dawns by which morning was led in.
The sprig of your youth bent at that waist
> Was like the curve of a soft breeze on a dewy branch.

[8]

I was consoled for Musa by Mohammed's love;
> I was guided and, but for Allah, I would not have been so;
And this was not out of hatred, but because
> A way to Musa's oasis was barren of Mohammed.

[9]

As if the mole on Musa's cheek
> Was a black blame in the light of love,
He wrote a "w" with his curls for beauty,
> And there was some ink voweled on his cheek.
His glances were exciting but
> By them sorrows were guided to my heart.
His mole was just a bit of an eye's wink;
> Beauty produces it with a great miracle.

It comes to an eye like a visitor to the cheek;
> Drink thins it out, and it avoids a return.

One beauty loves another sadly; they
> Think how a coquette can desire a bull.

Judgment comes as I grieve for you.
> You are given your wish, O Musa, by fate.

If you're far away, still hate is in a well-rope,
> Or if you bore me darkness, there are moons.

I die with love and I call from afar;
> I am as sick as one who is blindly one-eyed.

I'll have my due from you at resurrection
> When heaven's stars will repay my greeting.

I am one poor in gifts who will be rewarded.
> Would that poverty were driven off by lisps or buns!

I have published verse but have stopped at poems;
> I was blamed at night for that at great length.

[10]

I strayed in the full moon because of his light;
> People want to be guided by the full moon.

Musa empties the magic of the past
> And yet Musa brought the magic for today.

Fine descriptions are a protection,
> So do not take him except in thought—

Like water in a cloud or a pearl
> In the shell or a fawn in the desert.

If he appeared to one of heaven's *houri,*   *[nymph in Moslem Paradise]*
> She'd hit him *between his lungs and throat.*   *[on the nipples that she's drawn to]*

If he called the dead by his words,
> Then they'd come to him from the grave.

Pearls are his teeth and his words;
> So they call him the pearl of the stars.

They can't keep their eyes from him; no,
> By his eyes, they guard men in love nightly.

As if the mole on his cheek were
> My heart's core in the glow of coals,

My blood flows onto his cheeks in red hues
> And the *place of sin* is blackened by it.   *[genitals; anus]*

I kissed his cheeks with my tears
    The way a rose is picked beside a pool.
I drank and confirmed in return
    The tale of hearts far from breasts.
I kissed his breast-bone as he went away
    And discerned the perfume of an ointment.
O Musa, you trouble my sweet sleep.
    My night after you is a worried night.
My sleep is far from my eyes
    And desire's tale stays in my mind.
Parting adds no distance from you except for
    The sun's rays on high or setting.
I drove hope away from my thoughts of you
    But watch over it in these changing times.

[11]

Why did we decide to break off and nothing stayed
    Of the good of passion but only the trifles?
I wept for a river hiding tears
    And its color changed them literally.
If my party knew my desire then
    They'd not go with me on the journey.
When my breath moves in the sails,
    My sighs send them back toward port.
We stood at dawn; I conquered my
    Passion; grief called beauty: Who aids?
O fire that my sighs have lit,
    The morning passed like noontime.
Parting gave his farewell, and
    I compared my far death to good news.

[12]

O Musa I do not flee you, by Allah;
    I flee sleep and mind and good, all pastimes;
I left you not to break faith; no, I see
    My life as sin after your going or betrayal.
I'm content in spite of all in your memory;
    Alone I offer wine for that and bloody tears.

I kiss the bubbles of the saqi's cup
>   When they portray those teeth I desire.

[13]

You rose to my eyes; they forgot sleep;
>   You plucked me from your cheeks in love.

Can my passion take solace without a kiss?
>   Offering an end of patience by a broken seal,

O Musa, O part of me and all in reality
>   And not excessive in my words, all or part,

You humbled my place when you cut me off.
>   Why did you join the cut and the lowering?

I stretched the sun's rope from you with
>   Fingers to my joy, and the joy cut it off sharply.

[14]

O Musa, you gave me an evil drink.
>   I am not Pharaoh, the clever infidel.

You bewitched my heart when you sent me
>   A downy snake; you drowned me in tears.

I didn't fear that you'd be my death
>   With both your hands in those days with wonders.

By Allah, my ears and eyes didn't enjoy
>   Other men, and that wasn't to my profit.

You made patience a kind of glue.
>   You forbade my coming to intercede.

I don't care if I die; I am only
>   Wary lest you cast the blame upon nature.

[15]

Heart's parting expands,
>   And the lover nurses me.

He comes with calm heart.
>   So ask him: How did it go?

Did men find any
>   Soul trusted afterward?

O vision not given

Until I picked passion,
Magic often glows and
Stays in Musa's glances.
O strong burdening,
My love in Musa's burden,
May Allah not heal me
If I pray to him for a cure.
I submit that if he wrongs me,
Judgment is not made weak.
Base love and the power of
Beauty are a tale made known—
No sin but a lover
Submitting to half desire
I am not, as he flees me,
And my traces are erased,
The first of lovers to die
Or the first of lovers to fight.
O you, I swore that I'd see
Toil, and the oath was true.
O you, stingy to resurrect
By words a perished lover,
I fear your crime as
You claim spent beauty.
My parting nears, so weep
And with tears and sweating,
I do not blame our parting.
I say: It parted dead ones.
I was not embraced as
A liar hard on past unions.
Distance does not add to
Distance or anger, praise Allah!
Your love was a food,
And today it is an affection.
O welcome to your love
And to your chaste patience!

ABŪ ḤAYYĀN (1256–1344)

Abū Ḥayyān, Athir al-Dīn Muḥammad ibn Yūsuf ibn ᶜAlī ibn Yūsuf ibn
Ḥayyān al-Andalusī. Born in Granada, he became famous as a commenta-

tor on the Koran. He left Spain and traveled in Tunis, Egypt, and Syria. He
wrote the first Turkish grammar and a grammar of Persian. His love poems
are addressed to women as well as to men. See Wormhoudt Arab Transla-
tion Series, No. 120 (1989).

[1]

On the white waist darkness rustles—
    Cool desire, coyness, not cool breezes,
Tender, except for heavy dunes that jest:
    Fruitful buttocks responding to a pulled belt.
Full moons rise and pass, but only you
    See in them black hair like a dark night.

[2]

Your absence for a week sets two in grief,
    And two days away kill a youth in sorrow.
Grant that you're present in my heart; my eyes
    At the sight of you enjoy quiet peace in trouble.

[3]

I went out walking when my heart
    Told me to, and would not deny someone I met.
I came and saw his swaying branch,
    His thick stalk; a full moon watched.
He knows a heart whose place is love
    Where the secret I knew drew me to him.
I used to deny any knowledge of the hidden
    Until I saw that my heart perceived the divine.

[4]

What a life for a little sheikh!
    He has an existence the way a corpse does,
Lacking friends from afar,
    Abandoned by people of the house.
He has a soul that calls on
    The fates: "Come on, come on!"

He hopes and desires
>A second drink; I'd like it.
My candle is not for him;
>Only a drop of oil remains;
He'll be named in my tale
>In that he's only so-and-so.

[5]

By a fawn's heart whose faith is lost,
>Would that he, while I live, hated and fled
The Turkish; if you see a full moon rising
>In part, or if you quarrel, then a wild lion's
Nature is beloved by him; his legs
>Become branches bearing the fruit of new moons.
He points a spear at me from his waist
>And the head of his lance is brown-eyed.

[6]

A fawn hit me with an arrow,
>Aiming with it toward my heart
With a musky eye, and in it
>Were rays that destroyed my sleep.
My eyelids were watchful,
>And my side full of open thorns.
My tears flowed in a stream,
>Moving to bring me to a valley.
The heart in my bosom was full of coals,
>Like sparks from a flint.
My patience for him was short,
>And my love began to increase.
Why did he seem a solace
>To a youth whose ills were plain?
A cure for sickness is a healing
>That includes sweet honey from the comb.
When he tastes the sweetness,
>He finds an end to other intentions.
He lives the best of lives
>And is safe from others' hostility.

[7]

Allah, save a moment mixed for me

    With my lover, for we mingle like honey.

Allah, curse the hour that we parted!

    My bosom had the hottest fire in it.

I was like a candle burning bright,

    And he was like dew poured on the rose.

[8]

By my father! he is a fawn at parting;

    His eyes attract my heart by their strength;

All handsome men see his likeness in them

    Except when my lover is importunate.

He said: "What do you want?" I: "A kiss

    To fill the heart that feels torn to pieces."

He said: "Take it," but he would not

    Take one from me, and so I was not taken.

I sucked sweetness from his locks.

    He allowed me this honey and pleasure.

I asked favors that are meant to enchant.

    They made me like a *jinn* who will steal.   *[spirit lower than angels]*

He said: "Enough, no jinn in him."

    But my share in him had been exhausted.

When my glance struck him, the arrow

    Pierced up to the feathered butt-end.

No illness in love is cured by charms.

    No, no strong refuges are then of value.

Yes, love's cure lies in speedy union:

    A fuck with a unanimity that seeks pleasure.

[9]

I was in love with a silken black—

    There was nothing white in him except ivory teeth.

The Creator endowed him with black eyes,

    And every eye on him was enriched in its vision,

As if he was a mirror to reflect images

    From men like a soul that stores pictures . . .

The Nubian kind saddens my heart.

He is an exile in his poem, an eloquent image
Of Ham's folk; brother to Shem and
    Japhet, he served the Semite and Khazar.
He has a perfect nature from top to bottom, and is
    Humbly submissive when his temper is hidden.

[10]

Exchanging glances with languid ills,
    A healthy heart is broken by them.
His sighs and lips and saliva
    Are produced by musk, wine, and pearls.
His torso, hair, and face are
    Like a willow, night, and the full moon.

[11]

O waking and tears and sighs—
    Some of these for a lover are many.
I only recall my lover's embrace;
    My heart nearly flies to his passion;
My own passions quiet him and then depart in desire,
    Wondering at his paradise and flames.

[12]

We sucked our saliva like wine.
    I smelled it, excited by the unguent.
We climbed a dune, pouring on him,
    Tender in the shining of the moonlight.
The braids of his hair fell down.
    Behold the viper coming toward a pool!
With fearful eye, it changed all
    To shame as the belovéd fawn cried out.

YŪSUF III OF GRANADA (r. 1408–1417)

Yūsuf III, Abū ʿAbdillāh ibn al Aḥmar ruled Granada from 1408 to 1417, the year of his death. In his lifetime Arab holdings in Spain were already falling to the Spaniards. See Wormhoudt Arab Translation Series, No. 120 (1989).

[1]

I wrote; my heart melted for you;
      Love as passionate desire will melt.
The dream was as strong as waking;
      It held tears as love's memory flowed.
O full moon which does not rise
      To any height, can sunset hinder me?
Maybe you'll heal my heart's grief
      And free me from my strange desire's need.

[2]

O lightning showing on the heights, which
      Like a glance in dark night flamed for him,
Often you drew your sword to pierce the borders;
      You spoke, but boldness is not just fine teeth.

[3]

He appears to the eyes
      Like a coolness and a stalk,
A king with eyelids
      That assault the heart
Till with hard service
      His beauty is a wonder.
Justice turns away from him;
      His glance is my uncertainty.
My eyelids are hot
      With burning sorrows.
He is like a fawn in flight
      Or an antelope of the dunes.
Glory to one who made
      Him from the clay of hearts!
He is a full moon sans secrets,
      A sunshine without a setting.
Would that he showed me some sin!
      From his fine cool teeth
I never endured any filthy
      Food or any frowns from him.

Yet my soul is sick
    Since he is my belovéd.

[4]

I went early to a garden of pure joy
    As the dawn looked down from rifts of clouds—
The way desire drives a lover when
    Pangs of illness urge him onward,
Veiled as the eye looks long and hard,
    Wary of the guard and not replying.
The dew was weaving pearls on the branches,
    Bending to beauty and to amazement.

[5]

What excuse is there for deceptive teeth
    Lighting sparks and flames in the heart?
Every time I scorn him in passion,
    It aids pride and denial and hatred.
Can one hope for union with you
    When the heart waits for an embrace?

[6]

Pain in the far west, long his absence;
    In the east his people, friends complain.
Fate judges him, since his home is far away.
    One avoids anyone who covers his sides,
Blames anyone harshly as long as fate rules.
    One seeks him who hopes for rewards;
My heart throbs for what I have hoped for;
    One blames him who fears his blame.

[7]

Often grief returns with his visit;
    If I visit him, our eyes and hearts are cooled;
Your memory brings the soul joy in grief.
    O would that the joy of the eye from you were near!

[8]

Many a cheek flames,
    And the piss is amazing.
If his look is silver,
    Still gold flows from it.

[9]

By your life, he brings us fine wine,
    Leaving one who gives while a friend is dying;
If I'm drunk, I am in the *Garden;*   *[of Paradise]*
    If I'm inebriated, it's the resurrection.

[10]

O wonder at his picture—
    My meadow and his Paradise.
There is water where he comes from
    And manure from his pathway.

[11]

O my breath on empty lips,
    For they are golden with hot wine.
Some men in open transgression
    Reveal to the enemy our holy place.
I will not search for a caliph's day
    Of victory in the desired peace of pride.

[12]

If I deny my grief and despair,
    Look at the blackness in his calm eye.
Look at the curls on his cheeks,
    As if musk were written on ivory.
How will it end as the fawn's eye stares?
    Where is my rescue, since I can't avoid him?
Let me rave on, you who know my state.
    My eyes flow and my heart lacks hope.
If I once loosed my reins, it isn't now.
    Let them excuse me for taking the high road.

[13]

Many a fawn tricked me
    With a generous promise,
With whiskers on his cheeks
    Like a rainbow in shape.
His face dripped the water
    Of life when it glistened.
His lips tasted of *Salsabil*   *[the River of Paradise]*
    To heal all the wounded.

[14]

Friend, has a heart any peace
    When the one I love leaves or denies me?
His face offers gifts to me
    But drives love and folly away from me.
Don't think I am seeking solace if
    He hides when breaking a vow.
My faith and love, nature knows,
    Fear no denial and dread no distance.

[15]

Narrow-waisted with a fat ass,
    He plays fugitive in jest and earnest.
I have no need of wrongdoing
    But the wrongs include wine and honey.
O beloved, grant my heart some favor;
    Yield contentment in Allah, O moon of joy!

[16]

O bright new glance of unknown love,
    Eager for a beloved's sweets and denial!
When I thrust in, his eyelids broke;
    The touch of his torso watered my bosom.
My cheeks knew his steely look,
    His necklace of curls like fresh cheeks.
Don't you see a bloody sacrifice
    If it is only the wound of his passion?

What a stay in a soul, O top of joy!

    Your glance is keen in its heart's aim;

Either you take a love you know

    Or you taste death as a friend to passion.

[17]

Flight keeps good sleep from my eyes;

    Tears and waking cling to my eyelids;

Pain worries my ribs harshly;

    Passion by love's decree goes on.

Flight is only death unending.

    What excuse is there for my heart in denial?

Mohammed always trusted in journeys.

    Keeping vows or guarding friendships.

You fled, but I did not, O my best gift!

    I feared my loss when my bond showed;

My heart increased in grief and love

    Even when I had pain and long waking.

I was lacking sweet, dear visitors,

    And so my eyes tasted no food in my sleep.

Would that my time yielded some favor!

    I'd spend for it all my new and old wealth.

I'd cross deserts forbidden to you

    By all my polished keen swords,

And I would not keep any gifts away from you

    Nor fear any blades or brave enemies.

O would that I saw some favors from you!

    My heart could be healed by your wanted lips.

If gossips and blamers spoke up,

    They'd only, by Allah, hear denials.

[18]

I value your glance, O my desire,

    For I am the lover who inclines to you.

Your heights are a refuge to turn to;

    My heart unites with you in eternal flame.

You were my Paradise of Love,

    Though my bowing and prostration to you were long.

Why block the path of our meeting,
      Why forbid my immortal soul a way to you?

[19]
You speak while heaven's moon envies us
      With its rain-stars hovering between heart and joy
Your longed-for bounty, as I return
      To what unites us—not envy's revenge.
The night is long between you and me.
      Will my happiness see dawn's union?

[20]
Say to a lover who wants to deny you:
      Beware lest you cut my love's bond.
By Allah, I love only a moon
      Whose shirt is rosy and whose cheeks
Appear like the sun with clear rays;
      And a full moon shines, rising in joy,
Like a fawn in favor and warning,
      Like a branch with softness and a torso;
I hurt in earnest as he plays,
      Plays like the wind on red aloes . . .
Why is he too proud for union
      As I thirst for denial in drinking?
What if I revive my condemned sin
      With a taste of his beloved lips?

[21]
My patience for you is poor.
      I die of grief and of distance.
O my heaven and my hell,
      And O my hope of rescue,
If I could own my fate
      I'd never cease to serve you!
I'd fulfill my vow to you,
      And perhaps you'd keep your promises.

You hit my heart with the arrows
Shot from between your eyes.

[22]
O thirsty lips, rescue me!
Patience and courage abandon me.
His distance is near me, but
The way of union is blocked.
People say in a riddle:
How can a child console a father?

[23]
Who excuses the eyes of a gazelle?
Men are mad for beauty as he comes.
His looks are as keen as Indian blades
In my heart—though those wounds could heal!

[24]
Soft full moons take me by their beauty.
My tears are seas in desire's heaven.
I want to quench my thirst in them.
In the heart of them are groans and sighs.
I'm in heaven when I see fine cheeks;
Flowers glow in them as in his lips,
Smiling at winds that are at peace,
Stirring and urging sorrow's parting,
But when his kiss offers contentment,
He scorns love's pleas dangerously.
Wherever he wants it, there is our love.
When the day for me is a threat,
I say: O keen glance in a heart,
Do you come like rubies in the heart?
I am Yūsuf, my sorrow is great.
Can the sun shine favorably in you?
I share what passes as solace,
Though events fall after calamity,

My blame is for a heart, not me;
>I reject time's doubts with patience.
An evil tongue says of his sighs:
>Parting points to the saddest claim.
I found a loss not in ennui or hatred;
>I am fit for embraces with the blame.

[25]

I complain to Allah of hard evil;
>Magic eyes enslave me in silence.
I ask a lover's question but
>He vows proudly in drink's deceit.
If I come to fulfill my vows,
>He turns his eyes away from me in reproach.
No despair ends or heart heals;
>No embrace is given, nor does he visit me;
Never does he trifle with me,
>Though he's in my mind and thought.
O what a wonder that kings fear me,
>And yet my heart is scared by a nearby fawn.
My love begs me with all the kings' goods;
>Then his look turns, and he goes away.
This is the only passion for him;
>The bond I want is my heaviest chain.
Purity feels no pity for my state;
>I ransom my heart by yes and no.

[26]

In love evils demand a humble soul
>In one forbidden by his people and tribe;
Tall trees offer an embrace in the shade.
>My friend guides me but by what way?
>Love comes just as flight creates distance.

[27]

Time judges me with evils by chance;
>Patience is put off, and love's coat is worn-out.

He who loves chooses either good or evil.
Neither state is separate from sorrow.
Suddenly in both, life lies in ruins.

SECTION V

HEBREW POETRY

Norman Roth

Jews in the medieval world of Islam, which was centered in Mediterranean lands (especially in al-Andalus or southern Spain) usually lived in harmony and enjoyed a shared culture with their Muslim neighbors. Quite naturally they took part in the all-night wine parties with Muslim men, enjoying the singing girls and dancing boys and the young male cupbearers who poured the wine. They also composed the first Hebrew secular poetry, borrowing many of the themes as well as the meter of Arabic verse. But this poetry is not mere imitation. Much in it is original and a progression beyond its model.

Like men everywhere in medieval and other times, many of the Jews of Spain loved boys as well as women, and although they were usually married, they shared the sexual pleasures of boy-love, which in no way was condemned or considered degenerate. The Hebrew language, unlike Arabic, contains no explicitly sexual words, so that much must be hinted at or expressed in metaphorical allusions.

The translations included here are only from the "foremost" poets of the "classical" period in Muslim Spain, and they are a representative selection. The beloved boy was called a "gazelle" (Hebrew ṣevi, which is similar in sound to Arabic ṣabi, "boy") or sometimes "fawn."

For texts and further information, references are made to my articles "'Deal Gently with the Young Man': Love of Boys in Medieval Hebrew Poetry of Spain," which appeared in *Speculum* 57.1 (1982), 20–51; "'Fawn of My Delights': Boy-Love in Hebrew and Arabic Verse," in *Sex in the Middle Ages*, ed. Joyce E. Salisbury (Garland, 1991), pp. 157–72; and "The Care and Feeding of Gazelles: Medieval Arabic and Hebrew Love Poetry" in *Poetics of Love in the Middle Ages*, ed. Moshé Lazar and Norris J. Lacy (Fairfax, Va., 1989), 95–118.

Another primary textual source is: Ḥayim Schirmann, *Shirim ḥadashim min ha-genizah* (Jerusalem, 1965), as well as the various *divans* or collections of poets.

13 . Medieval Spanish Selections

Isaac Ben Mar-Saul (eleventh century)
   Apparently the first Hebrew poet to have written a poem in this genre. He
lived in Lucena in the eleventh century. The text is from Schirmann, *Shirim*
hadashim, p. 157; my translation is from "Deal Gently," p. 31, which con-
tains explanatory notes.

Gazelle desired in Spain,
       wondrously formed,
Given rule and dominion
       over every living thing;
Lovely of form like the moon
       with beautiful stature:
Beautiful curls
       upon shining temple,
Like Joseph in his form,
       like *Adoniah* his hair.   *[actually Absalom, son of David]*
Lovely of eyes like David,
       he has slain me like Uriah.
He has enflamed my passions
       and consumed my heart with fire.
Because of him I have been left
       without understanding and wisdom.
Weep with me, every ostrich
       and every hawk and falcon!
The beloved of my soul has slain me—
       is this a just sentence?

. . . .

Because of him my soul is sick,
    perplexed and yearning.
His speech upon my heart
    is like dew upon parched land.
Draw me from the pit of destruction
    that I go not down to Hell.

ANONYMOUS

This poem combines many of the elements of Arabic and Hebrew love po-
etry: the "rebuker" or "censor," who criticizes the lover and sometimes, as
here, is jealous of him; the lovely boy, who is said to be a "slayer" of his
would-be lovers because he rejects them; and sadness over the parting of the
beloved. The poem also shifts from Hebrew to Aramaic in lines 15–25; and
it concludes with a final couplet in Arabic, since it is also a *muwashshah* or
strophic poem in which the final couplet is written either in Arabic or
Hispanic Romance or a mixture of the two.

How shall I live if my beloved is not?
And who will heal, without the lovely of eye, my pain?
    When I remember my fawn near me,
    A burning flame blazes in my soul
    And I consider as darkness my *brightness.*   [or *"cheerfulness"*]
From the time when, like Cain, my slayer
With his lips, without a weapon, went to my rebuker.
    The day he fled from me to my oppressor,
    I cried, "Do not, please, be rebellious,"
    And he answered me mercilessly:
"Drunk of water without wine—
My prey is upon the mountain and *fountain,* like a lion cub." [also, *"eye"*]
    When I saw that he flew without wing,
    And I despaired of seeing hope,
    I changed the expression from the Hebrew language—
"Do not exchange the head for the feet;
Kiss me on the mouth and hands; blot out my obligation."[1]
    [But] he abandoned me and fled like a cloud in the wind
    To his house, and speaking in the street,
    I am distressed and grieved on a day of trouble:
"Good looks are exchanged and are changed.
Appearance is confounded and liars are neighbors."[2]

Before me the pelican and night-bird are silent
When I complain of new and old [sorrows].
Separation severs my heart in blood.
"You who are brown, delight of [my] eyes,
Who is able to bear separation, my beloved?"[3]

[1]These lines, written in Aramaic, have the sense of "don't remove your 'head' from me by fleeing; kiss me and I will have fulfilled my obligation to you."

[2]Sense difficult; perhaps, "beauty is gone—appearance confounded and false-hoods become real."

[3]The translation of the first line of the Arabic couplet is from S.M. Stern, *Hispano-Arabic Strophic Poetry* (Oxford, 1974), p. 150. The second line is a mixture of Spanish and Arabic, and the translation is from Stern, *Les Chansons mozarabes: les vers finaux . . . en espagnol dans les muwashshahs arabes et hébreux* (Palermo, 1953; rpt. Oxford, 1964), p. 20.

IBN ḤASDAI

The first name of the poet is unknown; possibly it is Abū Yūsuf or even Abraham, but it cannot be Yūsuf, since Yūsuf Ibn Ḥasdai is known to have written only one poem, which is translated later.

The text is from Schirmann in *Yediʿot ha-makhon le-ḥeger ha-shirah ha-ʿivrit* 2 (1936), 145–46; there he attributed the poem to Judah Ibn Bilʿam, but in *Shirim ḥadashim*, p. 298, note 8, he attributed it to Ibn Ḥasdai. An English translation appears in T. Carmi, *The Penguin Book of Hebrew Verse* (1981), pp. 362–63, but the translation here is my own, except for the final Arabic couplet.

The gazelle gives me to drink spiced wine with his eyes—
    if only he would kiss me with his mouth!

By my soul, the gazelle has oppressed my heart and made me ill
With his face like a lily and lips like a scarlet cord.
When he begins to play a song upon his instrument,
    There is instruction in his song which he lets me hear;
        if only in his mercy he would give me life!

My heart moans like the sea, my friends, at his parting,
And I am like the jackals in my crying on the day of his wandering.
For what shall a man, for what, continue to live without his beloved?
    And from the day he was taken by separation, I am killed;
        by wandering I am consumed.

Until then must I wait, like one standing watch,
And I am pained and do not find a cure.
Would that I could begin and place mouth upon mouth,
    And by his will mix grape and rose,
        bell and pomegranate.[1]

Well-wishers and eloquent ones, judge this fawn
Whose eyes he prepared like arrows to slay me,
But on his cheeks are pleasant blossoms, unchanging;
    And every time I see his face,
        the light of his cheeks overwhelms me.

Blessed is the gazelle; I conceal his name because of oppressors,[2]
But he is the one who put to shame the luminaries of heaven—
Beautiful gazelle who has completed his fifteenth year.
    We shall set in motion that which impregnates.
    He who is like a [willow] branch
        [has come back to me entirely].[3]

[1]Mingle our love together; bell and pomegranate were found on priestly robes.
    [2]The poet's spies or rivals. Concealing the name of the beloved is a common feature in Arabic poetry, as well as in Greek and Latin.
    [3]Brackets indicate my uncertainty with Carmi's translation; for the last line, perhaps: "he has set me on fire" or "aroused jealousy in me."

JOSEPH IBN ṢADIQ (ca. 1075–1149)
    A great scholar, Joseph Ibn Ṣadiq was born in Cordoba around 1075 and died there in 1149. He was a religious judge and the author of an important philosophical work. The two poems that follow are among numerous Hebrew *muwashshaḥs*, in which the final couplet *(kharja)* mixes Arabic and Hispanic Romance. Text is from Schirmann, *ha-Shirah ha-ʿivrit bi-Sefarad u-vi-Provans* (Jerusalem-Tel Aviv, 1954), I, 547–58, No. 2; my translation is from "Deal Gently," pp. 32–33.

[1]
Desire remains in the heart like fire
Because of the eyes of a beloved ever since I first saw him.
As he hates my soul, I hate it,
    For it is the counsel of wickedness to love what the gazelle hates!

My beloved does not favor me when I speak
Graciously to him, and answers me harshly; when I kiss his foot,
He only afflicts me without cause, but my heart will not
    Consider it to him a trespass that he has afflicted.
Lo, I am sold to you, my fawn, without redemption.[1]
Take a present—my heart—and do not in vain tread
On me until I drink from your palate the honey I shall take.
    Also, when I thirst, I find coolness in your saliva.
This alone is my sun—the beloved who has enslaved my heart;
From being free, he has pierced my heart and profaned it.[2]
My soul knows that in you to slay me there was no guile,
    But God brought it to your hand.
From weeping for brothers the tears on my cheeks
Descend moistly, warm like the coals of a furnace.
Please let the wretched one couch among apple trees, and to the pomegranate
    Of a maiden's breast for a shield direct my heart.[3]
The day when at her door the gazelle waits and knocks,
In the chamber of her dwelling she lifts her voice and leans
Upon her that bore her—I am not able to restrain myself.
    "What shall I do, Mamma?
My beloved stands before the gate!"[4]

[1]Cf. Leviticus 19.20.
[2]As the ear of the perpetual slave was pierced (see Exodus 21.6); "profaned" possibly because the poet, a renowned rabbi, was a Levite.
[3]The poet proposes to find comfort from his frustrated pursuit of the boy with a woman, and in the following line the "gazelle" in this case is the poet himself (though hardly young, yet a lover).
[4]The final couplet of this *muwashshah*, mixing Arabic with Hispanic Romance, says: *"Que faray, mamma? / Meu'l habib estad yana!"* The translation is mine.

[2]

The following poem was formerly attributed to Judah ha-Levy, but has since been newly attributed by Yonah David in his *Shirey* (Jerusalem, 1982), pp. 33–35; all his references to supposed previous editions are wrong, however. For the final couplet, see Stern, *Hispano-Arabic Poetry*, p. 140; in my translation I have used the transcription suggested by Cantera Burgos in *Sefarad* 9 (1949), 219.

Enough for you, my admonishers, of contention!
    How long will you reprove a man *heavy*

Of *ear* about a gazelle with the stature of a pillar   *[who does not listen]*
        of cypress waving like a bough?
        Deal gently with me for the sake of the beauty of the age;
        Slacken his anger lest I be destroyed;
        For he is more faithful than the winds,
        And my soul is *deposited with him.*   *[as a surety, ransom]*
        His lips are honey; his face like *manna*   *[clear and white]*
        Which the sun has never left—
It rises and sets;
        His beauty is like the sun in equal parts,
Or it is possible to say: the sun at Gibeon
        is silent—at his words it trembles.   *[cf. Joshua 10.12ff.]*
        The fawn who tarries from coming with me,
        I shall suffice with mention of his name.
        My soul is his ransom; would that he would
        Make a ransom of the *honey* of his loveliness!   *[saliva]*
        He delights every day in the ornament
        Of glory, and his cheeks are as if
Hair begins to embroider round about
        their lilies, an embroidery of woven work.[1]
"There is none like him" is written about him;[2]
        he alone is the king of beauty.
        My Torah is the Torah of love
        And against it I shall not rebel,
        For a soul of myrrh is breathed into me
        Which I have desired from the days of my youth;
        If it is bitter, its waters I shall draw;
        Or if it is sweet, I long for it.
The day when there burns in my ribs a flame
        of sorrow, I have no foothold[3]
Except wine and a gazelle generous
        of heart, in whom there is delight for the heart.
        Arise, sing, my fawn—arise, sing, perfect
        Beauty, by name "father of a multitude,"   *[Abraham]*
        Gold refined in a crucible—
        For my ears delight in tumult.
        The fame of [one who] wears beauty like a cloak,
        I shall make for it [of] my poem a bell.
If sorrow causes me to languish,
        My heart, in the pleasantness of his memory, be comforted!

Or if in his wandering he grieves
>my soul—ah, fear the day!
My heart is torn because of
Its fawn; to see him it thirsts,
And tears on the cheeks moist and clear
Against heaven it raises
The day it was told saying: already
Your beloved is sick—bitterly it calls:
"My heart goes out from me;
>O God, shall it return to me?
How bad is my suffering for the beloved;
>He is sick; when will he get well?"

[1] Either literally the hair of his head (perhaps the sideburns just beginning to grow, or the appearance of down on his cheeks).

[2] This line quotes words from the Aramaic translation of 1 Samuel 10.24, which refers to King Saul; thus the boy is the "king of beauty."

[3] Cf. Psalms 69.3 (2).

YŪSUF IBN ḤASDAI (ELEVENTH CENTURY)

He lived in Zaragoza. The following poem, sent to his friend Samuel Ibn Naghrīllah of Granada, was the only poem he wrote, and hence was known as a *"Shir yetomah"* in Hebrew ("orphan poem"); this is similar in sound to Arabic *"yatimah"* ("unique"), for it was considered so beautiful as to be unique. Here I give only the opening part of the poem, which describes a "night vision" or dream of a boy who appears from afar in sleep and permits his lover to do what he would never allow while awake.

Text is from Samuel Ibn Naghrīllah, *Divan Shemuel ha-nagid,* ed. Dov Jarden (Jerusalem, 1966), pp. 161–64, No. 51. I have translated and annotated the entire poem, and also Samuel's reply to it, in my article "Satire and Debate in Two Famous Medieval Poems from al-Andalus: Love of Boys vs. Girls, the Pen and Other Themes," *The Maghreb Review* 4 (1979), 105–13.

Has the boy charm, strength of power and might
>to envelop himself in a veil of darkness as a garment
And shepherd the evening stars and wander amid ruins
>of the desert, dwelling place of fear and dread,
To go from hearth to heath and from sound
>of lutes to tumultuous noise?

Until he is seized by the ropes of dreams
    and captured in the traps of slumber
And I pluck, while he slumbers, at will
    What he refuses, when awake, with anger.
He kissed me in sweet dreams,
    the wine of mouth in *cups of red*.   *[his lips]*
I lay—and on my breast his scented locks
    on ruddy temple;
My right hand embracing the moon,
    and my lips kissing the sun.
The bed is perfumed with frankincense,
    the couch fragrant with spices.
The vision was pleasant to me
    until I awoke—and lo, there is nothing.
But a scent revises the spirit
    and flowing myrrh the soul. . . .

SAMUEL IBN NAGHRĪLLAH (993–1056)

The first major Hebrew poet in Spain and author of three large volumes of poetry; he was also the prime minister and commander-in-chief of the army of the Muslim city-state *(taifa* kingdom) of Granada.

[1]

Text from *Divan,* ed. Jarden (Jerusalem, 1966), pp. 221–22, No. 75; translated in my "Deal Gently" with additional notes, p. 34.

Lovely gazelle, heaven-sent blessing
    on earth, remove me from *the snare*.   *[of passion]*
Satiate me with *beneficence* from your tongue,   *[saliva]*
    like a jar filled with good wine.
What advantage have you that you crush hearts,
    with shining face and dark hair
And roving eye, black as night,
    on ruddy cheek?
How do you ply your craft upon the feelings
    and hearts—without knowing craft?[1]
You prevail over heroes, and not with weapons,
    and over swords, without an army.

You cure the mortally wounded without medicine
　　or any healing on the wound.
Tell me, is there an end to your *roaming*,　　　　*[from man to man]*
　　and how long? How, oh how,
Can you stand among friends and shoot them
　　with your arrows and bent bow?[2]
And how can you choose death for the righteous,
　　when their life or death is in your hands?
You exult in their ills like an enemy—
　　why does one like you to do so?

[1]How does a boy apparently so innocent behave in such a seductive manner?
　[2]Arrows as usual refer to glances from the eyes; the "bent bow" may refer to
the eyebrows, but usually refers to the penis.

[2]

Text from *Divan*, ed. Jarden, p. 297, No. 162; also in Schirmann, *ha-Shirah*,
I, 154, No. 2; translated in my "Deal Gently," p. 35, with commentary. The
poet has fallen in love with a boy who is picking roses in the garden of a friend
who rebukes him, but the poet says that if the friend noticed the boy's beauty,
he would abandon his own beloved. The boy asks for the honey of religious
teaching, and the poet audaciously suggests that the boy give him his own honey
(saliva).

True, the gazelle who gathers roses in your garden I have loved—
　　therefore you turn your anger against me.
If you would see with your eyes the one whom I have loved,
　　then your beloved would seek you and not find you!
He who said: "Give me, please, the honey of your words"—
　　I answered: "Give me the honey from your tongue."
He became angered and said with wrath: "Shall we sin
　　to the living God?" I replied: "On me, sir, be your sin."

[3]

Text from *Divan*, ed. Jarden, p. 301, No. 171; Schirmann, *ha-Shirah* I, 155,
No. 5; my translation. The poet addresses a boy for whom he is lusting, and
tells the boy that he could arouse the same feelings in him by showing him
another beautiful boy.

I shall show you a fawn, and he shall melt your heart
  with his eyes, as your eyes melt my heart.
Praised be He who made your heart cold as snow
  to my entreaties, and placed you in my heart as a flame.
And praised be He who gave greater power to your arrows
  and to you [to resist] than to armed soldiers and warriors,
Who kill but a few with many arrows—
  but you with just one arrow kill thousands!

[4]
Text from *Divan,* ed. Jarden, p. 301, No. 172; see my "Deal Gently," p. 36.

God, change, please, the heart of the dove who stole
My slumber—and restore to my eyelids a little sleep!
The beloved who came by *Thy oath* and gave me   *[God's permission]*
His heart's love, without force, as a gift
Has been treacherous, and so every boy is treacherous.
But now, forgive his sin—or if not, punish me.

[5]
Text from *Divan,* ed. Jarden, p. 303, No. 176; see "Deal Gently," p. 36.

O moon, created to rule the earth
  by day and night, gently rule over hearts!
How do you judge the *star,* whom I thought a brother,   *[boy]*
  yet through no fault of mine he turned cruel to me?
Buy me a boy whom all boys will envy for his beauty
  for all the wealth I have acquired,
And I will see if he has eyes like the eyes of the boy who fled
  after he twice came willing and slept with me.

[6]
Text from *Divan,* ed. Jarden, p. 296, No. 160; Schirmann, *ha-Shirah* I, 165;
see "Deal Gently," which offers comparisons with Arabic poems.

Where is the stuttering boy, where has he gone,
  gazelle perfumed with pure myrrh and frankincense?

The moon has concealed the light of the stars—
    the graceful beloved conceals the light of the moon!
He chirped with soft speech and relied upon
    Him who gave voice to the turtle-dove and swallow.
He meant to say "bad," and he said to me "touch";[1]
    I touched him as his tongue had declared.
He desired to say "go" and said "belly";[2]
    I hastened to his belly, fenced with roses.[3]

[1] The boy mispronounces *Hebrew ra'as ga'.*
[2] He mispronounces *surah* as *sugah.*
[3] Cf. Songs of Songs 7.3; the reference is to the pubic region, surrounded by hair.

[7]

Text from *Divan*, ed. Jarden, p. 305, No. 183; my translation. The boy suggests to the poet that he should drink the saliva from his mouth rather than the wine he is drinking. The curved form of the moon is compared to the curved Hebrew letter *yod*, which is written as if in gold upon the night sky. It might also refer to the boy, whose first-appearing sideburns curl upon his face.

I shall be a ransom for the fawn who arose at night
    to the voice of the lute and flutes sweetly played.
He saw in my hand a cup and said:
    "Drink from between my lips the juice of grapes."
And the moon like a *yod* is written upon
    the covering of dawn in golden liquid.

[8]

Text from *Divan*, ed. Jarden, p. 291, No. 147; translated with commentary in my "Fawn of My Delights," p. 167 (see introduction).

I see in you beauty like the sun in its brightness
    and splendor like the heavens with its moon shining.
How goodly and how pleasant if it would be given you
    that your figure should last forever:
Beautiful form, beauty and fortune and pure
    body, as the very heaven in its purity.
Not good is the beauty of one who lies in the night of his death
    and is not aroused, and does not see evermore the dawn.

There is no good except a good name and good wine and singing
    well and a good companion to drink his merchandise.
Bow to God by day, and bow down to the cup
    at night, and drink it and forget sorrow.

[9]
Text from *Divan*, ed. Jarden, p. 302, No. 175; translated in my "Care and
Feeding of Gazelles," p. 102 (see introduction). Here the poet writes about
a woman he loves who is jealous of a beautiful boy.

Healing is in her face and upon the ribbons of her lips,
and death in her eyes and under her dress.
I play when she pleases, and she plays when I am angry;
her desire gladdens me, my anger gladdens her.
As though I placed the boy—she imagines, unjustly, he is
Her enemy—beside her to anger her.

Solomon Ibn Gabirol (early eleventh century)
A contemporary of Ibn Naghrīllah, though younger, Ibn Gabirol was also
a renowned philosopher and author of 24 books, not all of which are ex-
tant. His *Well of Life*, which was written in Arabic and translated into Latin
as *Fons Vitae,* was an important Neoplatonic treatise. He was also called
Avicebron.

[1]
Text from Schirmann, *Shirim ḥadashim*, pp. 175–78; translated with com-
mentary in "Deal Gently," p. 37. Unable to describe the boy, at the end the
poet takes refuge in wine and praises God for the boy's beauty.

He steals the sleep of my eyes and I'm unaware—
    the like has never been seen or heard!
I draw his heart, slowly, lest he be weary—
    and he draws my heart, slowly, lest I pine away.
If dawn comes to me—gently,
    take pity on me—perhaps the evil will end.
Although I had not embraced you, nevertheless
    for you is my love—

strangers devour what I embrace.
I was asked to describe his form and said,
    "Your soul has torn the spheres of the earth!"
Come, let us sing to the vine a song
    and in it bow to God and to Him bend down.

[2]

Text from *Shirey ha-ḥol le-rabbi Shelomoh Ibn Gabirol,* ed. Jarden (Jerusalem, 1975), p. 362, No. 206; also in *Shelomoh Ibn Gabirol, shirey ha-ḥol,* ed. Schirmann and H. Brody (Jerusalem, 1975), p. 72, No. 123. Translated in my "Deal Gently," p. 41.

Branch[1] who has exalted my heart with its blossoms,
    and bough of myrtle which passion has planted
        in its thoughts,
Standing as a pillar of ivory, lovely in the eyes of every
    lover, and like a lover very poor are his gifts.[2]
The secret of love he understands from the hearts: when
    you raise your heart to him, he will raise his eyes to you.[3]
Lovers have wept for me but have not [truly] wept;
    for like the cooing of a dove I will moan
        before his eyes.
His cheeks are like apples of gold in a setting
    of silver, and a word fitly spoken.[4]
The moon is shamed when it sees the light
    of his cheeks, and the sun sets in his face.
His breast is like golden pomegranates fastened with silver;
    would that I could suck his pomegranates!

[1]The boy (but see other possibilities in my article).
[2]See note 4 in "Deal Gently."
[3]When you raise your heart, hoping to love him, he raises his eyes haughtily.
[4]Proverbs 25.11 (it is audacious to apply religious verse to love).

[3]

This poem is even more audacious than the preceding one. Text from *Shirey ha-ḥol,* ed. Jarden, pp. 135–36, No. 64; also Schirmann-Brody, p. 143, No. 116. My translation is from "Fawn of My Delights," pp. 167–68.

Lily upon a stalk, like foliage
>are you upon a pillar, a capital of gold.
Sun upon its sphere slowly walking—ah!
>stealing gently the heart without breaking in.
A fawn, embarrassed because of you—see
>the pearl change its appearance to [a reddish stone].

. . . .

Write, brothers of instruction, my words
>upon the ark of testimony as a token
For his heart—which, if the sons of Aaron find it,
>before it let them offer incense.
If Aaron wrapped himself with a holy mitre, lo!
>the lock of your cheeks is a diadem of beauty:
The form of a golden cherub with stretched-out wing
>as the cherubim upon the covering.

[4]

Text from Jarden, p. 361, No. 205, and Schirmann-Brody, p. 62, No. 110; translated in my "Deal Gently," p. 40.

He wounds me, whose necklace is the Pleiades[1]
>and whose neck is [white] like the light of the moon.
In opening the loops of his mouth he reveals
>the light of his pearls[2] like the sun from its abode.
I answered him: "Take my soul and slay [it];
>or if not, heal me, please heal!"
He replied with the sweetness of his mouth:
>"There is no cure for an old wound."—
"Is my wound old, my friend?
>It is fresh—not more than a year old."[3]
He answered: "Drink my cup, and sing to me
>as on a day of parting; let there be no exaltation."
And my beloved sang to me in Arabic:
>"In memory of the man whose appearance I love."[4]

[1]The constellation; his neck is so lovely as to be adorned by the stars.
[2]His loops are his lips; his pearls, his teeth.
[3]His "wound" or love of the boy is only a year old.
[4]Although the last line is in Arabic, the poem is not a *muwashshaḥ*.

Moses Ibn ʿEzra(h) (1055–ca. 1138)

Born in 1055 and dead at some point between 1135 and 1140, he is usually considered the greatest of the Hebrew poets of Spain. The following poems were edited in the *Shirey ha-ḥol* by Brody (Berlin, 1935).

[1]

The following poem is addressed by the poet to a boy whom he loved; note the almost breathless quality of the various lines. Ed. Brody, pp. 15–16, No. 11; see my "Deal Gently," p. 43.

To every man our wondrous love
shall be an example in the world to all.
I strengthen myself against my oppression, and you
are more perverse than all gazelles.
I shall hide from men what is in my heart,
lest they say it is a disease of folly.
Know that the sickness of love is in my heart,
and you increase the illness in keeping away;
And the world is like a firm seal because of your wandering,
and its breadth, without you, like a prison;
And that men, were they most noble,
without sight of you I consider wild animals.
In your mouth are streams of flowing honey,
and I faint in my pain among the thirsty.
Your scent is myrrh in the nostrils of strangers, and I pant
like the jackals in the dry wind of the desert.
To you—youth who understands hidden things,
and a fawn, but who hunts, gently, lions;[1]
Who gives life to all lovers, and my life
without fault makes hang before me—
To you, greeting: Know that my love
greatly increases while you increase sin,
And that your dwelling is in my eye and heart;
although men who dwell in them fear,
since in this[2] a flame burns,
and from that[3] clouds draw water.
And that your wrath is like the favor of God in my eyes,
and though my illness is strong, I do not envy the healthy.

I will not turn from my path until the ground
pours out dew, and the heavens bring forth vegetation.
Revive me, my fawn, as is the desire of my heart,
while the swallow yet twitters among the branches.

> [1]He is young, but he "hunts" (arouses passion in) noble men, "lions."
> [2]My heart.
> [3]My eyes.

[2]

The following short poem is about a Muslim boy (a son of Qedar) he fell in
love with. Text from Brody, p. 351, No. 49; see "Deal Gently," p. 44.

My heart mourns because of a son of Qedar,
A fawn lovely of appearance, young of years.
His cheeks are like scarlet, and black his hair,
And his lips are like crimson.

[3]

Cupbearers at all-night drinking parties were often the object of amorous
attention; ed. Brody, pp. 158–59, No. 159; see "Deal Gently," pp. 44–45.

By my soul! The night of companionship there rose in him,
     in spite of fate, the sun of my joy.
In the night the word of my fawn was my choice fruit,
     and his mouth was my cup, and the wine
       of his saliva my drink,
And the beauty of his face my lilies, and the rows
     on his cheeks were considered as
       branches of my myrtle.
When his eyes pierced my heart
     quickly to the balm of his breast [I took] flight.

[4]

This is one of the finest boy-love poems in Hebrew; text from Brody, pp.
161, No. 149; also Schirmann, ha-Shirah I, 367; my translation is from "Deal
Gently," p. 45.

Desire of my heart and delight of my eyes—
A fawn beside me and a cup in my hand!
> Many admonish me, but I do not heed;
> Come, O gazelle, and I will subdue them.
> Time will destroy them and death shepherd them.
Come, O gazelle, rise and feed me
With the honey of your lips, and satisfy me.
> Why do they hold back my heart, why?
> If because of sin and guilt,
> I will be ravished by your beauty—God is there!
Pay no attention to the words of my oppressor,
A perverse man—come and try me!
> He was enticed, and we went to his mother's house,
> And he gave his shoulder to my burden.
> Night and day I was only with him.
I undressed him and he undressed me;
I sucked his lips and he sucked mine.
> When I left my heart as a pledge in his eyes,
> He sought enmity and inflicted his anger,
And angrily cried, "Enough; leave me!
Do not force me, and do not entice me!"
> Do not be angry with me, gazelle, to destruction—
> Extraordinary is your will, my dear, extraordinary!
> Kiss your beloved and fulfill his desire.
If it is in your soul to give life, revive me—
Or if your desire is to kill, kill me!

[5]
Text from Brody, p. 178, No. 179; see my "Care and Feeding of Gazelles,"
pp. 108–109.

The gazelle is like a branch of spices, and almost
> because of his delicacy and tenderness
> the wind shakes him,
But a heart of stone is in him, pitiless for
> the captive of lust, faint and weary of heart,
Who rides without a boat the sea of his love—
> and his eyes prevent him from going ashore.

He seduces me with the fresh lily of his cheek,
    and the hand of my eye plucks it from afar.
In my heart he dwells, and my fire does not burn him,
    and in the pupil of my eye, and my tear does not flood him.
I asked of him to kiss his lips
    in a mouth fragrant like spice, or like his body.
He answered me: "Kiss my mouth and I will satiate you
    from my tongue, with its pleasant wine and honey."
With his mouth he healed what he had wounded with his eyes,
    and he said that his deeds were smiting and healing.

[6] Selections from the "Tarshish"

A section of his *Divan* is a separate book called the *Tarshish* (Necklace),
which consists of short epigrams divided into chapters according to subject.
The chapter on "wine-drinking and the changing seasons," as well as that
on love, contains poems about boys.

[A] ED. BRODY, p. 329, No. 2
Fawn, make the red of your lips my fruit
    and your breast a present.
And pour for my mouth always, and give me to drink
    the goodly wine of your palate until I am drunk.

[B] ED. BRODY, p. 329, No. 4
Take a cup from the hand of the fawn—
    the light of his face alone shines forth—
Who pours in Spain
    and spreads light to the extremes of the earth.

[C] ED. BRODY, p. 331, No. 13
The appearance of the apple is like the appearance
    of the pale face of the fawn when it is ashamed.
I shall weep for the separation from this upon the beauty of that
    until the fire of his wandering by my weeping is dried.

[D] ED. BRODY, p. 344, No. 1
Ah, for the time when its years
    in my eyes were, with the gazelle, a few days!

Days when a fresh and an old body were united
　　by the girdle of night until they were as one.

[E] ED. BRODY, p. 344, No. 4
My heart longs for my death;
　　of all boys I choose him!
I desire to be clay in his hand,
　　and he the creator,
And I shall pray and fast to him
　　and of the honey of his mouth I shall eat.[1]

　　[1]This poem is an example of real audacity, since clay in the hand of the creator (Jeremiah 18.4 and 6) usually refers to God, not a boy.

[F] ED. BRODY, p. 373, No. 42; SCHIRMANN I, 375
My heart, my heart sighs for the gazelle—
　　before he was created, it was his companion.
From the day of his roaming, its eye has not tasted
　　slumber, and it is companion to the stars of heaven.[1]

　　[1]Sleepless, the lover is often compared to a "herder" of the night stars.

JUDAH HA-LEVY (1075–1141)
　　Born in then Muslim Tudela in Navarre, ha-Levy as a young man journeyed to Granada, where he was a protégé of Moses Ibn 'Ezra(h). He became a renowned poet and later set out to live in Palestine, but the ship sank in a storm, and he died before reaching his destination.
　　His *Divan* was edited by Brody (Berlin, 1894–1930).

[1]
Text from Brody, II, 14, No. 11; see my "Deal Gently," pp. 46–47.

Inquire of my fawn my well-being; he will say what profit
　　there is in my blood.[1]
　　Speak to him flattery
　　That he should despise the gain of oppression.
　　His—to my weakened eyes—
His to restore a bit my well-being, perhaps my dream
　　will behold him,

The gazelle whom I ransom with my soul;
    Let the death of man seize upon me;
    He is the keeper of my paradise and my fire.
From his cheeks in the garden of my spices, as from
        his eyes my poison.[2]
    So with the arrows of his eyes he oppresses;
    The heart of his fellow he smites once and again.
    [But] those who rejoice at calamity I answer:
Even if my companion is changed into my enemy, the yoke
        of his love is dominion to my shoulder.
    With all the delights of the world I will ransom
    The night when my lust was fulfilled
    By the gazelle of loveliness, and I scraped
From his lips the flowing wine of his vineyard, and I
        kissed his ruddy cheeks:
    Of the bdellium[3] of his mouth he gave drink,
    Blood of grapes in crimson lips—
    Until he awoke and answered me:
"How long, how long will I give you to drink wine
        from my mouth?"[4]

[1]What advantage to life when I am dying of love.
[2]His disapproving glances "slay" me.
[3]A fragrant gum, like myrrh.
[4]The last couplet is in Arabic.

[2]

As in Greek and Roman cultures, the boy was considered an object worthy of passion only until he emerged from adolescence, the sign of which was the beginning of a beard. Text from Brody II, 308, No. 91.

Childhood—ah!—has fled before adulthood,
    and the skies of my cheeks are clothed with clouds.
My lovers I ask: "Are you not
    slaves of my cheeks from the days of youth?"
And they say: "Thus it is, but they have sprouted
    and written us a document of manumission!"[1]

[1]According to biblical law, a slave was freed by the writing of a document of manumission. In this case, the sprouting hairs on the white cheek are compared to writing.

[3]

It was difficult to suddenly give up the love of a boy simply because a few facial hairs began to appear, as we see in the following poem. Text from Brody II, 218, No. 7.

Anxiety has broken my heart, and the contention
     of all men, because of pursuing love,
        has grieved it.
They contend with it because of lust for a lovely gazelle
     and because with the love of its soul it loves him,
And they rebuke it because of the abundance of its tears
     when it recalls him and whenever it speaks of him.
His fault they all find in having
     a face like the day, but with a circlet of night
        surrounding it.
Yet it swears by the life of love and passion
     not to listen to their contention,
But to conceal the burning of its passion and its love
     in its innermost chamber so that it not be haughty.

[4]

The following is an adaptation of an Arabic love poem concerning a woman, which ha-Levy makes far more believable about a boy. Text from Schirmann, *ha-Shirah* I, 446, No. 2; my translation is from "Deal Gently," p. 48.

The day when I fondled him on my knee
And he saw his image in the pupils of my eyes,
He kissed my eyes—little deceiver,
His reflection he kissed, and not my eyes.

ABRAHAM IBN ᶜEZRA (1092–1167)

A famous philosopher, scientist, and biblical commentator, he also composed many poems, although not all survive. The work of his son Isaac follows.

[1]

This is the introductory "love" section to a classical ode in honor of a Jewish notable. Text from Schirmann, *Shirim ḥadashim*, p. 272; my translation is from "Deal Gently," pp. 48–49.

Spy[1] of the lovely gazelle, heal me:
    let me see the glowing cheeks!
[But] he was angered, and his eyes keep watch
    like a serpent by the road.
Beloved, I desire that you turn to me;
    my weeping and misery do not forsake.
My heart comforts me: perhaps
    his hard heart will soften.
[Perhaps] he will not be angry at the words of my speech;
    but, because of his guardian, he is silent.
To him my words are strange, for
    he has become lame with the affliction of his age;
Winking to me by design, he acts humbly,
    and tears down the house of the proud.[2]
Consent, beloved, to meet in secret,
    for I shall love to lie with you—
And to the name of the "prince"[3] of all Israel
    we will drink and take a cup of wine.
I will ask that God show favor
    to the seller of wine.
Joy to my right and my left—
    a fawn and spiced wine.
Wealth or health for drinking
    I will give—and it will take all!

    [1]The spy objected on moral grounds to affairs with boys.
    [2]Thus he dashes the hopes of his lover; see Proverbs 15.25.
    [3]The Jewish notable for whom the rest of the ode was written.

[2]

In this short poem, an old man offers to return the boy's "bow" (penis) upon maturity. Edited by A.M. Habermann, *'Iyun be-shirah u-ve-fiyuṭ* (Jerusalem, 1972), p. 77; I prefer the reading of the Oxford manuscript cited there; see my "Care and Feeding of Gazelles," p. 112.

An old man of stooped stature, bent like a bow—
A youth asked him: "What is the price of your bow?"
He answered: "Quiet, my son, for if you live
Freely will I give it to you when your time comes."

The son of Abraham, he married a daughter of Judah ha-Levy and accompanied the latter to Egypt on a fateful journey to Palestine. Later, apparently, Isaac himself went to Palestine, where he died.

[1]

Text of this poem from *Shirim*, ed. Menahem Schmelzer (New York, 1981), pp. 143–44, Appendix A, No. 6; see my "Deal Gently," pp. 49–50.

The secret of love, how can it be contained?
The heart and the tear are tale-bearers.
The heart is restrained from what it seeks,
Shut up and by passion of him besieged,
Unable to obtain its desire.
If it presumes to attain to the stars,
Its pride is brought down, laid low.
Beloved like a hart, with the heart of a panther,
If you desire to slay,
My heart is in your hand as clay.
But do not summon wanderings upon it,
For in its midst your name is sheltered.
Beloved, like a scarlet cord his lips,
Burning like fire, for they are his censer,
And in them is the work of his signs.
Live by them, for the heart waits for them—
A heart long suffering because of them.
How my fate has hardened its spirit!
A while, and separation will cause it to be odious
To my friends who knew its thoughts.
If wandering has separated us,
It has increased love.
I will watch for the gazelle
To leave in the garden my pleasures,
Although my rebuker stands to accuse me.

[2]

Text from Schmelzer, *Shirim,* p. 23, No. 14.

Gazelle, whose appearance is [as if] carrying quivers,[1]
    Lust for him makes judgments in my heart.[2]
Before him[3] my spirit is made empty within me,
    and I consult, because of him, necromancers and magicians.
He draws at will my love
    to love him, without cords or bands.
My spirit is pledged with him and my soul
    is bound with him, like the king in the tresses.[4]
In the path of your passion my steps I will hold fast
    lest they turn aside and slip.
Investigate the words[5] that testify of my heart;
    accept them, although they are few.
I have made them a sign and proof of your fame
    and have sent them to you as shields.

[1]With which to shoot arrows or glances at his lovers.
[2]Punishes me.
[3]Schmelzer reads "at his wandering," but this does not seem to fit the context.
[4]Song of Songs 7.6.
[5]Of the poem.

[3]

This poem is a *muwashshah,* and the final couplet is in Arabic; *Shirim,*
p. 141, No. 1.

My gazelle has gently left me.
My heart he has stolen with his beauty;
Why should my tears flow after him
    When [only] yesterday he oppressed my soul.
    How can my heart lust after traitors?
Why do you hope, my heart, and why await,
Expecting a cure and there is [only] anguish?
Nor will complaining help nor ought avail.
    If upon your soul wandering has knocked,
    Be like the dust, my soul, and forbear.
Lovely was my beloved's neck;
But because of its loveliness many were its desirers,
For you can observe the tears of his oppressed.
    "From the multitude of lovers
    You would think the tears were a flood of rain."

LATE MEDIEVAL VERNACULAR LITERATURE TO 1400

James J. Wilhelm

One might expect that there would have been an explosion of homosexual verse in the Later Middle Ages as the power of the Church began to wane. It is true that after the death of Chaucer in 1400, especially in Italy, many writers started to imitate the Greeks and Romans, including gay and lesbian verse. This was to be expected as the Renaissance developed. But before that, there is relatively little, as specialists in such areas as Old Norse, Polish, Byzantine Greek, Galician, and Sicilian have assured me. One needs only to look at the entries for Spain and Germany in the *Encyclopedia of Homosexuality* to see the dearth of material until the Renaissance.

There was, however, especially in German and Portuguese literature, a kind of poem in which a male poet speaks behind a female persona, but this can hardly be classified as homosexual. After all, almost every playwright does this.

As a result, the selections offered here are by two male writers who are creating portraits of gay men and a poem by a female troubadour of southern France that can be characterized as lesbian, even though several critics contend that it is simply a strong expression of female friendship or that it was written by a man or to the Virgin Mary.

14. The *Trobairitz* Bietris de Romans

(ca. EARLY 1200s)

Bietris (often less correctly spelled Bieris) is a mystery figure; she may have had some connection with the town of Romans, which is in the Rhone Valley, not far north of modern Die, a place associated with the well-known Countess of Dia.

Bietris was a *trobairitz*—a lady troubadour who wrote *cansos* or love songs in the Provençal language of southern France. These were female counterparts of the male troubadours, of whom we have more than 400 names. The women are not quite as numerous—we have about 22 names and 26 poems that can be assigned to them—one with music. These poems are usually love songs (as opposed to satires or other genres), and, except for this poem by Bietris, are all clearly directed to men.

Although it is possible that the love expressed here is Platonic, it is every bit as emotional as anything that can be found in other love songs. See Marcelle Thiébaux, *The Writings of Medieval Women: An Anthology* (Garland, 1994), pp. 241ff. My translation is from *Songs of the Women Troubadours*, ed. Matilda T. Bruckner, Laurie Shepard, and Sarah White (Garland, 1995), pp. 97–100.

"Na Maria, pretz e fina valors"

Lady Maria, the worth and outstanding value,
The joy, the intelligence, and the refined beauty,
The hospitality and excellence and honor,
The noble conversation and charming comfort,
The sweet face and the gay companionship,
The gentle look and loving appearance
That are all in you—without any dissembling—
Make me drawn toward you without a deceiving heart.

And so I beg you—if it pleases you that my refined love
And joyful bearing and sweet humility
May let me obtain from you the succor that I need—
That you should give me, lovely lady (if it pleases),
That which would give me the most of joy and hope,
Because in you I place my heart and my desire,
And through you I receive all of my happiness,
And for you I go most of the time with sighs.

And because beauty and worth put you forward
Above all other women, so that none supersedes you,
I beg you, if it pleases—and this would bring you honor—
Never to give your heart to a lying suitor.

Beautiful lady, whom worth and joy advance,
And noble speech, to you I send my stanzas,
For you are the source of gaiety and happiness,
And all the good that one can ask of a lady.

15. DANTE ALIGHIERI

(1265–1321)

Considered by many to be the greatest medieval poet Dante was not homosexual, but he did create one of the most sensitive portraits of a homosexual in world literature: that of his belovéd teacher Brunetto Latini. This occurs in Canto XV of the *Inferno* section of the *Divine Comedy,* an epic that follows Dante the Pilgrim as he visits Hell and Purgatory with the help of the guide Vergil and courses through Heaven with his lady, Beatrice.

Canto XV treats the third round of the Seventh Circle, a place where the souls of the violent are punished. Dante and Vergil encounter tyrants in the boiling river of Phlegethon in round one. Round two consists of a forest where the souls of suicides are imbedded inside the trees. Round three consists of a desert where the violent against God (blasphemers), nature (homosexuals), and art (usurers) are punished.

As Dante walks in this round he is on top of a dike where he can see the "sodomites" running below to escape a fiery rain. There he spies his old teacher friend, who is the author of the Italian *Tesoretto (Little Treasure)* and the French *Livres dou Tresor.* The scene is fraught with intense feeling as the student, who once sat at the feet of his master, is now in a reversed position.

It is important to add that Dante did not put *all* homosexuals in Hell. On the top of Mount Purgatory he sees them running in an opposite direction from the heterosexuals, and if one can make any rung of Purgatory, then the way is ultimately open to Paradise. Why was Brunetto consigned to Hell? This we will never know, but the scheme of the *Comedy* suggests that he was too violent in his sexual passions—although there is nothing in the excerpt to indicate that.

I have added the beginning of Canto XVI, which completes the portrait because it shows how widespread homosexuality was in Dante's Florence (as is borne out by Section VII in this volume on the Renaissance). Also, the

Greco-Roman imagery of the gay athlete, which is tragically described at the end of Canto XV with Brunetto as a winning track star, is continued with references to wrestlers and gymnasts, showing how the Greek world remained as a haunting memory in the mind of Dante and his world. It is noteworthy throughout how Vergil pays such great respect to this group, but we have to remember that he had the reputation of being gay himself, thanks in a large part to *Eclogue II*, and Dante was acutely aware of this fact.

My translation is from the text edited by Giorgio Petrocchi for the national edition of the Italian Dante Society (Milan: Mondadori, 1966).

INFERNO XV, 13ff.

We had removed ourselves from the forest
So far that I could not have seen where it was
If I had turned myself around to look—
When suddenly we met a band of souls
Who came along the side of the bank, and each
Was looking at us the way that in the twilight
One man stares at another under a new moon;
And they puckered up their eyebrows at us   20
Just the way an aged tailor threads his needle.
Eyed in this fashion by such a family of souls,
I was recognized by one, who grabbed the hem
Of my robe and cried out: "How wonderful!"
And I, as he held out his arms to me,
Fixed my eyes upon his well-cooked features,
So that his scorched face did not prevent
My mind from recognizing him,
And, bending down my face to his,
I replied: "Are *you* here, Ser Brunetto?"   30
    And he: "O my little son, may it not displease you
If Brunetto Latini hangs back here with you
A little while and lets the pack move on."
    I said to him: "I beg you with all my heart—yes.
And if you want me to sit down with you again,
I'll do it—if it pleases him who leads me."
    "O little son," he said, "anyone of this flock
Who stops just a moment has to lie a century
Without being able to flick off the piercing fire.
And so, go forward. I'll follow after your gown,   40

And then I'll go back to my herd, who go
Forever mourning their eternal loss."
    I didn't dare to descend from the highway
In order to move equally with him, but with head
Bent down, I walked like one who walks with reverence.
    He began: "What kind of destiny or fortune
Brings you down here before your final day?
And who is this man who leads you on your way?"
    "Up there above in the life serene,"
I answered, "I lost my way in a dark valley   50
Before the limit of my life was full.
Just yesterday morning I turned my back on it;
This man appeared to me as I was heading back,
And he is taking me home along this road."
    And he to me: "If you follow your star,
You won't fail to come to a glorious port—
If I judged rightly in the beautiful life up there—
And if I had not died in an untimely way
Seeing that the heavens are so kind to you,
I would have supplied comfort to your work.   60
But that ungrateful and vicious race of men
That descended from Fiesole of old,
And still retains something mountainous and hard,
Will act in terms of your welfare as your enemy;
And it's right, because among the bitter berries
It's wrong for a delicious fig to flourish.
An ancient worldly reputation calls them blind.
They're a people who are greedy, jealous, arrogant.
See that you keep yourself clean from their doings.
Your fortune reserves for you such honor   70
That both political parties will be ravenous
Against you; but let the grass elude the goat!
Let the beasts of Fiesole make fodder
Of themselves, and not touch the plant—
If any still springs up on their manure-heap—
In which there still survives the sacred seed
Of those Romans who stayed on there
When the place became a nest of iniquity."
    "If my prayers could be completely answered,"
I replied, "you would not now be banished   80

So soon from the human race.
For in my mind there is fixed—and in my heart—
That dear and kindly, fatherly image
Of you when in the world from hour to hour
You taught me how a man makes himself eternal.
And how greatly I am grateful, as long as I live,
It's right that my tongue should publish it abroad.
What you tell me about my future course I'll write,
And I'll keep it to be glossed with another text
By that lady who'll interpret it—if I reach her.   90
And I want this much to be very clear to you,
So that my conscience can never chide me:
Whatever Lady Fortune may will—I'm ready!
Your dark prophecy is not new to my ears.
However, let Fortune turn around her wheel
Any way she wants, and the peasant wield his hoe!"
          My guide then turned his head around
On the right side and eyed me closely
And said: "A good listener always takes note."
          In any case I went on talking   100
With Ser Brunetto, and I asked who among
His company were the highest men of note.
          And he to me: "It's good to hear about some;
About the others, it's more laudable to keep silent,
For the time would be too brief to mention all.
In short, you should know that all were clergy
And great and well-known men of learning,
Who were all defiled by one worldly sin.
Priscian goes there with a miserable crowd
And Francesco d'Accorso, and you could see there   110
If you had any craving for such filth
That man who was transferred by the Pope
From the Arno River to Vicenza,
Where he deposited his lust-strained sinews.
I'd tell you more, but our going and our talking
Can't go on any longer; no, I now see
A new cloud rising up from the desert sand.
Some people are coming who are forbidden me.
Let my *Treasure* be recommended to your keeping,
For in that I live on—I don't ask for more."   120

Then he turned around, looking like one
Who races for the green cloth in Verona's games;
And he looked like one who wins—not one who loses.

[*In line 109, Priscian was the sixth-century writer of a much-used Latin
grammar; Francesco d'Accorso (1225-94) was a famous Florentine law-
yer; the man in line 112 was Andrea de' Mozzi, Bishop of Florence, who
was sent by Boniface VIII to Vicenza, where he died around 1295. The
games in Verona during the first Sunday of Lent were run in the nude,
imitating the games of the ancient Greeks.*]

INFERNO XVI

I was already in a place where I could hear the reverberation
Of the water that was falling into the next sphere,
Similar to that hum that beehives make,
When three shades separated together
Running toward me from a crowd that was passing
Under the rain of bitter suffering.
They came toward me, and each one shouted:
"Stop here, you, who in your clothing seems
To come from our depraved territory!"
O me, what wounds I noticed on their limbs,   10
Burned in both new and old from the flames!
It hurts me even now when I remember.
My master paid attention to their cries,
And, turning his face toward me, said: "Wait!
To these people you have to be courteous.
And if it wasn't for the fire that licks
The nature of the place, I'd have to say
That it would be better for you to hurry than them!"
As we rested a bit, they began again
Their previous pace, and when they had reached us,   20
They made a wheel—all three in one—
The way that champion athletes do, nude and oiled,
Watching for some change that is opportune
Before they exchange their thrusts and blows.
And as they kept up their gymnastic wheel, each
Kept his face riveted on mine, as they kept their necks
And their feet going around in a continual gyre.

One said: "If the misery of this desert waste
And our well-cooked and dried-up features
Make you look despisingly on us and our prayers   30
May our former fame incline your mind
To tell us who you are, and why you move
Your living feet so securely through this Hell.
That one, whose footsteps you see me follow,
Who goes naked now and peeled of skin,
Was once of a greater rank than you might think.
He was a relative of the good Gualdrada;
His name was Guido Guerra, and back in life,
He acted both with good sense and the sword.
That other one, who presses on my flanks,   40
Is Tegghiaio Aldobrandi, whose every word
Should have been listened to in the world above.
And I, who am placed with them on such a cross,
I was Jacopo Rusticucci; certainly my bitch of a wife,
More than anything else, brought me harm."
        If I had been protected from the fire,
I would have thrown myself down toward them,
And I do believe my master would have let me.
But because I would have been burned and baked,
Fear overwhelmed that good will of mine   50
That made me desirous to embrace them.
Then I began: "Your condition fixed in me
Not loathing but such compassion that it will be
A long time before I can slough it off—
As soon as my lord here told me
Words of the kind that made me think
That men such as you of such a class were coming.
I'm from your city, and I have always heard
And passed on with affection words
About your deeds and your honored names.   60
I'm leaving behind the gall and am now seeking
The sweet fruits promised to me by my true leader;
But before that I have to descend to the depths."
        Jacopo said: "In the hope that your soul
May long lead on your limbs, and that
Your fame may long shine after your going,
Tell us if courtesy and nobility still linger

In our city, the way they used to do,
Of if they have completely abandoned it;
Because Guglielmo Borsiere, who has suffered   70
With us a short time and goes with companions over there,
Torments us greatly with his words."

     "The *nouveaux riches* and get-rich-quick gains,
Chutzpah and lack of measure, my dear Florence,
Have generated in you what makes you weep!"
These words I howled with face uplifted;
And the three, who took them as an answer,
Stared at each other the way you stare at truth.

     "If other times cost you as little
In satisfying others," those three said,   80
"You will be happy speaking in your place.
And so, if you live through these darkened depths
And go back to see once more the lovely stars,
When you are happy to say 'I was once there,'
Mention our names to the living people."

     Then they broke up their wheel, and in fleeing,
Their swift-footed legs resembled wings.
You couldn't say "Amen" as fast
As it took for them to vanish.   90
And then my master decided to move away. . . .

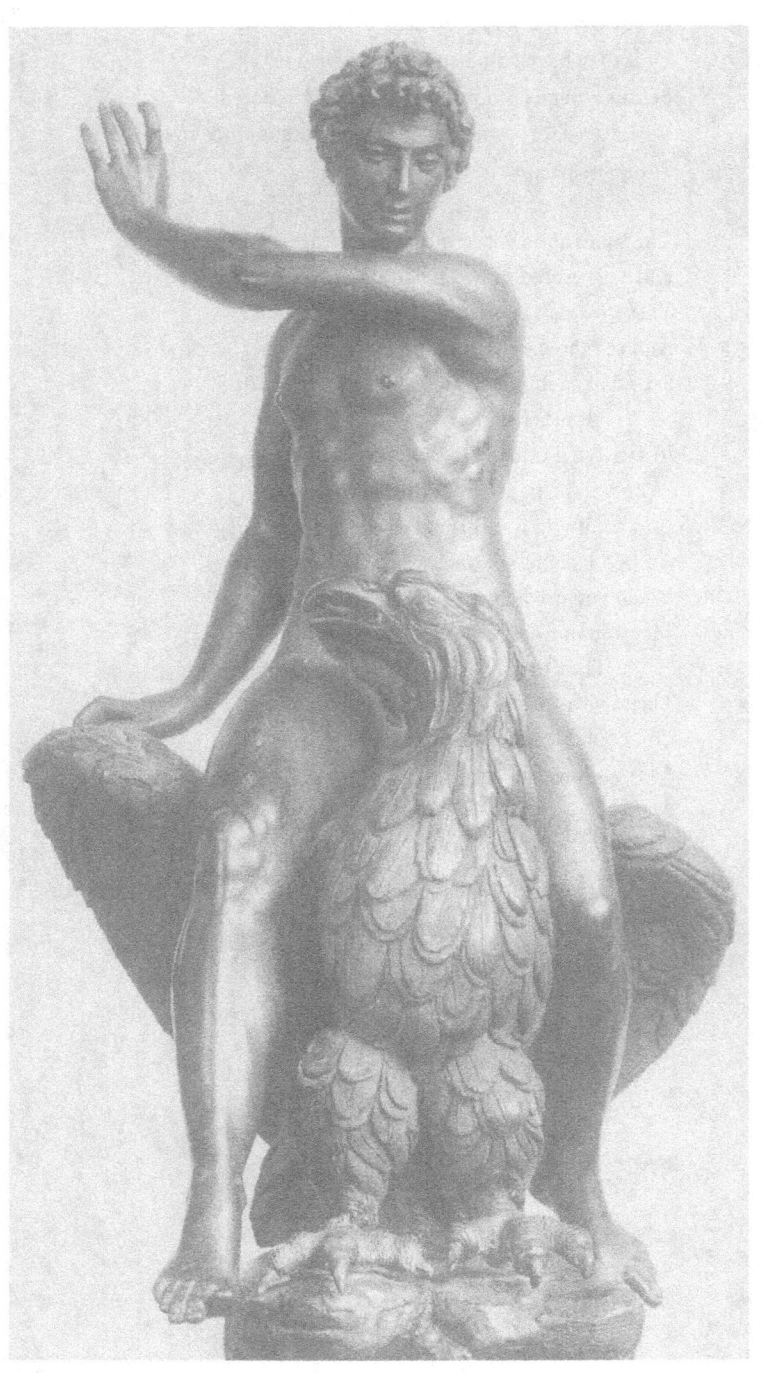

Ganymede Astride the Eagle *by Benvenuto Cellini. (Alinari/Art Resource, New York)*

16. Geoffrey Chaucer

(ca. 1341–1400)

Geoffrey Chaucer is considered the father of English literature. His master-work is undoubtedly the *Canterbury Tales*, a collection of stories told by a variety of pilgrims en route to the holy city of Canterbury in the springtime. One of this group of about thirty is a man called the Pardoner, who sells official pardons for sins from the Church. He is clearly a scoundrel who rides at the end of the group with the Summoner, with whom he may be having a lecherous relationship.

Although Chaucer does not specifically say that the Pardoner is gay, there are many indications of it, ranging from the portrayal of him as being effeminate and his close attachment to the reprobate Summoner. The two men sing together ("Come hither, love, to me"), and the Summoner "bar (bore) to him a stiff burdoun"; the latter expression has a musical meaning, like supplying a bass, but it can also be read in a sexual way. Chaucer the Pilgrim's own judgment of the man consummates in the line: "I believe he was a gelding or a mare." But in typical good humor, Chaucer then goes on to try to paint the Pardoner as a noble clergyman.

On the other hand, the tale he tells is extremely moral, concerning the way that three thieves murder each other, therefore canceling out the value of their crime. But after telling it, he transgresses the bounds of decency by offering to sell the company, especially the Host, his worthless relics and is put down, although the Knight eventually restores peace to the group and orders the two antagonists to kiss.

I have emended and to some degree normalized the text for the general reader.

With him [the Summoner] ther rood [rode] a gentil Pardoner
Of Rouncivalle, his freend and his compeer,
That straight was comen fro the court of Rome.
Ful loud he song [sang] "Com hider, love to me."
This Somnour bar to him a stiff burdoun;
Was never trompe[t] of half so greet a soun[d].
This Pardoner hadde heer [hair] as yelow as wex [wax],
But smoothe it heng as dooth a strike [piece] of flex [flax].
By ounces [wisps] heng [hung] his lockes that he hadde,
And therwith he his shuldres overspradde [spread over];   680
But thin it lay, by colpons [strands] oon and oon [one by one];
But hood, for jolitee [fun] , ne wered he noon [he wore none];
For it was trusséd up in his walet [pack-bag].
Him [He] thought he rood all of the newe jet [latest fashion];
Dishevele[d] , save his cappe, he rood al bare.
Swich [Such] glaringe eyen hadde he as an hare.
A vernicle hadde he sowed [sewn] on his cappe;
His walet lay biforn [before] him in his lappe,
Bretful [Brimful] of pardon[s] come from Rome all hoot [hot].
A voys [voice] he hadde as small as hath a goot [goat].   690
No be[a] rd hadde he, ne [nor] never sholde have;
As smooth it [his face] was as [if] he were late[ly] y-shave[n].
I trowe [believe] he were a gelding or a mare.
But of his craft, fro Berwick unto Ware,
Ne was ther swich another pardoner,
For in his male [bag] he had a pilwe-beer [pillow case},
Which that, he sayde, was Our Lady['s] veil;
He sayde he hadde a gobbet [piece] of the sail
That Saint Peter hadde whan that he wente
Upon the see, till Jesus Crist him hente [took in].   700
He hadde a croys [cross] of latoun [brass] full of stones,
And in a glass he hadde pigges' bones;
But [And] with these relickes, whan that he fond [found]
A povre [poor] person [parson] dwelling upon lond [land],
Upon a day he gat [got] him more moneye
Than that the person gat in monthes tweye [two].
And thus, with feinéd flatterye and japes [tricks],
He made the person and the peple his apes.

But trewely to tellen atte [at the] laste,

He was in chirche a noble ecclesiaste.   710

Well coulde he re[a]de a lessoun or a storye,

But alderbest [best of all] he song an offertorye;

For well he wiste [knew] that whan the song was songe,

He moste [must] preech, and well affile [smooth out] his tonge

To winne silver, as he full well cou[l]de:

Therefore, he song the murierly [more merrily] and loude.

Epilogue to "The Pardoner's Tale"

"But, sirs, o[ne] word forgat I in my tale:

I have relickes and pardon in my male,

As faire as any man in Engelond,

Which were me yeven [given] by the Popes' hond.

If any of yow woll, of [out of] devocioun,

Offren, and han [have] myne absolucioun,

Cometh forth anon, and kneeleth heere adown,

And meekely receyveth my pardoun;

Or elles [else] taketh pardon as ye wende,

All newe and fresh at every miles' ende   600

So that ye offren alway newe and newe

Nobles [coins] and pence which that be goode and trewe.

It is an honour to everich [everyone] that is heer

That ye mowe have a suffisant [competent] pardoneer

T'assoille [to absolve] yow, in [the] contree as you ride,

For aventures which that may bityde [occur].

Peraventure [Perhaps] ther may falle oon or two

Down of[f] his horse, and breeke his necke atwo [in two].

Look what a seuretee [security] is it to yow alle

That I am in your fellowship y-falle [fallen],   610

That may assoille [absolve] yow, bothe more and lasse [less],

Whan that the soule shall fro the body passe.

I rede [advise] that our Hoste heer shall biginne,

For he is most envoluped [enveloped] in sinne.

Com forth, Sir Hoste, and offre first anon,

And thou shalt kisse the relicks everichon [every one].

Yea, for a grote [groat] ! Unbokel [Unbuckle] anon thy purs!"

"Nay, nay," quod [said] he, "it shall nat be, so thee'ch [may I thrive]!

Thou wouldest make me kisse thyn olde breech[es],   620

And sweere it were a relick of a saint,
Though it were with thy fundement depaint [bottom besmirched]!
For by the croys [cross] which that Saint Eleyne [Helena] fond [found],
I would I hadde thy coillons [balls] in myn hond
Insteede of relickes or of seintuarie [sacred things].
Let cut 'em of[f] ; I woll thee help 'em carrye;
They shall be shrinéd in an hogges' turd!"
　　　　This Pardoner answerde nat a word.
So wrooth [wrathful] he was—no word ne woulde he saye.
　　　　"Now," quod our Host, "I woll no lenger [longer] playe　　　630
With thee, ne with noon other angry man."
　　　　But right anon the worthy Knight bigan,
Whan that he saugh [saw] that all the peeple lough [laughed]:
"Na more of this, for it is right enough:
Sir Pardoner, be glad and merry of cheere;
And ye, Sir Host, that been [are] to me so deere,
I pray yow that ye kisse the Pardoner.
And Pardoner, I pray thee, drawe thee neer,
And as we diden [did] , let us laughe and playe."
Anon they kisste, and riden forth hir [their] waye.　　　　　　640

Italian Renaissance Literature to Michelangelo

James J. Wilhelm

Homosexual literature blossomed in the Renaissance, even though it was often concealed. As poets rediscovered the treasures of Greco-Roman antiquity—thanks in a large part to the fall of Constantinople to the Turks in 1453—the Greek language became more accessible than it had been for centuries. The new gay poetry tended to fall into two classes: an idealized, ethereal kind of love song that was based on the philosophical works of Plato—especially his *Phaedrus* and *Symposium*. The leader in the vindication of homosexual love was the Florentine philosopher Marsilio Ficino (1422–1499), who nevertheless insisted that his love for young men such as Giovanni Cavalcanti (ca. 1444–1509) was "platonic" in the best sense (i.e., non-erotic). He thus avoided the calumny and even persecution that fell on many others such as Benedetto Varchi (1503–1565). The sonnets of Michelangelo (1475–1564) present the best of this tradition.

The other major trend was realistic and satiric, following the themes of the *Greek Anthology* and the poems of Martial and Catullus, who was emerging from a long period of neglect. The pastoral tradition of Vergil also reappeared, although the truly homoerotic quality of its nature in the Renaissance is highly debatable.

Most of the works in this chapter have been suppressed or neglected, for in the sixteenth century the Counter-Reformation put an end to literary gay works as homoerotic expression went underground into forms of coded popular poetry. Homosexual love was pulled down from the heights of Parnassus and vilified as "sodomy," punishable in most places as a crime.

An important introduction to this era consists of the articles by Giovanni dall'Orto in the *Encyclopedia of Homosexuality*, ed. Wayne R. Dynes, et al., 2 vols. (Garland, 1990), beginning with "Renaissance, Italian." Although Dall'Orto is often overly zealous in his classifying of works as homosexual, he nevertheless opens up a treasure trove that is yet to be made public outside of Italy. Another key work is the two-volume *Lirici toscani del quattrocento* (Rome, 1973) by Antonio Lanza (abbreviated Lanza), which supplies many of the texts that follow, except in the first section, where Lanza's *Polemiche e berte letterarie del primo quattrocento* (Rome, 1971) is employed.

17. Selections from 1400 to 1550

Early Developments

Except for Dante Alighieri, there are very few references to homosexuality before 1400. The only sample cited from the 1200s in Lanza's *Polemiche* (107) is that of Granfione Tolomei:

> Sir Lici is a bugaboo who feeds on boys,
> And Muscia a witch who turns into a cat at night
> And goes around and sucks off the masses.

In the 1300s there are many accusations of sodomy raised by one man against another, such as that of Jacopo da Lèona against Rustico di Filippo, or that of Meo de' Tolomei against the cleric Mino Zeppa, who:

> Because he gave Branca such a cudgeling-over
> Now has to be called a fag. *(Polemiche,* 108)

Homosexuality did not have an easy course. Homophobes were present from the start, including Domenico da Prato (ca. 1370–ca. 1432), a notary who wrote *In Condemnation of Philosophy* (as opposed to Theology). This work consisted of two chapters in which Domenico attacked philosophy in the first and sodomy in the second (showing the way in which intellectuality and homosexuality were linked in the popular mind). Here is a sample from Chapter II, beginning with line 8:

> Whoever directs his mind toward this vice
> Is breaking the laws of God,
> Doing damage to both himself and Nature.
> This is not some debatable thing.

Woe to whoever won't correct himself!
One reads about a certain country
That perished entirely with Sodom and Gomorrah;
Now more than ever people seem to transgress.
He who is guilty runs through a great stench. . . .
Ah, what a filthy, disgraceful yearning this is!   31
Is the human mind reflected here
In the way that God mercifully raises up our eyes?
He didn't give Adam a boy—no, he gave Eve
For companionship under decent laws,
And that's the way everyone should act.
Let all the rest of them weep and be miserable!

This kind of "poetry" continues to line 94.

With the appearance of a mystery figure known as Lo Za, whole groups of gay people were fiercely burlesqued. Lanza identifies the actual writer as Stefano Finiguerri (dead after 1422). His three longish poems probably appeared between 1406 and 1409. Two of these are directed against homosexuals.

One is titled either *La Buca di Montemorello* or *Monteferrato*. Lanza prefers the first title, which could mean either *The Cave on Montemorello* or, since *double entendres* abound, *The Hole on Browning Hill* (text in *Polemiche*, 309-25). The plot concerns the author, Lo Za, being led in a vision by a bankrupt banker named Tier Tornaquinci to the nearby mountain, where they believe a treasure hoard is hidden. There he sees a host of fellow Florentines, who are all corrupt, many of them sodomites:

[Anton Guardi] through poverty looked hoary and beardless [impotent];
He was a buddy of that guy of the Fracassini
And they did a lot of buggering together. . . .   (Chapter I, 55–57)
[Meo] without his pal Lombei desired
To whip around a pretty page who just arrived,
And didn't give a damn about anything else. . . .   (I, 163–65)
I saw Ser Anton, head of the Marchi clan,
Who was carrying Vergiglio on his shoulders,
Who had eyed him coyly at Montevarchi. . . .   (I, 250-252)
I saw the sodomite named Corso Cei. . . .   (I, 262)
I saw Tony di Naddo, handsome brute. . . .   (I, 310)
[Bartolaccio] wanted to enter the hole without ado.
"That isn't right," said Anton Guardi,

And Taddeo della Rosa joined in
By saying, "I'm the guardian of this hole!"   (III, 106–109)
[I saw] Doctor Giorgio, who examines the sick minutely,
And gives excellent treatment to any who bend over.   (III, 158–59)

The poem continues to line 67 of Chapter IV and abruptly ends. It is clear that Lo Za was in some ways imitating Dante, especially with his use of "I saw," as in *Inferno IV,* but the poetry seldom rises above the level of invective.

The same holds true of his poem *Il Gagno,* which is supposedly the name of an island and can mean three things: gain; slimy swamp; or penis. This work takes place at Pisa, where Lo Za, again in a dream vision, sees himself transported to this island, where he meets a man named Buiano, who introduces him to a crowd of people who have come here to be free of taxes and to make big gains. The text of this truncated poem is in Lanza's *Polemiche,* 348ff. A sample of lines 118 to 123 shows a similarity with the previous poem:

"Tell me, Buian, who is that man who walks
Beside Ser Giusto, who looks so short?"
And he to me: "I've already told you;
His name is Michael Pestellino, and he
And his brother run along the wasteland
Looking for my *gagno* to store in their cesspool."

Another important figure of the early 1400s is a mysterious person who was called L'Acquettino (Croucher/Squatter), since his work was given that name. He has been identified by Lanza and others as Giovanni Gherardi da Prato (ca. 1367–ca. 1446), whose poem follows, but that identification is highly debatable. *L'Acquettino* opens with a narrator giving a pious account of the glories of Rome, and it then shifts to Florence, with its outstanding vice:

This is that damnable sodomy,
Which vilely offends nature
And annoys Him who sent us here,
And although the world is found to be
Full of such filth, it is even less fitting
For you, Florence, who have risen so high!

(118ff.; *Polemiche,* 163)

The author wanders around, meeting a handsome young man who rejects the advances of a beautiful girl, claiming that he worships Diana and therefore will have nothing to do with women. After other encounters, including one with Giovanni da Prato, it trails off.

Another mystery figure is Il Burchiello, who gave his name to a whole genre of popular poetry known as burchiellesque. He (or his leading practitioner) seems to have been Domenico di Giovanni, a barber who was born in Florence in 1404 and died, after some associations with Siena, in 1449 at the age of 45. The adopted name derives either from the word *burchio* (barge), which was a symbol that Domenico placed above his barber shop, or from *alla burchia,* which means "haphazard, careless."

His poems show a very broad range of themes and tones but many of them lend themselves to erotic interpretations. As Giovanni dall'Orto has said in his article on Burchiellesque Poetry in the *Encyclopedia of Homosexuality,* they "use coded language . . . bristling with obscene double meanings which offer a certain parallel to the famous poems in *jargon* by François Villon (1431–ca. 1463)." Villon's *Jargon Poems* are indeed extremely complicated and, although gay motifs have been observed in them, for the most part they deal with robbery, thievery, gambling, and drunkenness—the main fabrics of the poet's life; no decent translations have been made into English to date, although there have been some attempts in French.

The same aura of mystery surrounds Burchiellesque Poetry, which faded away in the 1500s, being replaced by the less ambitious Bernesque Poetry and by the Roman *pasquinate* (see Francesco Berni and Roman Pasquinades below). Until some key has been devised, most of Il Burchiello and his followers must remain uninterpreted and untranslated.

NANNI PEGOLOTTI (ca. 1345–1431)

Nanni Pegolotti was born and died in Florence, but wandered widely in Italy. His most important work, the so-called *Opera,* is a historical poem attacking the powerful Malatesta family of Rimini. The following poems were all written for a young Florentine named Andrea Ferrantini.

[Lanza 11]
Thanks to you, my angelic figure,
There is a light that without you wouldn't shine;
Even Phoebus is guided by your light.
Nature created you in the Empyrean.

Faith, hope, and charity securely reside
In you, and prudence radiates there
With strength and temperance; pure justice
Returns with you, along with other virtues.

Heaven made you so worthy of great praise
That I could not describe you in just a few lines,
But your virtuous acts show the honor in you.
And I—poor thing!—can only disparage myself.
I thank you that you didn't refuse my proposal,
And so I'll be your slave with you my master.

[Lanza 10]
From the time of your promise and my acceptance
The new moon has ten times returned,
And still that time can't quiet my desire
But kindles it to heavy passion
In my thoughts and my imagination;
But the hope of having you as the doctor
For this terrible wound also comforts me,
Since no one but you could ever heal it.

I know that you will keep that promise made
So that you won't lose any credit with the masses
And you will keep your virtues alive.
I was yours and will be if you want me;
And so I beg you not to further delay,
For time is fleeting, and we cannot regain it.

[Lanza 9] On the Death of Andrea Ferrantini
Dead is the desire, lost is the hope
That used to make me happy in this world;
For me every comfort is lacking;
For me there is no joy or happiness;
All that I grieve for are my failures;
I grieve for myself and repose with grief.
Grief assails me so hard that I don't dare
Or even want to have good spirits again,

Because through vileness I have lost that one
That the heavens and fate and world gave to me
In order to lend peace to my troubled heart.
What shall I do, what say, my beautiful friend?
I can't die, and yet living aggravates me
If your loving flower doesn't spring up again.

[Lanza 14]
I can no longer be content
Any more in this world
After Death undertook the undoing
Of my once happy lord.
I've become completely depressed,
No longer in any way happy!
I wasn't aware of the ambush
Treacherously laid in my path—
Not as long as I enjoyed my happiness.
Only God perceived it   10
And made a fool of me
To everyone around me.
Andrea and I always spent our time
Together in fun and games,
And we were in each other's
Thoughts all of the time.
We were always together
At balls, song-fests, and banquets.
This way our noble lives moved on,
And both of us were always happy.   20
When we were most content
And were basking in our love,
False, disloyal Lady Death
Sneaked out in a treacherous way
And stabbed my friend so brutally
That he was forced to leave me.
He departed in the flower of his youth,
Leaving me bereft in this bitter world.
I asked that jealous bitch
Who so violently divided us   30
To be gracious enough

To turn my tears to laughter;
I asked her if she would strike me
With the bow that had transfixed him
To banish me from this world
So that I could join my happy master.
Go away, my song, and travel
Up to the sixth heaven;
Find my companion there
And tell him this for me: 40
"Andrea, as you know,
Your Nanni suffers pain for you
And is struggling to rejoin you
But Death spitefully holds him in this world."

GIOVANNI GHERARDI DA PRATO (ca. 1367–ca. 1446)

As was mentioned earlier, Antonio Lanza tries to identify him with a poet known only as L'Acquettino. Lanza says in his anthology that Giovanni was known in his day as an "unabashed sodomite" (Vol. I, 610), but he nevertheless addressed the bulk of his songs to women. His style is heavily indebted to Dante and Petrarch, to whom he wrote tributes. In the following poem, the adjectives describing the beloved are masculine.

[Lanza 25]
O troubled heart, O tempest-torn soul,
O sorrows and woes and tears and sighs,
O powerful laments and vain desires,
O foolish thoughts and anxious burden,
O futile mind and cries with frequent blows,
O pungent wails, O heaving sighs,
O eyes of mine, O guilty sufferings—
Will they never have a truce, peace, calm or victory?
No, because I've had a taste of bitter honey
And war instead of peace, and so I
Struggle constantly and burn and freeze.
Alas! even the one who kills me I hold dear;
I adore the one who consumes and drags me down,
And I see no escape from this grave evil!

Antonio Panormita (1394–1471)

Born Antonio Beccadelli from an old Bolognese clan, Panormita soon called himself by an ancient name for the city of Palermo, where he lived for a time. He was in Siena in 1420 and then moved on to Florence, where he met Cosimo de'Medici (1389–1464), whom he praised in his works and to whom he dedicated his salacious *Hermaphroditus*, which was published in Bologna in 1425.

By 1434 Panormita was working as the secretary and archivist for King Alfonso V of Aragon and the Two Sicilies (1396–1458), where he became a good friend of many other Renaissance humanists, such as Giovanni Pontano. We are told from various sources that his poems pleased many powerful men, but they shocked the general public so much that an effigy of him was burned at least twice in his life.

My translations of the *Hermaphroditus* are taken from the revised edition of his works by F.C. Forberg (Leipzig, 1908; rev. 1986). I often use Latin names, although obviously they had Italian counterparts.

Book I, Poem 3

Cosimo, have you read the title of my book?
　　On the side is the title *Hermaphrodite*
Because inside, you will find both a penis and a cunt,
　　And therefore the mixed name is very fitting.
But you may call it *Anus*, since it sings of that too,
　　And thus that title would also be appropriate.
But if you don't like the first name or the second,
　　Whatever name you give—don't make it "nice."

I, 7 Epitaph for a Limping Pederast

Traveler, if you want to know my name,
　　I am Pegasus who lies here beneath this soil.
And knowing my name, now hear and listen to me:
　　When you have a young man that you want to bugger,
Do it, I beg you, right here on my tomb!
　　This way through your coitus—and fuck your incense!—
You can lend some peace to my soul, O I beg you!
　　Yes, this is the best way to make peace with the shades
Of Hell; that's what our ancient fathers told us.
　　This way Achilles placated the ashes of Chiron;

And, blond Patroclus, your bottom also experienced this rite;
　　And Hylas knew it when Hercules pierced him on his father's grave;
So make this offering to me, which our elders have bequeathed!

I, 12

If you had as many cocks dangling outside you as you've swallowed in your ass,
　　Dear Mamurianus, your shoulders would be massive enough to
　　　　overcome any bull.

I, 13 Answer to Lepidinus on the Popularity of Pederasty
Why is anyone who browns or is browned, my dear writer
　　Of pleasantries, never able to give it up?
In this way the stupid Briton who's once tasted this delight
　　Struggles to surpass even the Sienese in his savoring.
Naples takes second to the French, and the Florentines whip the North Germans
　　If Fate just one little time lets them sample the ass of a boy.
If anyone by chance bends over the back of a young-'un,
　　It's extremely hard for him to ever abandon that task.

I, 14

Lentulus, you alone covet your money and your many books;
　　You alone control your many queens and your clothes;
You alone possess brains and feelings and regular friends,
　　And keep everything to yourself—with one exception:
And that's your asshole, which doesn't belong to you alone,
　　Dear Lentulus. O no! It's common property.

I, 18 To the Evil-Tongued Hodus
Hodus says that my life isn't politically correct;
　　He thinks that he fathoms my mind from my works.
Hodus has apparently never read Catullus,
　　And he's never set eyes on Priapus' bulging prick.
What was all right for Marcus and Marsus and Pedo
　　And all those others—is that forbidden for me?
Let me wander the same paths as the great poets,
　　And you, Hodus, believe with the rabble what you want to believe.

I, 25

Minus, you think that I should remove all the cocks
    From my poems, and this way I'd be more popular.
Minus, I don't want to castrate my book;
    After all, Apollo had a prick and Calliope a hole.

I, 19 *Lauridius Writes to the Author*

My boyfriend from Perugia is driving away the one from Siena;
    O, how he overwhelms me, and how he torments me!
I pray that Perugia's offspring may please the Thunder-God,
    That Perugia's sprouts may gain the grace of the gods!
My Carlo, with his magnificent body and inborn charm,
    Captivates me, and his tender little soles press down my neck!

I, 33 *To Mamurianus, a Hypocritical Tuscan Cocksucker*

You're a Tuscan, and Tuscans always are drawn to the cock;
    And my book, dear Mamurianus, comes from Tuscany too.
Nonetheless, I'm going to cut all the cocks out of my opus
    As soon as you tell me that this should be done.
But I'm not going to make the operation until you promise
    That you won't run around and gather up the excisions.

I, 34

Bugger the boy who brings you this book, Amilus,
    And then tell me: which has the better end.

I, 36

When Lupius is browning an untaught young man,
    He says, "Hey there, my beautiful baby, open up!"
He says this, and the boy replies: "I'll do it if you tell me in a single word."
    He says: "Swivel!" and the opening is complete.

Book II, Poem 16 *To the Pederastic Teacher Mattias Lupius*

Poor Matthew has only three students
    In his enclave—and one is his partner by night.

II, 17 *To the Boy Maura on Behalf of M. Soccinus*

You are more lovely than silver, more gorgeous than gold
    If you send me back some kind words, you kindly young man.
Your household is warmly devout—your brothers, and your sister and parents.
    Since your household is so lovable, you should be too.
Your figure is magnificently shaped, and your mind should be too;
    Let your words, when you answer, be fitting to your form.
It's a magnificent thing to rescue men who are perishing.
    This raises the rescuer to a level with the gods.
And I will lead forth the Muses from the Castalian fountain
    To hymn your outstanding figure and your virtues.
What better than a Muse can I offer? What better in song?
    If you demand something superior, ask—and I'll supply it.
Any man whom the sacred poets favor enjoys eternal fame.
    You also, unless I err, will be celebrated by my song.
For in my learnéd verse I shall offer you a lively and pious
    Friendship—as long as our lives shall last.
Indeed, refined youngsters will always follow your example,
    And they will often rejoice in retelling your deeds.
O light of my life, Maura, be well! I offer myself
    And Thalia the Muse for whatever you want; so thrive!

II, 18 *To M. Soccinus Concerning the Above*

Soccinus, I pray that the gods will help our undertaking,
    And that Venus will patronize us with her Cupid;
May a suitable response match our young man's wonderful figure,
    And thus a beautiful boy may return us beautiful words.
His whole house is full of love—his brothers, sister and parents;
    I don't know why you shouldn't be sanguine with a house so mild.
And he far surpasses his relatives in his gentleness.
    So why should Maura be any different from his dad?

II, 20

Lentulus, you don't screw around with widows or brides,
    And no whore and no virgin attracts you.
Yet you keep insisting you're the world's biggest, hottest fucker.
    Dear Lentulus, tell me: what on earth do you fuck?

Giovanni Pontano (1426–1503)

A friend of Panormita who even composed an epitaph for him, Pontano was also a major courtier for King Alfonso of Aragon and the Two Sicilies, although he finally delivered the city of Naples over to the French. He is famous for discovering Donatus's commentary on Vergil. His writings in Italian and Latin, though numerous, are almost entirely heterosexual. The following attack is translated from the edition of Liliana M. Sabia, *Poesie Latine* (Torino, 1977), I, 102ff.

Parthenopaeus or Amores; Book I, 29 Against the Faggot Antonino

O little faggot of an Antonino,
I want you to come back to me so that, by Hercules!
If I get hold of you, I want to work over
Those nasty little buttocks of yours
With some wicked rods
So that your punishment will fit your crime.
Did you really dare in the middle of the street,
With me present, to confront my girlfriend?
You actually had the gall to snatch
Some white roses from the bosom of my Cinnama?
And after that to pull down her mantle
And to forcefully grab her snowy breasts
With your sweaty hands?
If this wild anger compels me onward,
You're going to learn a little later what it means
To feel up beautiful women with those hands!

Pacifico Massimi (ca. 1400–ca. 1500)

Very little is known about the facts of Massimi's life, as the dates indicate, but he tells us a lot about himself and his family in his poems. We do know that he was born in Ascoli, and he lived widely in Italy, including Naples, where he wrote verse in honor of Alfonso of Aragon and the Two Sicilies. His *Hecatelegium (One Hundred Elegies)*, written in Latin, were published in Florence in 1489; they were dedicated to Francesco Soderini, the Bishop of Volterra. Massimi wrote some poems to Pope Sixtus IV, but later Massimi's relations with the Church grew worse, for although the prelates were at first taken by Massimi's easy handling of Latin elegiacs, they later resented his antipapalism and frank humanism.

His 100 elegies, divided into ten books, have been well edited by Juliette Desjardins (University of Grenoble, 1986), who includes a facsimile of the first edition.

Book I, 9 *Advice to Paulinus*

That man is pleasing and worthy of praise who shuns vice and always,
  Always follows virtues and beautiful deeds.
He who wants to be a companion of the wicked
  Will eventually pick up the same bad name that they bear. . . .
The only taint on my morals came from the tutor   13
  That my father and mother unwittingly wished upon me.
He was the king of the pederasts; no prey ever
  Escaped his hands, since he was a master of that art.
O yes, I learned a lot of things I'd have preferred not to.
  I learned a lot about using my mouth—and my asshole.
Now you, my Paulinus—don't you want to avoid all this?
  Don't you see the appearance of that man you associate with?   20
I'm wondering in fact if you're not being sucked down in the same filth,
  Because, as we know, like is attracted to like.
Already some not very pretty stories are circulating about you.
  A lot of people are ripping you apart with their teeth.
You might as well cut off the long prick of your dog
  Because your old reputation is going to give way to the new.
If you're not careful, if you don't move away from that guy,
  No water of the ocean will ever wash you clean.
That guy could steal an egg from under a sitting hen;   30
  He could sneak away with a sandal from a woman who's watching.
If a pederast once gets a young kid in his clutches,
  He knows how to drill the recruit in his art.
He will handle you with his hands and his tongue so expertly that he
  Could overcome Hermogenes in thievery and Battus in fraud.
Just recently I happened to be sitting at the theater,
  And that guy slid away a soft cushion from under my butt.
He didn't touch a boy who was there or utter a word to him;
  In fact, he didn't even seem to see him, yet he took down one's breeches.
The boy's grandpa and dad were bamboozled as the kid was buggered, 40
  And that's the way the kid will end up his life.
Have no doubt! the same punishment will be reserved for you.
  Look and see if a noose isn't already dangling around your neck.

You don't think my words are worth a damn. That's why they say this
about you:
"Nobody ever gets back a sheep that's fallen into the mouth of a wolf."

II, 10 A Love Song for Marcus
You couldn't find a better time to meet me, Marcus,
    Or a place that was more convenient.
May my soul disappear and my senses fail
    And a blast of cold sweep over my limbs
When I look at you and when I picture
    Your honeyed lips bitten by my teeth!
Often I wanted to talk to you, but the words
    Choked in my palate and a chill overcame my tongue.
O how many times my tears and my sighs
    Have offered a sure proof of my passion!   10
What do they mean—this thinness, pallor, moisture and fasting
    That flees my lips—o, but you don't care!
The devout simplicity of your tender years causes this;
    Your snowy-white virginity makes you rude.
Don't you know the power of Cupid's golden weapons,
    And doesn't your heart tell you what love is?
Nothing is harsher than that, nothing more bitter;
    I would undergo a thousand deaths to have it taken away.
I'd like to know if you want to be totally rid of me
    Or if there is ever some hope for ending my pain.   20
Either give me some life or remove the time that is left to me;
    Now I've decided to live—yet now to die.
I have no arbiter for either choice; I totally lack a judge.
    No woman or man could tell me anything right.
Let the matter lie between some willows and green pastures.
    Let a shade-tree cover us over with its leaves.
Let a brook lull us to sleep with its dulcet murmurs
    Along with the songs of many a bird from the branches.
Come here and gradually glide down over my bosom,
    O you cause and cure for my desires!   30
Now I'd like to exhale my breath; now I'd like to die
    Among all these blandishments and pleasures.
No man on earth or in heaven would be happier than I am,
    No one would consider Jove a greater being than I!

III, 2 Hymn to Priapus, the Phallic God

. . . "Priapus, if you don't hurry and cure my prick,   19
     It will die. Alas, its strength won't come back!
O, I'd rather be deprived of my two eyes! I'd rather
     Have my nose cut off from my deformed face!
No girl will ever look at me or want me again,
     And even the boys will spit contemptuously at me! . . .
I commend myself to you with all of my heart, Priapus.   37
     Let my rod be cured; let it be healthy like before.
And here is how I'll show my gratitude: I'll rear up
     A wax column for you—as big as my own."
As soon as I finished my prayer, he gave a sign to my words,
     And that was the major cause of my being cured.
And, what is better, my cock now feels no pain.
     I'm completely cured; it does its job better than before.
It will perform for any girl or boy who is present,
     And they're sure to appreciate the purgative power of my tool.

IV, 2 To Sleep

. . . Let me speak the truth: we like to talk about what we've done;   33
     Just as we take pleasure in doing, so we take pleasure in speech.
I am happy when a new desire captivates me,
     And I'm totally unable to conceal my delight.
Let other men run after coins and palaces and acres,
     Gold vessels and clothes and wine and the finest food.
I have only one thing I care about: my penis.
     As long as I'm fucking well, let the gods take all the rest!

V, 4 An Invitation to All Boys and Girls

Come, all of you—a hundred boys and girls—
     If any or all of you want to be mine.
Come and visit me while my heart's not in love,
     While it's free, and no frenzy possesses it.
Seize this chance and take your places outside my door.
     If you blow this, you'll never get the chance back.
Right now I'm not asking for money; all I request
     For my work is simply a pussy or a prick.
The time has come for you thousands of boys and girls.

What are you waiting for, girls and boys?   10
Believe me: you're going to wait too long, my friends,
    For soon I'll belong to another and follow their yoke.
If you boys and girls aren't alone, come anyway—
    All of you thousands together! Even that's not enough!
In the courtyard I saw one male bird servicing many,
    And I've seen thousands of ewes mounted by one male.
I don't need any magic herbs; no, go away from me,
    All of your hocus-pocus aphrodisiacs!
I remember that in one single hour I've made love
    Ten times, and right now I'm ready to do the same.   20
But what can I do? I'm so controlled by my savage lust!
    I could fill three or four times any stinking hole.
It's been a long time since my pecker knew a cunt,
    A long time since I wrecked somebody's rectum.
My cock is stiff night and day, yes all night long; never
    Does it sleep. Night and day it is hard.
But not a single boy or a single girl is listening.
    Nobody comes. As usual, the right hand ends the job.

V, 6 To a Cute Young Hustler

May fire and wind blow away all the earnings
    Of anyone who sells tender love at a venal price,
Because it is wrong to sell anything that Nature freely grants.
    It is shameful to offer for silver what has been given as a gift.
It is right that anyone who offers filthy lucre for his pleasures
    Should lose the beautiful boy granted to him.
Fortune will call him ungrateful if he asks for payments
    And if he stingily refuses to help out the poor.
He who wants to strangle travelers should lurk away
    In deep, dense forests, inhabiting lairs without light.   10
He who exchanges his flesh and his hide for a sum
    Should market his wares in a dirty whorehouse.
The crime of greed will make him lose his beauty and charm
    And lower the value of what once rose above any price.
What I want is almost nothing: if you give it, you'll lose
    Nothing there; I ask you to give what costs you nothing.
You aren't smiling at me or looking happy—in fact, you dare

To brassily beg me for silver with outspread hands.
Yes, if some admirer doesn't open his bosom to you,
    He'll never cross the thankless threshold of your home.   20
And yet there isn't anyone who plies some god-forsaken craft
    Who will be denied if he just offers you some trinket.
Any cocksucker can have you, any ass-greaser,
    Or anyone who licks the cracks of the foulest whores.
In you there is none of the intelligence that runs the whole world;
    In your being there is not one ounce of mind.
You're a vain, silly little piece painted over with a slight charm;
    You're something entirely different from what you imagine.
In fact, you are nothing, and you're not going to find anyone
    Who will offer a penny of your price—if he gets to know you.   30
Do you want to change your habits, you nut, and stop acting
    So trashy so that you can live decently and become good,
To follow virtue and do what wins praise and
    What never at any time will perish in death?
Then lend me your ears and listen a little. Lilies on their stalks
    And roses with their thorns very quickly lose their beauty.
I was once like you—don't laugh!—I was the envied object—
    You'd better believe me!—of a thousand johns.
But nevertheless that was all like a cloud in a thunderstorm:
    It blew away, like a bubble in boiling water.   40
Now I've got nothing except what I can get for nothing;
    What I once gave away free—that I call my own.
A lover should be valued higher than gold or jewels,
    Higher than all of the wealth that the world possesses.
To that man you should be able to open the recesses of your heart
    And confide your words with full confidence.
But you won't get away from me entirely unrewarded;
    The hope that you sense from my kindness won't be vain.
You'll be celebrated for your merits in every country
    Because of my poem, and your fame will survive your own death. 50
You'll be known in the West and known in the East
    And be known on the axis of the two Poles.
This is far more precious than any silver or gold,
    Far more than any pearl an Indian finds in the Red Sea.
Ah, but you're lowering your head, little fool, and turning away your ears!
    O hell! Go ahead! May your asshole make you a millionaire!

Happy is the day which saw me when I was joined to my boyfriend
 On some grass that supplied us with a delightful bed!
Happy was that place, happy the waving branches and the tree
 That made me feel greater than Jupiter himself!
When was there ever anyone happier on earth than I,
 Or who could be considered an equal to me?
I was swimming in joy; I could scarcely hold myself back.
 The earth could scarcely sustain my swift-running feet.
Even if Croesus had given me great riches or wealthy Alcinous
 His gold, I would not have exchanged this for anything— 10
Not if I were given what the Tagus River carries in its current
 Or what the Pactolus and the Hermus have hidden,
Or what the dusky Indian searches for in the Red Sea
 Or what Danaë or Midas once controlled.
Let wealth incline to the happy! Who, if he's sad,
 Is truly rich? Only a happy soul has wealth.
I possess everything; my mind wishes nothing more,
 Except what I hold and will always enjoy;
May that never end, may it never be lacking,
 And may Fortune never envy me my pleasures. 20
May no day ever separate my sweet lover from me
 And no day ever cut me off from my love.
May high noon always see me happy in its brief shade,
 And may the rising and setting sun see me the same way.
May a propitious stone mark that continuous hour
 As only white stones issue out of the divining urn.
As an object of envy, may I seem miserable to no one,
 And may everyone always see me heaped with goods.
May the heavens nod yes to me, or if there is anything greater,
 May that god absorb my prayers with a willing ear! 30
Shall I speak to anyone? No, I say. Arrogantly
 I move forward with an obdurate face. Pride orders me to do so.
Let the passive crowds give way. I want to march down Broadway.
 Who would dare to touch my nose or finger my hair?
If anyone interrogates me, I'll say: No! Nobody will know
 If my grain or my greens support my great claim.
No one will know this—not as long as the rivers
 Run down to the sea or the fish adore their flowing waters.
I would die before anything fell from my lips that told

When this all happened and how—that love that blessed me.   40
That man, that is a sage who reveals his love to no one.
    A man who gabs about his joys in love is a damned fool!

VII, 3 On a Budding Disciple

When a Tuscan friend brought me a boy of the kind
    That you might find superintending Jove's table,
He whispered in my ear: "This kid I've brought you
    Will cling to your side night and day.
The gods and the goddesses want you to cling to his love.
    If you bugger him, he'll become an expert there."
I said: "I like this freedom that gives way to shame.
    Your kind offer forces me to hold myself back.
You'll see that I'm very different from the usual hungry dog.
    If you give most people a finger, they'll open to a hand.   10
I don't know what god shines out of his face.
    He certainly seems to have more than a human power."
"Don't doubt if he's good that he'll get better; you will see
    That he's drained every drop of my doctrine to the dregs."
My friend went away happy. Happily I claimed my joy.
    Every day of my waiting seemed too long.
O father of great virtue, the only one to be praised,
    Who alone in such a large city is known to be wise,
You joined the ass of this boy to the cock of his master!
    Foolish people, do you think you could learn this right away?   20
O lucky boy that Fate chose me as your master,
    And gave you to me as a loving dad!
Alas, how slowly the sun descends into the shadows!
    Alas, how slowly the somber night descends!
When will the marriage bed join us in its embrace?
    When will this hour be witnessed by my eyes?
Someone will sing on a guitar all night about our misfortunes;
    Another will sigh, and two others hymn our woes.
Then, as you lie in my arms, I shall tell you some stories,
    And you can give me long kisses while I talk.   30
As the wind blows outside, we shall lie happy in sleep,
    While the raindrops beat downward upon the roof.
I'll delight in running my tired body down from your neck
    And to rub my tired limbs against yours in the lamplight.

Let others lust for riches, a chest full of coins;
  Let them take up the yoke like some crazy bull.
If you want to learn poetry, I shall teach you the art:
  Whether to compose with four or five feet to a line,
And how to turn a short syllable into a long one,
  And how something can artfully be lengthened or cut.   40
Often I'll stretch out the chords as I move the plectrum;
  Often I shall make you hold fast to my lyre.
You'll become a true poet, circled by a sacred crown,
  And on festival days, a laurel will be placed on your door!

IX, 2 To My Cock

Cock, why are you rising up, burrowing a hole in my pants?
  Why don't you lie hidden in your nest in my shorts?
Why is your head on fire as you send off sultry heat-waves?
  Why are you swelling, lifting your ruby head upright?
Are you once again daring to go back to tender boys
  And girls, not satisfied with all your past mischief?
To what cunning will your perversity not descend?
  To what crime won't your frenzy drag you down?
You've now lived to see your seventieth consul,
  And you've already seen twice seven lustral rites.   10
At this age all other cocks usually loll around half-dead,
  But you stand more sturdy than any iron rod or oak tree.
That's the way young men act, driven by their fun-loving years
  Who are just beginning to scatter their seed in the furrows.
No incantation or magic art can hold you back.
  No sparrow hops around this way; no love potion does this.
It's true that vicious habits that are formed in one's early years
  Often last to the very end of one's days.
You're true to your customs; this habit arouses you.
  The throat cries out for the food it is used to.   20
I foolishly used to think you'd get satiated or tired,
  That you wouldn't be able to keep lifting your head.
You're not ashamed of your past; in fact, you desire worse things
  So that you can heap one dirty deed on another.
There's nothing left for me to offer you; you've devoured everything
  That my father and mother and grandfather left me.
You always demanded anything I spied in this whole big city,

And I never denied a thing to your wishes.
I never turned anyone down as long as you were content.
    I offered you the fork to my choicest meats.   30
And you, dear traitor, never cut me in on your profits,
    Even though a rigid dick has enriched many a man.
You never wanted any old ladies or widows or one-armeds;
    O no! only the choicest birds could appease your taste.
I'm stupefied that you haven't been worn out by excess use.
    You must have been forged from iron or from bronze.
If you're wise and not totally lacking in sense
    See how shameful it is for an old man to rise up so much.
Why not instead control your fury with a little reason? Master yourself!
    Throw the spurs away from the stallion running wild!   40
Divert your time to something else; don't persist in what's useless.
    Today I have nothing; maybe tomorrow you'll find something.
I'm talking, and yet you don't show any sign of calming down;
    No, you keep rising; you want to spew out your food.
Wait a little and I'll go and lie on a soft cushion;
    Then I'll spit on you and polish you off with a hand!

IX, 3 To an Aging Pretty-Boy

You're no child any more, my boy, but with the increasing years
    A noxious beard is invading your tender cheeks.
You're wearing the toga of a man now, not of a child;
    And your short hair is not as pretty as your long locks.
You can't fool around with nuts in a childish way;
    No, your life has to be directed to a different course.
A tender age allows a lot that a harsher one doesn't;
    You used to do a lot of things you can't do any more;
If you act like a foolish kid, you will have to pay for it.
    What you once called the vices of the old are now yours.   10
Achilles gave up guitar-playing when he became a man,
    And he stopped gathering flowers and thinning the distaff.
And they say that Paris, when he became a man, stopped
    Plowing the fields with yoked oxen.
Everyone knows what you used to be. You yourself know
    You were the foulest, filthiest thing on earth.
I fear that, like a plant, you put your roots so deep in dirt
    That no scythe or no fire could ever uproot them.

You can wash a stinking garment in fast-flowing water,
        But it will still retain a trace of its stains.   20
You can take a dog and bathe it, perfume it, wipe it clean,
        And yet your nose will tell you it's a dog. . . .
But maybe you'll be able to turn good and live uprightly;   29
        Maybe you can pull back your feet after a false step.
You would not be the first; many have done it; but only one
        Out of the many, you know, ever regains control;
And I seriously doubt that after him you will be the second.
        At no time do you show any sign of getting well.
Your decadent parents bequeathed you this life style.
        You still wear the bridle that your tutor put on you. . . .
All hope and any cure for healing have to be abandoned   55
        Unless some god from the heavens takes you by the hand.

IX, 6 *On an Unappealing, Persistent Hustler*

What does he want—that shithead? He's always saying hello
        And smiling at me and making some sign with his fingers.
He's always at my back or just up ahead; if I'm leaving
        One place, he's already been there before.
I never saw anything like it in all my life!
        You wouldn't believe it unless you saw it too.
In short, I don't know what he's after, but I suspect
        He wants something; he wants to be one of the boys.
He saw me the other day with a lot of cash and right away
        He cunningly set out his nets with a shyster skill.   10
I have the reputation of being kind to tender gay boys.
        So now he's after anything he can get.
But he's wrong if he thinks he can roll me on the sly.
        I'm not the kind to get trapped in his kind of net.
He doesn't know me at all, has barely met me; well, if he
        Wants to be browned, he's going to have to pay *me!*
And even if he shells out well and begs me, that's not
        Something I'd do easily. His face is so jaded!
I'm afraid he might collapse during the job between my legs!
        Why, a fly or a mosquito has more energy in him!   20
Like a hen who gathers her chicks underneath her wings,
        I believe that he too emits a saffron-yellow shit.
He has no vitality, no sap, and is poorly endowed.

He has no real meat anywhere on his body.
He looks bloodless; paleness and sluggishness dog him.
     He's about as graceful as a crawling cricket.
I'd rather have sex with a magpie or starling
     Or the ancient bones exhumed from some cemetery.
If he keeps tossing himself and darting in front of me,
     I'm going to kick him like a ball to the stars!   30
Look at how badly the gods above are treating me,
     And how fortune has turned evilly against me.
He's drawn to me because he's ugly; if he was smart
     And had a heavenly body, he'd ignore me!
I confess that very often I'm given to buggering; I won't lie.
     But nevertheless I only feed off the choicest chicken.
I like a boy who is juicy, rounded, warm and white,
     And yes! one whose asshole is filled with fire!

X, 2 *On a Pair of Twins*

Cupid, look! Once again I'm expiring; once again I'm your prey.
     I submit my hands doubly cuffed to your orders.
There will be no respite from this insane rage.
     One throb scarcely dies when another arises.
But what is this new kind of love? What name shall I give it?
     Under what title shall I place this furious flame?
Alas, I sense a new fire, a passion never known before.
     I've never before experienced this kind of frenzy!
Who could believe you can burn for a pair of gay twins?
     And, what's more, at the same time desire both?   10
When I praise one, the other seems more worthy of praise.
     The more I like number one, the more number two appeals.
I sigh for this one, and that one yanks sighs out of me.
     The former wears down my heart and the latter takes the pieces.
As one single torch burns me that issues from the two,
     Who would believe that the torch divides but stays one?
My mind is always imagining one of the two,
     And yet at the same time seeing two in one.
Locks of hair cascade down both snow-white necks,
     The like of which neither Bacchus nor Phoebus had.   20
Their faces are virginal, their flaming eyes like Greek gods,
     And their lips contend with the roses of Paestum.

O what shoulders they have, what fingers and hands!
What thighs surrounding rippling abdominals!
Dignified in their bearing, their movements show moderation.
But why list specifics when the wholes are extraordinary?
If I could embrace the two together in my loving arms,
I would lose all sense of where I was!
If I could plant some kisses between their lips,
I would lose my mind entirely with my senses!   30
If I could do even more—if more could be done—
In the midst of my rapture, I'd give up the ghost!
Twins, who make up my life, why are you torturing me?
Why do you both roast me over a slow flame?
What great glory is there for two of you to torment one?
I've surrendered my neck and hands to your every whim.
Cruel ones, stop acting with such savage fierceness!
Stop letting your hearts revel in this cruel slaughter!
You are going to lose more from my ill fate than you think.
Yes, the loss will exceed your furthest imagination.   40
If I perish, your reputations will perish too.
There won't be anyone alive in the world to hymn you.
The miserable cause of my death will be engraved on my tomb:
The cause is you both, who will then be infamous.
These are the words that I order my heir and successor
To engrave on the marble that encloses my bones:

HERE LIES PACIFICO, WHO WAS UNDONE BY A DOUBLE LOVE;
THE TWO WHOM HE LOVED BOTH ALLOWED HIM TO DIE.

ANTONIO BONCIANI (1417–ca. 1485)
Besides this severe attack on his rival Antonio di Guido, Bonciani left a hand-
ful of poems, including the stilted, precious *Garden,* with a mythological
theme.

[Lanza 4] To Antonio di Guido
O you stinking, poisonous toad
Of a Master Antonio, outstanding emperor
Of every vice and all kinds of evil-doing,
In which you have made yourself a full professor.

You are the reason that Florence will be corrupted
And destroyed if you're allowed to stay here.
After dinners, you grab any gluttonous thing
With greedy hands, in order to keep dining on;
And to fill up that insatiable throat of yours,
Even a worm wouldn't be lowly enough.
You slobbering creep, ungrateful and always guilty,
You could even educate Semiramis in lust
By using your dirty sack for sodomy,
Surpassing even Capaneus in your pride.
    God send a pox upon your head,
You clumsy pig, you atrocious *mule*,   [also, bastard]
Who uses your mouth the same way you do your ass.

ANTONIO DI GUIDO (d. 1486)

Antonio di Guido was a famous and beloved folk-singer who sang publicly
in Florence as early as 1437, when he was very young. He was a good friend
of Poliziano and left more than 20 poems, some of which were love songs
to women and some which were religious.

[Lanza 3] To a Friend Named Antonio
Tony, this excellent lord of yours,
Whose head is resplendent, is so genteel
That no other word would be capable
Of sounding his praise except "divine."
He stands out among emeralds and rubies;
His every act is serious, measured, and mature;
His aristocratic face is like an eastern pearl;
His pupils shine like nickel, his hair like gold.

And so, by his manners, deeds, and movements,
You can easily see what nature creates
Within its eternal and ever secret realm
If you survey his very radiant figure.
For this reason, please try hard to direct yourself
To be very kind to him, exceeding every measure.

[Lanza 11]

You can take away the glint that diamonds have
And make sacred Apollo with his shiny locks
Follow his usual sun-track somewhere else;
You can take away the rainbow from navigators,
Turn bitter into sweet and laughter to tears,
Put fish in the Alps, remove waves from the seas,
Take seed from the soil with grass and flowers and leaves
And force the birds to give up their songs . . .
Before I'll ever leave you, my dear lord.

MATTEO FRANCO (1447–1494)

A poet-priest, Franco engaged in a famous exchange of scurrilous poems with
the noted poet Luigi Pulci, author of the *Morgante maggiore*, an amusing and
well-written burlesque of heroic poetry that was published in its final form in
1482 and dedicated to the mother of Lorenzo de' Medici, Pulci's patron. Pulci's
success irritated Franco, and he initiated an exchange of bitter *tenzoni* which
appeared from 1474 to 1475. In these Franco is always homophobic, accus-
ing Pulci of sodomy, even though from the little we know of the man, Pulci
married one Lucrezia degli Albizi in 1474 and had four children by her.

The poems are written in a difficult jargon with multiple meanings;
they were poorly edited by Giulio Dolci as *Il Libro dei Sonetti* (Milan, 1933);
though called sonnets, the poems contain more than fourteen lines and are
highly irregular. My translation is from Dolci, No. 36.

Listen a little, you who listen to no one;
When you walked among the scholars of Padua,
You unjustly bad-mouthed an awful lot of them
Because they didn't offer you an upright tail.
Couldn't you do something more worthy of praise?
When you came back from Pisa not long ago,
Didn't you curse the saints and all of Heaven
Because some horse embroidered you with its slop?
The emperor included you among the wicked
After you were canonized among the saints of Sodom
When you held a big banquet of blowhards.
Now I'm addressing myself to your trials
Following the writs of a thousand citizens,
And the charges aren't dreamed up; they're quite explicit.

So you and your trouble-makers won't believe
That I really stole that altar cloth to dice on,
I want that cloth to be given to you on stakes.
    You little bark for the depraved,
For vices and for scandals and their like,
If anyone wants to call you, he should say "Luigi"—
    Or rather, poisonous little Gigi,
Cheater, screwer-upper, big-mouthed buffoon,
A man who'll subject any tenderloins to his fork.

FILIPPO SCARLATTI (ca. 1442–AFTER 1487)
    Little is known of his life, despite the fact that he left over 100 poems with
    an amazing variety, ranging from Petrarchan love songs to comic and scur-
    rilous burlesques.

[Lanza 51]
O beautiful adolescent, O young man,
Cupid has opened my eyes to you,
So that I (though undeserving) appeal only to you
As my master with me your chosen slave,
And I see beneath your outer look
So many good things you offer me,
Kindnesses and favors that indeed
Have carved my very heart out of my breast!
But you needn't look down on my presumptions.
I praise you, my excellent young man,
To please show some compassion toward your servant,
Who comes before you timidly, with head bent down.
Please exercise some discretion with him,
So that he won't wander vagrantly through the world.
    He, poor wretched thing,
Has seized the courage to make a frail proposal,
And he would be overjoyed if you respond.

[Lanza 52]
You have to show a strong upper hand
If you want to keep good standing with a boy

To make him rational in anything he chooses,
And yet not go off at cross-purposes with him;
And if at times you see him acting freakishly
And a dispute arises about a certain question,
And you're sure that he doesn't have a reason,
It's very important for you to keep your patience.
Any other foolish action won't succeed.
However, their love will only last as long
As a lot of money keeps flowing from you.
As long as you're giving, the value lasts.
As soon as you stop, your person is distasteful
Since he no longer tastes the savor of your wealth.
       Then he becomes an assassin,
And he'd willingly gouge out your eyes.
Pay him first and he'll welcome your advances.

[Lanza 57]
O buddy of your buddy-body,
You know all about what I'm going to say:
Because you've received your little pet
In exchange for a pussy!
You were well fucked-out the other evening,
When you went with a happy face
To the house of your buddy,
Even though you found yourself
The butt of humor.
You found yourself as the guest   10
Of a nasty creep,
Because by the morning
You had to take
About twenty enemas,
But that medicine
Made you happy and well.
You used to be the whore
Of the sack-lovers,
And for year after year
You were hungry for it;   20
You sucked them off again and again,
I do believe.

And your lustful little arsehole
Made its appearance everywhere,
And in the jousts
You broke down every lance,
Which would be a great feat
In a hard rain.
Even though you had great luck
That time, 30
You still responded
To every young kid's cry;
And you have for your amusement
The fact that Brother Cock
Can open up your hole for any impaling.
I don't know if you can hold
The shit back
Or if it issues
Liquid from the pounding.
You've split the rind 40
Of your little bunghole
And your rectum
Looks like a container
For little berries,
Mixed with the mustard
Of little babes. . . .

[The poem continues for 44 lines in this vein.]

ANGELO POLIZIANO (1454–1494)

Born as Angelo Ambrogini in Montepulciano, Poliziano at an early age was taken to Florence, where he studied under such important teachers as Marsilio Ficino. While still very young he translated part of Homer's *Iliad*, thereby attracting the attention of Lorenzo de'Medici, who made him the tutor of his children. In 1477 he became the Prior of San Paolo, and thus had time for his voluminous writing. Later he fell out with the Medicis.

The place of homosexuality in the works of Politian (as the English called him) has been hotly debated. Many of the mentions seem to be mere imitations of Greek and Latin verse. There are passages in his *Stanzas for the Tournament* (which was sponsored by Lorenzo de'Medici) that praise Lorenzo's brother Giuliano, but there is nothing beyond ordinary panegyric there. In his drama *Orfeo*, the hero, Orpheus, renounces the love of women after losing his wife Eurydice; this follows a theme that Ovid and others had treated, but with some passion. The closest things to homoerotic (and homophobic) verses are his *Greek Epigrams*, edited by Anthos Ardizzoni (Florence, 1951), with his numbering. Other selections are translated from *Il Poliziano, il Magnifico, Lirici del Quattrocento*, ed. Massimo Bontempelli, new ed. (Florence, 1978).

A. Greek Epigrams

2

You say, O Corydon, "I'm a boy"; I should say it too.
>But you're a man. Your beard has spoken against you.

7 To Giovan Battista Buoninsegni

As much as pilots are happy when they are traversing the sea
>When they hear the halcyon birds proclaiming a safe passage;
As much as a king delights when he's razed to the ground a hostile city,
>As much as a sick man rejoices when he's escaped a grave illness,
As much as a newlywed full of love feels as he enters the virgin's bed—
>This much my heart exults within my breast when I see
Your face and I suddenly hear your words.
>O day that's worthy of a sign of white and incantation!
O day that's worthy to be remembered for many years!
>O friend who is sweeter to me than honey, O lovable face!
May you always be happy and may Zeus yield to you all good fortune!
>And please conserve in your breast our mutual love!

21 To Popes Paul II and Sixtus IV

Paul was once a very good pope, but an evil man.
>Now Sixtus is a "groovy" man, but a lousy pope.

23 On the Love of Two Boys

A double love torments me; I strain because of two boys
>Who are equally resplendent in their eyes and equally appealing.
The one is hard and insolent; the other virginlike in his face;
>Both arouse in me an equally sweet desire.
One of them has dark locks cascading from his head,
>While the other has billowing blond tresses.
The rest of them is not the least bit similar—except for their lack of pity;
>Neither of them overcomes by his graceful charm.

It's not possible, Aphrodite, to hold on to both; so counsel me:
    Which of these two flames should I try to hold on to?

26 Love Song for Chrysokomos (Goldenlocks)

Watch over me from heaven while within my arms I hold my boy,
    And don't envy me, Zeus, because I envy no other.
Be contented, Zeus, be contented with your Ganymede, and leave to me
    My shiny Chrysokomos, who to me is sweeter than honey.
O how happy I am—three and four times! O yes, I have kissed—
    Truly kissed your mouth, you delicious boy-love!
O mouth, O locks, O smile, O light from your eyes!
    O gods, truly you are mine, you delightful boy, yes mine!
I say you are truly mine, my little lover boy! How much I have anguished,
    How much I have suffered and undergone to receive this prize!
My heart, why now are you suffering torment, as you did before? There's no
    Danger now; you shouldn't be trembling, O heart!
Because the thing that once destroyed us and made us fearful—look!
    I now hold him vanquished between my arms.
So take this, my goddess, take this dove to place on your altar,
    And arrange for me that this joy shall be eternal!
And you, rise up! How much more gently you inspire my love
    As you hold my tongue intertwined in your mouth, O my boy!

29 To a Boy

Don't inflame me with your whirlwind winks, my boy,
    As you're always hurling burning arrows into my heart.
In fact, my love for you, which you deride, lights torches in my eyes,
    O you who have laid me living on a burning pyre!

36

Don't try to kiss me, you drinker of piss! In fact, I'm accustomed
    To kissing the savory lips of young boys—so screw yours!

B. Orfeo

[Orpheus speaks after the loss of Eurydice:]
When will there ever be such a miserable song
That can equal the grief of my great loss?
Or how shall I be able to cry so much
That my crying will match my mortal grief?

I shall remain sad and disconsolate in my sorrow
As long as the heavens maintain my life.
And since so cruel is my fortune,   280
Never do I want to love a woman any more.
From now on, I shall go plucking new flowers,
The springtime of the superior sex,
When they are all light and slender;
This is the sweeter and gentler love.
Let there be nobody who talks to me about women,
Since that one is dead who held my heart.
Whoever wishes to have commerce with me in talk
Should never discuss the love of women.
O how miserable is the man who changes his will   290
For a woman or who ever is happy for her or grieves!
O how he is stripped of his freedom for her,
Or believes in her appearances or her words!
Because always she is lighter than a leaf in the wind;
And a thousand times a day she wants this or doesn't want that;
She follows what flees her, and hides from those who want her;
And she comes and goes like the waves on a stream.
Jove makes a complete testimony about this,
For, bound by a sweet and loving knot,
In heaven he enjoys his lovely Ganymede,   300
And Phoebus Apollo on earth enjoyed his Hyacinth;
Hercules yielded to this sacred love,
Who conquered the world and was conquered by cute Hylas.
I'll take comfort in divorcing myself from the married,
And I'll run away from every female contact!

PIETRO ARETINO (1492–ca. 1556)

Aretino was an Italian satirist who was called "The Scourge of Princes" by
Ariosto. He accused Michelangelo and others of being gay, and was him-
self accused of that vice by Niccolò Franco in his *Rimes Against Pietro
Aretino* (1541); however most scholars consider him straight because of his
numerous erotic heterosexual writings, including a sonnet sequence on "Six-
teen Ways of Making Love" (with drawings), pp. 104 ff. in Vol. I of his
Opere, ed. G. Aquilecchio and A. Romano (Rome, 1992). The following
poem is one of the few that might be considered homosexual (p. 61), but it
can also be viewed as merely extravagant panegyric.

Sonnet 65 To a Young Poet

Let Orpheus' raucous cithara and songs
Cease! To sing your praises with your eloquence
Human speech is not enough—only the divine—
To describe your lovely style resonant and pure.
Wingéd Pegasus for you would be submerged
In the Fount of Hippocrene on Helicon;
Dante would fail, along with our pure Serafino
For, compared to you, their style is lost.

You'll wear a fillet free of fraud
That every great poet bears on his sacred head,
And in life and death you'll be always praised.
Mount Parnassus is preparing for you
Its vase and water so you may rejoice on high,
Since your works are already close to being prophetic.

FRANCESCO BERNI (1496/8–1535)

Berni continued the burchiellesque tradition, but was much easier to under-
stand. A priest who was born near Pistoia, he lived most of his rather brief
life in Rome, where he was a friend of Popes Leo X and Clement VII. He
was imprisoned for some kind of sex scandal in 1523, but Clement arranged
his release. He moved to Verona in 1528 and died later under mysterious
circumstances, possibly being poisoned.

Of the numerous editions of his poems I have used *Rime,* ed. Danilo
Romei (Milan, 1985), which has excellent notes for puns. Poem 48 is an ex-
tended sexual spoof written to the "abbots"—the three sons of Francesco
Cornaro of Padua, who invited him to live with them in 1531. Poem 8 is
one of many praises of objects with sexual undertones; similar phallic poems
include the goby-fish (7), artichoke (9), and needle (13); anal poems were
written to the peach (10), urinal (11), and gelatin (12). See the article
"Bernesque Poetry" in the *Encyclopedia of Homosexuality,* ed. Dynes, for
more information on him and his many followers.

48 To the "Abbots" of Padua

. . . O what pleasant, what beautiful company you'd make,   43
Wonderful for me and the same for you, I know,
And the beauty from it would not just be mine.

We can make a living arrangement among us;
After we've been together for a little while,
Everyone can tend to his own business.
But often we'll play "the brothers' game" together,
Which is fabulous when it's done with taste,   50
As is practiced in convents where there are lots of abbots.
Every morning we'll perform our holy offices.
You'll surge up and warble, and I'll take it all mutely
Because I'm not very good at that kind of job.
And yet, not to be uselessly passive,
I'll perform any special services you ask,
Like those who play organs in the church's rear.
What grander feasts, what gayer parties,
What happier times, what greater bonanza,
What smoother comforts could there be?   60
He who admires honor likes to do any job.
I consider the highest good in all the world
To be among a band of close buddies—
In winter, before the fire in a big circle
Where we exchange our tales; in summer, *au naturel.*
These pleasures have no end; they know no bottom.
Just thinking about them gets me all heated up!
I think I'll die if I don't get over there!
Just thinking about them in vain depresses me.
I wrote you the other day that I was rushing   70
To see you, and I was suffering hammer-blows,
And now I'll write this to you again:
I left my top behind when I left Padua;
You have my heart clutched and locked
Under your keys with your sacred rings.
Get the bed ready for me right away,
That magisterial seat with its two little cushions
So that I can lie back in full delight.
O, and stay well, my divine little abbots!

8 In Praise of the Eel (1522)
. . . The eel is a lively beast that surges up in liquids   13
And lives on earth and in water and vice versa;
It penetrates where it wants to, then slips out,

So that you could call it the Combat-Conqueror
Because it forcefully shoots and then comes away,
Especially if you press it in a handlock.
Anyone who understands geometry
Can see that the eel corresponds   20
To the most capacious figure that there is.
It has everything that's long and round
Included in itself more perfectly
Than anything that has another shape.
That's why you can quickly see proved
That round holes and circles and rings
Are quite rationally formed to take it. . . .

[*The poem continues to line 72*]

BENEDETTO VARCHI (1503-1565)

Varchi was a prolific writer known today largely for his *History of Florence*, covering the period 1527–1538. He was notorious for his defense of homosexuality, although his Italian sonnets often employ the same kinds of Neoplatonic conceits that heterosexuals use. Many of these poems are addressed to a young man who is called Alloro (Laurel); although this sounds like an imitation of Petrarch's Laura, and it obviously was (like many of the features of Varchi's work), the masculine name dictates that all of the adjectives follow suit; hence the poems can sound frankly homosexual.

Many of Varchi's most moving poems concern the deaths of young men, such as Giulio (della Stufa), Martello, Luca, Lelio, Andrea, and so on. He suggests that there was a wide circle of homosexuals in Florence at the height (and death) of the Renaissance, addressing poems to Torquato Tasso (1544–1595) and his "Tribol" and "dear Davitte," and to Pietro Bembo (1470–1547) and others. He wrote some famous commentaries on the poetry of Michelangelo, praising it for its celebration of "Socratic love and Platonic concepts"; the artist thanked him for these. When Varchi delivered a eulogy at Michelangelo's funeral, he could not keep himself from commenting on the artist's attachments to Gherardo Pertini and Tommaso de' Cavalieri.

Varchi also wrote a famous comedy, *La Suocera (The Mother-in-Law;* 1557–1560) and works on the Italian language. See the article on him in the *Encyclopedia of Homosexuality.*

Because of the neglect that Varchi has suffered, one is forced to consult the antiquated edition of G. Benzoni, *Sonetti* (Venice, 1555) and other inadequate texts.

[1] p. 33

What part of my holiest and most beautiful feelings
For the young man Alloro, while I was still young,
Did Love with his chaste torch and golden arrows
Light up and then engrave in a high and noble refuge?
If I walk or sit, if I'm quiet or am talking,
Whatever I see or hear or think or feel or smell
Is nothing except that extraordinary honor
Of that green, pure, noble, happy sapling

With whom (if I live) I hope one day to fly
Above, so that, far from the vulgar crowd,
I'll have no cares about the final assault of death,
But always, seated in a happy place
High up in the third heaven with my handsome Giulio,
I'll extol my Giulio above all the rest.

[2] p. 63

See now this new grief that comes unforeseen
To my eyes and heart, and it's so grave
That I fear, alas! that I will die of weeping,
Indeed if a man has ever died this way,
Because my good Lelio, a young man who rose up
To the highest rank of every honor,
Like some frail flower battered down by the rain,
Is sick and is losing all his strength and color.

And so will it happen that this happy sprout
In his full flower and just now bearing fruit
Will wither, leaving me to mourn his green?
O Lord, who sees and hears and rules the universe,
Don't allow this blessing that you gave us
To be seized by something else, with your grace infirm!

[3] p. 63

Already the golden horns of the nearest star
Have been kindled and then spent,
And now appear less glowing, for what

Departs from us will never return again.
Already Phoebus goes back to his happy dwelling
With Taurus, and the sweet sigh
Of a gentle zephyr is felt as the laughing season
Adorns the world with all its grass and flowers;

Already whatever Apollo and Aesculapius
Ever knew about the art which cures the ill
And what noble Medicine has proved is true—
Not without the usual moans and groans,
My good Lelio lies sick, and I'm past the fear
Of lying myself gravely ill, and I'm feeling vile.

FRANCESCO COPPETTA BECCUTI (1509–1553)

Beccuti was a poet from Perugia, which had a lively tradition of homosexual poetry, although he also traveled widely. His one gay romance seems to have been with a young man named Francesco Bigazzini, who is called Alexis after the shepherd in Vergil's *Eclogue II*, although Beccuti vehemently denied that their relationship was anything but Platonic; nevertheless he wrote many poems of despair on their break-up, although he also in Rime 163 wrote a noble poem to Alexis's future bride. Rime 191 paints perhaps a more realistic description of Beccuti's own situation and that of Perugia. Texts from *Rime,* ed. E. Chiorboli (Bari, 1912).

Rime 60 To Alexis

One could certainly say Great Jove was blessed
If it's true that he was kindled by love
When, changed into an eagle, he held close
Handsome Ganymede suspended in loving air
And, flying aloft, often said to himself:
Soon we'll enjoy this dear, belovéd weight;
Frequently he deviated from his flight-course
As his wings clung closer to the young man's thighs.
I could also call myself blessed
If you weren't the prey I'm praying for;
I don't love you any less, and to my eyes you are
Every bit as sweet and pretty as Ganymede,
But I don't have the power of the gods;

I can't become a bird and whisk you away.
Don't be annoyed if, in my greed to embrace you,
I am sometimes thrown off track by my modesty.

Rime 79 A Nymph Addresses Corydon, the Poet, about his Alexis
Stanza 2:
It was bad for you to be obsessed
By handsome Alexis, you poor miserable lover!
Yes, he had the hair and voice and face of an angel—
But the heart of a tiger and a breast of stone.
Under his sweet and gentle laughter
Lurked so many nooses and flames—O so many!
And his tranquil eyes, where Love was lodged,
Now promise yours a continual rain.

Rime 163 To Alexis's Bride-To-Be
Stanza 16:
To save his life and rescue your honor,
You'll find a thousand ways, a thousand ploys;
You're a wise woman and he a savvy lover;
You don't have to teach a fish how to swim.
You both radiate a beautiful splendor
And you're both deserving of each other.
Time and beauty never run backwards!
And with those words I'm ending; I am mum.

Rime 191 "In Praise of Pederasty"; To Messer Bino, His Friend
. . . In order to take disaster off your back,   52
I tell you that these young men of ours
Are all without any stains or blots.
If you like a mind that's sharp and learnéd,
There's Crispolin, who's always content and cute,
Who has a bevy of young boys around him.
Contino is charming, neat, and slim,
And always acts very kindly and humbly;
It wouldn't be wrong to make him be your brother. . . .
The best is Valerian, but he stays with his own,   64

And there's one who has a name very much like mine,
Who pleased me, pleases and will forever please.
Turno should thank his very God above
That he's so happy-go-lucky and so gracious
That everyone yearns for him—and so do I. . . .

ROMAN PASQUINADES (1500s)

In the sixteenth century in Rome there arose a form of anonymous political lampoon called a *pasquinata*. The name was based on a mutilated pagan statue that became known as Pasquino; this had been set up in 1501 in an angle of the Orsini Palace by Oliviero Carafa, Cardinal of Naples. It soon became known as a place where one attached brief satires in Italian or Latin to the breast of Pasquino; the statue is now in the Braschi Palace facing the Square of Pasquino.

Most pasquinades attacked political figures, and churchmen were especially favored targets. The following selections, which name actual men, are taken from the massive two-volume *Pasquinate romane del cinquecento*, edited by V. Marucci et al. (Rome, 1983). The patron mentioned at the start of the first poem was Cardinal Andrea del Monte, who was in charge of an annual Pasquino festival in April. The so-called "Tough-Drinker" at the end was a German-Dutch prelate named Wilhelm Enckvoirt, who was notorious for his wine-drinking.

356 What Really Goes on in the College of Cardinals
My patron has truly opened up my eyes:
Cardinal Francesco Pisani's ass is always open;
I've seen Innocenzo Cybo, who fucked Cardinal Trani
And then Fernando Ponzetta, plugging it into Ercole Rangone.
I've seen in the College of Cardinals a big question
About who's a buggerer, browning queen or pimp.
I've seen Niccolò Ridolfi hoisting up his robes
Like a kneeling slave waiting for his turn.
I've watched Andrea della Valle get behind Franciotto Orsini,
And seen Brother Egidio Canisio with full hypocrisy
Doing battle with cute Alessandro Cesarini.
I've seen that crazy Archbishop of Siena
Wanting to rub his thighs with Francesco Armellini,
As Cardinal Aracelli does with that heretic De Vio.

Every cardinal quite courteously
Joins in fucking every other one—
Except for old Tough-Drinker, who only rams it down his throat.

176 *On Pompeo Colonna, Who Wants to be Pope*
A lot of things made me laugh of late,
But I'm afraid that this one's going to bust me;
Pompeo Colonna's got it in his head
To try to be our Pope at this particular time,
Even though he's considered a monster and a madman
With a head full of crickets—a big bag
Of wind who every hour or so changes
His promises, oaths, rules, and agreements.
He's vainer than the Cardinal of Santa Croce
And more two-faced than Alessandro Farnese,
And more arrogant than the Bishop of Ancona,
More vicious even than the Bishop of Bologna,
More bull-headed than Flisco or Grumano,
And more of a pig than any of those Frenchies;
      Why, he's even more a flagrant
Fag than Cardinal del Monte, a bigger gangster
And evil traitor than Francesco Soderini.
      O poor Pasquino! He runs around
Saying in shouts that he wants to be Il Papa,
And do you people blame me now for laughing?

329 *Advice to a Young Man*
Young man, before time flies further away,
Devote yourself, I tell you, to having a good sexy time,
And if it enters your heart, don't be afraid
To find out where Sodom and Gomorrah are located.
Don't enter into projects where the sperm should run
And then try to hold it back—
Because ejaculation is just like pissing.
Wherever you're heading, let it flow and fly!
Don't ever worry about what the nuts will say:
If she's your aunt and you're her relative,
Screw on, and get to wherever you're bound to come to.

If you're afraid that you're committing a sin,
Aren't jubilee celebrations held for all the living
And the dead? Two thousand for a single sin!

MICHELANGELO BUONARROTI (1475–1564)

Although renowned as a sculptor, painter, and architect Michelangelo was also a poet of note. Raised in Florence he created many of his best artistic works in Rome, as his *Pietà* and the Sistine Chapel show. It was in Rome in 1532 that he met a young nobleman named Tommaso de' Cavalieri, to whom he wrote many of his love poems. It was to Tommaso that he sent the famous drawing of the eagle carrying away the beautiful Ganymede. However there were always deep tensions between the physical and the spiritual in Michelangelo's life, as well as his poetry, which is often tormented in its syntax and grammar.

Later in his life the artist also wrote poems to the lady Vittoria Colonna but she remained a woman of lofty, unassailable virtue. Although the gossipy historian of art Pietro Aretino indicated that Michelangelo was openly gay, his friends denied this, and there is no clear proof, except perhaps from his art, where gay motifs related to Ganymede and Orpheus occur, and where the male nudes predominate over the often muscular ladies. For the connection between his writings and his art, see Chapter 1 in James M. Saslow's *Ganymede in the Renaissance* (New Haven, 1986), as well as Saslow's translations (New Haven, 1991). For a defense of Michelangelo's literary artistry, see Glauco Cambon, *Michelangelo's Poetry* (Princeton, 1985). I have translated from the edition of *Rime* edited by Enzo N. Girardi (Bari, 1960), following his numbering of poems.

31 Madrigal dated ca. 1525; on a sheet showing a sketch of a "putto" (nude baby boy)
Not just love but life and death together
My eyes have found
In your eyes, which alone are beautiful.
The less they offend me and inflict harm,
The more I am destroyed and burned.
And, on the other hand, love
Harms me, the more grace I find in it.
While I meditate and suffer
The evil, goodness surges in me in a moment.

O strange and novel torment!
Still, I don't shrink back;
If having misery and stress
Is sweet here, where there is seldom good,
Then I'll go seeking grief with greater pain.

58 The first poem to Tommaso de' Cavalieri; a sonnet dated 1532

If the desire for the immortal that raises and corrects
The thoughts of other men could draw forth mine,
Perhaps that hateful one who rules the House of Love
Could be converted into being merciful.
But because the soul through divine legislature
Enjoys a long life while the body briefly dies,
The senses cannot describe its praiseworthy value,
Which it can only very dimly perceive.

And so, alas! how can the pure desire
That burns within my heart be heard
By one who always sees himself in another?
And so a blissful time is denied to me
By *my lord*, who listens to every lie;   [*the usual epithet for Tommaso*]
To tell the truth, a liar is someone who doesn't believe.

72 Sonnet for Tommaso

If you can see the heart in someone's face by his eyes,
I am not showing any sign more manifest
Of my flames; and so, let this be enough,
My dear sweet lord, for asking mercy from you.
Maybe your spirit, which has a greater faith
Than I can believe in, and which sees the noble fire
That burns me, will be quick and kindly to me,
Offering that grace abounding for one who truly prays.

O happy would be that day if this were certain!
In one single moment, let time with its hours stop,
With the day and the sun in its ancient track,
So that I can have—though granted without merit—

My sweet and longed-for lord
Forever in my unworthy but eager arms!

76 Sonnet for Tommaso; summer of 1533
I don't know if it's the desired light
Of the First Maker that my inner being feels,
Or if some other beauty from my memory
Of people is glowing in my heart;
Or if some reputation or dream brings someone
Forth to my eyes and makes present to my heart,
Leaving with it some unknown pungent power
Which explains perhaps what causes me to cry.

The thing that I feel and search for and one to guide me
Are not part of me; I don't know in fact where
I could find them or who there is to show me.
All this, my lord, has happened since I met you:
I am moved by a sweet bitterness—a yes-and-no.
And there's no doubt that the causer was your eyes.

77 Sonnet for Tommaso, probably written in 1533 while the artist was back in Florence
If the fire of your eyes was equal
To the beauty that radiates from them,
Our Earth wouldn't have a frigid zone
That wouldn't burn when inflamed by your darts.
But the heavens, which are kindly toward our troubles,
Remove from us the capacity for seeing
All of that beauty that is a part of you
In order to pacify our bitter, mortal lives.

And thus my inner flame cannot match your beauty,
For a person is inflamed and falls in love
Only with the heavenly beauty that he encompasses.
And so it happens to me, my lord, at this time:
If it doesn't seem that I'm burning and dying for you,
My limited capacity has limited my fire.

80 Sonnet for Tommaso; written ca. 1533
I thought on that day when I first spied
All of your unique and singular charms
That, like an eagle staring at the sun, I'd keep
My eyes fixed on the smallest part I desired.
Then I recognized my fallacious error—
Because a wingless one who wants to follow an angel
Scatters seed on stones, throws words to the winds,
And in vain yields his intellect to God.

Therefore, if the infinite beauty dazzling my eyes
Won't allow my heart to come close to it,
But also doesn't assure or trust me far away,
What's to become of me? What guide, what escort
Exists who can help or avail me with you,
Since, when near, you burn—when far, you murder me?

81 Madrigal extensively revised
Every thing that I see counsels me
And begs me and forces me to follow and love you;
Because there's nothing good that doesn't come from you.
Love, which destroys every other miracle,
Wants me, for my good, to search and desire
You alone, my Sun; and thus my soul
Is deprived of every other high hope and power.
Love wants me to burn and live

Not only for you, but for anyone who resembles
You in your eyes or any part of your face.
And whoever diverges from you, my eyes
And life, no longer then has light,
For there is no heaven where there is not you.

82 Sonnet for Tommaso; written ca. 1534
I can't imagine any other figure
Either as a nude shade or in earthly spoils
In my highest thoughts that could force me
To take it as a weapon against your beauty.

For whenever I am far from you, it seems
I sink so deep that Love strips me of every power,
And when I try to diminish my suffering,
Love doubles it and comes to give me death.

And so it's no good to project a further flight
As I double the distance from my enemy, Beauty,
For the less quick cannot outstrip the more.
Love dries my tears with its own hands,
Promising that all my labors are held dear;
For anything that costs this much cannot be vile.

83 Sonnet for Tommaso; written ca. 1534
I see in your lovely face, milord,
What can only be ill described in this life;
The soul while still clothed in the flesh
Has often ascended with it up to God.
And if the malicious, stupid, evil rabble
Point fingers at others for what they feel,
My intense yearning is no less pleasing—
Nor my love, my faith, my noble desire.

Every beautiful thing that can be seen here,
More than anything else does to perceptive men,
Recalls that Fount of Mercy from which all come.
We do not have any other example or any fruit
Of heaven here on earth. Thus he who loves you
With faith ascends to God and holds Death sweet.

89 Sonnet for Tommaso; written ca. 1534
I see through your beautiful eyes a sweet light
That I could never see with my own blind ones.
I carry with your feet a burden on my back
That my lame feet aren't yet accustomed to.
I fly with your wings, though I lack feathers,
And by your genius I'm always impelled toward Heaven;
According to your judgment, I'm pale or red,
Cold in the sun, warm in the coldest blasts.

My desire is solely within your will;
My thoughts take their form within your heart,
And my words are created by your breath.
Like the lonely moon I seem by myself,
Because our eyes don't know how to view
The heavens, except for what the sun illuminates.

90 Sonnet; possibly for Tommaso

I'm much more precious to myself than I was before.
Now that I've got you in my heart, I'm more valuable,
Just as a stone that has an engraving added
Is worth much more than the rock it used to be;
Or, just as a page or leaflet written or painted
Is regarded more highly than any sheet or shred,
So I regard myself, since I've been imprinted
By the sign of your face—and it doesn't hurt me.

Secure with your imprint, I can go anywhere
Like a man who carries with him charms or weapons
That can make any peril seem the lesser.
I am strong against all water and all fire;
With your imprint, I bring light back to the blind,
And with just my spit, I can cure any poison.

95 Sonnet for Tommaso; written at some time between 1534 and 1538

O you streams and rivers, restore to my eyes
The waves from your sources, always flowing but not yours,
Which always make you rise as they increase,
With greater force than you have in your natural flowing.
And you, thick air, who eclipse the heavenly light
To my sad eyes, saturated with my sighs,
Return them to my worn-out heart and clear again
Your darkened face for my sharpened insight.

Let the earth return some paces for my feet, so that
The grass plucked from it may sprout once again,
And Echo resound, who is now deaf to my laments,

And your holy lights may restore sight to my eyes
So that I once more will be able to love
Another beauty, since you're not content with me.

99 Sonnet for Febo di Poggio
*The poet probably met this handsome young Florentine in 1534 before leav-
ing Florence and returning permanently to Rome. The name Febo is Italian
for the ancient sun-god Phoebus-Apollo, and "poggio" means "hill" as in
the third line.*

With such a happy fortune, I should have
Risen when I was able from earth upon his feathers
While Febo lighted all the hill, and thus
I could have made death sweet for me.
Now he's all gone; and if he promised me
In vain to shorten the flight of my happy days,
It's right that against my ungrateful and guilty soul
Mercy should deny her hands and Heaven its gates.

His feathers offered me wings, his hill a staircase;
Phoebus was a lamp for my feet, and Death at that time
Was no more a source of salvation as a miracle.
Now, as I die without these, my soul doesn't rise on high
And the memory of them doesn't restore my heart,
Because with lateness and damage lost, who can counsel me?

193 Sonnet written to Luigi del Riccio on the death of Cecchino Bracci, 1544
*Luigi wanted the artist to carve an effigy of Cecchino for a tomb. This is
the only sonnet Michelangelo wrote about Cecchino, but there are numerous
short epitaphs.*

Scarcely had I seen his gorgeous eyes
Open for the first time in this frail life
When, closed on his final day of departure,
He opened them to contemplate God above.
I know this and I weep, but the error wasn't mine
That my heart was slow in acknowledging his beauty—

No, it was early death, which caused my ardent love
To vanish—though yours goes on and on.
Therefore, Luigi, to carve the outstanding figure
Of Cecchino, of whom I speak, to live in rock
Eternally (now that he's only dust among us here),
If one lover can be transformed into another,
Since without a form my artistry will fail,
It's right that, to portray him, I portray you.

General Bibliography

See introductions to chapters and authors for specialized references.

Bailey, Derrick S. *Homosexuality and the Western Christian Tradition*. London, 1955.

Boswell, John. *Christianity, Social Tolerance, and Homosexuality: Gay People in Western Europe from the Beginnings of the Christian Era to the Fourteenth Century*. Chicago, 1980.

Bouhdiba, Abdelwahab. *Sexuality in Islam*, tr. A. Sheridan, London, 1985.

Bousquet, G.H. *L'éthique sexuelle de l'Islam*. Paris, 1966.

Buffière, Felix. *Eros adolescent: la pédérastie dans la Grèce antique*. Paris, 1980.

Carpenter, Edward. *Ioläus: An Anthology of Friendship*. London, 1902.

Curtius, Ernst. R. *European Literature and the Latin Middle Ages*, tr. W. Trask. New York, 1963.

Dalla, Danilo. *"Ubi Venus mutatur": omosessualità e diritto nel mondo romano*. Milan, 1987.

Dover, K.J. *Greek Homosexuality*. Cambridge, Ma., 1978.

Dronke, Peter. *Medieval Latin and the Rise of European Love-Lyric*. 2 vols. Oxford, 1965.

Dynes, Wayne R. et al., eds. *Encyclopedia of Homosexuality*, 2 vols. Garland, 1990.

Foster, Jeannette H. *Sex Variant Women in Literature*. 1st ed., 1956; Tallahassee, Fl., 1985.

Goodich, Michael. *The Unmentionable Vice: Homosexuality in the Later Medieval Period*. Santa Barbara, 1979.

Grimal, Pierre. *L'Amour à Rome*. Paris, 1980.

Kay, Richard. *Dante's Swift and Strong: Essays on "Inferno XV."* Lawrence, Ka., 1978.

Kempter, Gerda. *Ganymed: Studien zur Typologie, Ikonographie und Ikonologie*. Cologne, 1980.

Kiefer, Otto. *Sexual Life in Ancient Rome*. London, 1934.

Lanza, Antonio, ed., *Lirici toscani del quattrocento*. 2 vols. Rome, 1973.

Licht, Hans. *Sexual Life in Ancient Greece*. London, 1932.

Lilja, Saara. *Homosexuality in Republican and Augustan Rome*. Helsinki, 1982.

McCall, Andrew. *The Medieval Underworld*. London, 1979.

Monroe, James T. *Hispano-Arabic Poetry: A Student Anthology*. Berkeley, 1974.

Nykl, A.R. *Hispano-Arabic Poetry and Its Relations with the Old Provençal Troubadours*. Baltimore, 1946.

Paglia, Camille. *Sexual Personae: Art and Decadence from Nefertiti to Emily Dickinson*. New Haven, 1990; New York, 1991.

Percy, William A. *Greek Pederasty*. Garland, 1990.

Peyrefitte, Roger. *La Muse Garconnière*. Paris, 1973.

Raby, F.J.E. *History of Christian-Latin Poetry from the Beginnings to the Close of the Middle Ages*. 2nd ed. Oxford, 1953.

———. *History of Secular Latin Poetry in the Middle Ages*. Oxford, 1934.

Salisbury, Joyce, ed. *Sex in the Middle Ages*. Garland, 1991.

Saslow, James M. *Ganymede in the Renaissance*. New Haven, 1986.

Sergent, Bernard. *Homosexuality in Greek Myth*. Boston, 1986.

Tonelli, Luigi. *L'amore nella poesia e nel pensiero del Rinascimento*. Florence, 1933.

Waddell, Helen. *The Wandering Scholars*. Rev. ed. New York, 1966.

Wilhelm, James J. *The Cruelest Month: Spring, Nature, and Love in Classical and Medieval Lyrics*. New Haven, 1965.

Index of Authors and Longer Works

Abelard, Peter 159ff.
Abū Hayyān 221ff.
Alan of Lille 169ff.
Alcaeus 36ff.
Alcuin 142ff.
Alpheius of Mytilene 34
Anacreon 11ff.
Antipater 51ff.
Aquettino, L' 281
Aratus 58
Aretino, Pietro 310ff.
Asclepiades of Samos 38ff.
Ash-Sharīf at-Ṭalīq 195ff.
Ausonius 137ff.
Automedon 38

Baudri of Bourgueil 154ff.
Beccuti, Francesco Coppetta 315ff.
Ben Mar-Saul, Isaac 237
Bernard of Cluny 166ff.
Berni, Francesco 311ff.
Bietris de Romans 263ff.
Bonciani, Antonio 302ff.
Buca di Montemorello 280
Burchiello, Il 282

Callimachus 39ff.
Carmina Burana 185ff.
Catullus 87ff.
Chaucer, Geoffrey 273ff.

Dante Alighieri 265ff.
Diocles 38
Dionysius 54
Dioscorides 33ff

Ennodius 139
Evenus 67

Flaccus 33
Franco, Matteo 304
Fronto 67

Gagno, Il 281
Ganymede and Hebe, Debate of 187ff.
Ganymede and Helen, Debate of 176ff.
Gherardi da Prato, Giovanni 285
Glaucus 40
Godfrey of Winchester 150ff.
Gottschalk 145ff.
Greek Anthology 29ff.
Guido, Antonio di 303

Ha-Levy, Judah 255ff.
Hilary the Englishman 163ff.
Hildebert of Lavardin 157ff.
Horace 98ff.

Ibn al-Zaqqāq 211ff.
Ibn ᶜAmmār 200ff.
Ibn Arfa ᶜRa'suh 210ff.
Ibn Darrāj al-Qasṭallī 195
Ibn ᶜEzra, Abraham 257ff.
Ibn ᶜEzra, Isaac 259ff.
Ibn, ᶜEzra(h), Moses 251ff.
Ibn Gabirol, Solomon 248ff.
Ibn Hamdis 209ff.
Ibn Ḥasdai 239ff.
Ibn Ḥasdai, Yūsuf 243ff
Ibn Ḥazm al-Andalusī 199ff.

Ibn Joseph Ṣadiq 240ff.
Ibn Khafāja 201ff.
Ibn Naghrīllah, Samuel 244ff.
Ibn Sahl 213ff.
Ibn Shuhaid 198
Ibycus 12ff.

Julius Leonidas 34
Juvenal 129ff.

Latin Anthology 140ff.
Luxorius 139ff.

Marbod of Rennes 153ff.
Martial 117ff.
Massimi, Pacifico 290ff.
Meleager 35ff.
Michelangelo Buonarroti 319ff.
Mnasalcas 60
Musa Puerilis 29ff.

Notker Balbulus 148ff.
Numenius of Tarsus 36

Ovid 111ff.

Panormita, Antonio 286ff.
Pasquinades, Roman 317ff.
Paulinus of Nola 138
Pegolotti, Nanni 282ff.
Petronius 132
Phanias 37
Philodemus 67
Plato 21ff.

Poliziano, Angelo 307ff.
Polystratus 50
Pontano, Giovanni 290
Posidippus 40ff.
Prato, Domenico da 279
Prato, Giovanni da 285

Rhianus 38ff.

Salomo 149
Sappho 5ff.
Scarlatti, Filippo 305ff.
Scythinus 35
Serlo of Wilton 167ff.
Statyllius Flaccus 36
Strato 29ff.

Theocritus 23ff.
Theognis 13ff.
Thymocles 37
Tibullus 100ff.
Tolomei, Granfione 279
Tolomei, Meo de' 279
Tullius Laureas 35

Varchi, Benedetto 313ff.
Vergil (Virgil) 107ff.

Walafrid Strabo 147
Walter of Châtillon 168ff.

Yūsuf III of Granada 225ff.

Za, Lo 280

For Product Safety Concerns and Information please contact our EU
representative GPSR@taylorandfrancis.com
Taylor & Francis Verlag GmbH, Kaufingerstraße 24, 80331 München, Germany